OXFORD WORLD'S CLASSICS

A POCKET PHILOSOPHICAL DICTIONARY

VOLTAIRE was the assumed name of François-Marie Arouet (1694–1778) Born into a well-to-do Parisian family, he was educated at the leading Jesuit college in Paris. Having refused to follow his father and elder brother into the legal profession he soon won widespread acclaim for *Œdipe* (1718), the first of some twenty-seven tragedies which he continued to write until the end of his life. His national epic *La Henriade* (1723) confirmed his reputation as the leading French literary figure of his generation. Following a quarrel with a worthless but influential aristocrat, the Chevalier de Rohan, he was forced into exile in England. This period (1726–8) was particularly formative, and his *Letters concerning the English Nation* (1733) constitute the first major expression of Voltaire's deism and his subsequent lifelong opposition to religious and political oppression. Following the happy years (1734–43) spent at Cirey with his mistress Mme du Châtelet in the shared pursuit of several intellectual enthusiasms, notably the work of Isaac Newton, he enjoyed a brief interval of favour at court during which he was appointed Historiographer to the King. After the death of Mme du Châtelet in 1749 he finally accepted an invitation to the court of Frederick of Prussia, but left in 1753 when life with this particular enlightened despot became intolerable. In 1755, after temporary sojourn in Colmar, he settled at Les Délices on the outskirts of Geneva. He then moved to nearby Ferney in 1759, the year *Candide* was published. Thereafter a spate of tragedies, stories, philosophical works, and polemical tracts, not to mention a huge number of letters, poured from his pen. After the death of Louis XV in 1774 he eventually returned to Paris in 1778 for the performance of his penultimate tragedy *Irène*. He was acclaimed and fêted by the entire capital as the greatest living Frenchman and as one of the most effective champions of freedom, tolerance, and common sense the world had ever seen. He died there on 30 May 1778.

JOHN FLETCHER is Honorary Senior Research Fellow at the University of Kent.

NICHOLAS CRONK is Professor of French Literature and Director of the Voltaire Foundation, University of Oxford. He is General Editor of *The Complete Works of Voltaire* and editor of *The Cambridge Companion to Voltaire* (2009).

OXFORD WORLD'S CLASSICS

For over 100 years Oxford World's Classics have brought readers closer to the world's great literature. Now with over 700 titles—from the 4,000-year-old myths of Mesopotamia to the twentieth century's greatest novels—the series makes available lesser-known as well as celebrated writing.

The pocket-sized hardbacks of the early years contained introductions by Virginia Woolf, T. S. Eliot, Graham Greene, and other literary figures which enriched the experience of reading. Today the series is recognized for its fine scholarship and reliability in texts that span world literature, drama and poetry, religion, philosophy, and politics. Each edition includes perceptive commentary and essential background information to meet the changing needs of readers.

OXFORD WORLD'S CLASSICS

VOLTAIRE

A Pocket Philosophical Dictionary

Translated by
JOHN FLETCHER

With an Introduction and Notes by
NICHOLAS CRONK

OXFORD
UNIVERSITY PRESS

OXFORD
UNIVERSITY PRESS

Great Clarendon Street, Oxford OX2 6DP

Oxford University Press is a department of the University of Oxford.
It furthers the University's objective of excellence in research, scholarship,
and education by publishing worldwide in

Oxford New York

Auckland Cape Town Dar es Salaam Hong Kong Karachi
Kuala Lumpur Madrid Melbourne Mexico City Nairobi
New Delhi Shanghai Taipei Toronto

With offices in

Argentina Austria Brazil Chile Czech Republic France Greece
Guatemala Hungary Italy Japan Poland Portugal Singapore
South Korea Switzerland Thailand Turkey Ukraine Vietnam

Oxford is a registered trade mark of Oxford University Press
in the UK and in certain other countries

Published in the United States
by Oxford University Press Inc., New York

Translation © John Fletcher 2011
Editorial material © Nicholas Cronk 2011

The moral rights of the authors have been asserted
Database right Oxford University Press (maker)

First published as an Oxford World's Classics paperback 2011

British Library Cataloguing in Publication Data

Data available

Library of Congress Cataloging in Publication Data

Data available

Typeset by Glyph International, Bangalore, India
Printed in Great Britain
on acid-free paper by
Clays Ltd, Elcograf S.p.A.

ISBN 978-0-19-955363-1

10

CONTENTS

ABBREVIATIONS

D   Voltaire, *Correspondence and Related Documents*, ed. Theodore Besterman, *OCV* 85–135 (Geneva, Banbury, and Oxford: Voltaire Foundation, 1968–77). The letter D is followed by the number of the letter in this edition.

OCV   *Complete Works of Voltaire/Œuvres complètes de Voltaire* (Geneva, Banbury, and Oxford: Voltaire Foundation, 1968–)

SVEC *Studies on Voltaire and the Eighteenth Century* (Voltaire Foundation, 1955–)

INTRODUCTION

VOLTAIRE'S *Pocket Philosophical Dictionary* (*Dictionnaire philosophique portatif*) is not a 'dictionary' (in any ordinary sense of the term), nor is it 'philosophical' (in the way we now use the word). But, crucially, it is 'portable' (*portatif*) and meant for the pocket. Voltaire wanted to write a book which would shock and which would change minds, above all he wanted to reach out to a wide readership, so portability was essential: small books are cheaper—and easier to hide if the police come looking for them. The *Pocket Philosophical Dictionary* is one of the most explosive and controversial works of the European Enlightenment; and it is also, if this all sounds rather serious, one of the funniest. It certainly tested the sense of humour of those in authority. Published anonymously in Geneva, in July 1764, the book was promptly condemned by the Paris *parlement* and ceremonially burned by the public executioner in Geneva. It was also placed on the Index of books prohibited by the Catholic Church, where it remained until the Index was abolished in 1966. Voltaire's critique of the Bible and of Christian faith was certainly shocking—some believers still find it shocking—but many of the ideas he expresses in the work were commonplace in clandestine literature of the time. Why then did the book cause such an enormous storm from the moment of its first publication?

The Patriarch of Ferney

In 1764, Voltaire was 70 years of age, and the most famous living writer, not just in France, but in all of Europe. He was a living legend, a monument to be visited by gentlemen travellers on the Grand Tour.[1] Voltaire was also, at last, established, if not quite secure, in his imposing house; it had not always been so. His life until then had been full of incident and scandal, for he had a lifelong talent for upsetting people. Born in Paris at the end of the seventeenth century, as a young man he knew the Paris of the Regency and imbibed its spirit of libertine freethinking. But he went too far, and was exiled from Paris, then put in the Bastille on more than one occasion. He visited Holland as

[1] See the Appendix, 'Two Portraits of Voltaire in 1764'.

a young man, then spent two formative years in England (1726–8), an experience which led to one of his early masterpieces in prose, the *Letters concerning the English Nation* (1733). Later, with his companion Mme Du Châtelet, he would spend many years (1734–43) at Cirey in eastern France, and after her death he travelled to the court at Potsdam as the guest of Frederick the Great. When he left Berlin in 1753, he was almost a refugee, welcome neither in Berlin nor in Paris. He moved to Protestant Switzerland in 1755, living in Lausanne and Geneva, but eventually even this idyll faded: the Protestant pastors turned out to be as intolerant as their Catholic counterparts. In 1760 Voltaire moved into a château at Ferney in France, near Geneva, and it was here that he would remain for the remainder of his long life; he left only in 1778 to travel to Paris, where he died.

Voltaire was famous from an early age, and famously outspoken; his challenge was always to find a position of authority from which to speak. He was not welcome at the court of Versailles, he was no longer welcome at the court of Potsdam, and the image of the itinerant philosopher did not suit him in the way it suited Jean-Jacques Rousseau. Ferney was therefore the perfect solution. It was only just on French soil. After years of being abroad, Voltaire could now proudly boast that he lived in France (and he reacted strongly when it was suggested he was in exile). But the little village of Ferney lay hidden behind the Alps, very remote from Paris and the centres of power whom he continued to annoy. Ferney was close to the border with the Protestant republic of Geneva, a centre of commerce and culture, and crucially a city with thriving printers and publishers. Within the tiny village of Ferney—nowadays called Ferney-Voltaire in his honour—Voltaire was lord of the manor, enjoying seigneurial rights. He had considerable personal wealth, and relished the independence which that gave him; he was a generous host to his numerous visitors (many of them English), and they never failed to comment on his luxurious lifestyle.

After so many years of searching for stability, it was at Ferney that Voltaire's authorial voice finally became anchored, and after 1760 he acquired a new authorial posture, that of 'the patriarch of Ferney'.[2] His writing changed and developed in a new direction. Had he died

[2] See N. Cronk, 'Voltaire and the 1760s: The Rule of the Patriarch', in N. Cronk (ed.), *Voltaire and the 1760s: Essays for John Renwick*, *SVEC* 2008: 10, pp. 9–21.

in 1760, Voltaire would be remembered as a great poet and dramatist whose career had reached a climax with the publication of his novel *Candide* in 1759. The reputation that Voltaire enjoys today, as the ironist who campaigned relentlessly for liberty and freedom against the forces of intolerance, was forged essentially in the course of the 1760s. W. H. Barber sums up in this way:

> By 1760, one can see coming together all the main factors needed to give Voltaire the power to make a serious impact on public opinion, in France and even further afield, on any issue of political or social significance which he felt moved to take up. He was rich; he lived virtually beyond the reach of potentially oppressive governments but nevertheless at the crossroads of Europe; he was visited near Geneva by travellers of note from every country; he was famous everywhere as a major dramatist, poet, historian, freethinker, and wit. Nothing that he wrote could fail to attract public attention, and he was convinced that action to improve the human lot was both necessary and possible.[3]

Voltaire's political involvement grew in this period, and he even invented a campaign slogan: in many of the letters written at this time he signs off with the cryptic 'Ecr: L'inf'. *Écrasez l'Infâme* became Voltaire's rallying-cry, and it is not easy to translate: it means something like 'Crush the despicable', *l'Infâme* referring to the infamy of Catholic bigotry, intolerance, and stupidity. Voltaire was not growing old gracefully. As Mme Denis wrote to Voltaire's old friend Cideville in 1759, 'His petulance grows with age' (D8341). From the beginning, Voltaire had argued robustly for religious toleration. He made his reputation with his epic poem *La Henriade* which describes how France had been torn apart in the civil wars of the sixteenth century and how the conflict between Catholics and Protestants had finally been resolved by the statesmanship of Henri de Navarre who became king of France as Henri IV. In his *Letters concerning the English Nation*, Voltaire had proclaimed England as a country of toleration where different religions lived side by side in harmony. In a famous passage, inspired by Addison's *Spectator*, Voltaire had sung the praises of the Royal Exchange where traders came to make their deals: trade and commerce bring men of different cultures together, he seems to say, where religion needlessly divides them. The basic principles of

---

[3] W. H. Barber, 'Voltaire: Art, Thought, and Action', *Modern Language Review*, 88 (1993), p. xxxvi.

Voltaire's toleration did not change, but after 1760 they acquired new urgency as he applied them to specific cases.

The Malagrida and Calas affairs

In October 1761, Voltaire read in the *Gazette de France* about an auto-da-fé which had occurred in Lisbon the previous month, in which the Inquisition had executed some forty-odd people, including an elderly Jesuit, Father Malagrida. Voltaire had no reason to want to defend a Jesuit—especially a Jesuit who had become famous for arguing that the Lisbon earthquake of 1755 was God's judgement on man—but the spectacle of the Inquisition putting one of their own to death piqued his curiosity. Voltaire tried hard to find out more details of the case, which was a complicated affair: unable to find Malagrida guilty of attempted regicide, the court had eventually condemned the Jesuit instead for heresy, on the basis of extremely flimsy, even ludicrous, evidence. There were evidently political ramifications which Voltaire could not have fully known but which he suspected: in reality Malagrida was guilty of being an opponent of the prime minister, the future marquis de Pombal, who feared the growing influence of the Jesuits at the court of Joseph I. Whatever the precise facts, it is clear that Voltaire found the burning of Malagrida an excessive punishment, and the justification given for it utterly absurd—as fantastic and fanatical as anything in *Candide*. As Voltaire wrote to his Paris friends, the d'Argentals: 'Another auto-da-fé! In this century! What will Candide say?' (D10090). This was life imitating art. In late 1761, Voltaire published a fifteen-page brochure about the Malagrida affair, the *Sermon du rabbin Akib* (*Sermon of the Rabbi Akib*), in which he adopted the voice of a Jew in order to lament the cruelty inflicted by Catholics on one another. Voltaire's 'Jewish' speaker makes clear that intolerance is an invention of the Christians.

The 'Malagrida affair' was an important turning point. An event in far-off Lisbon became known to Voltaire at Ferney; it grew into a 'news story' thanks to the efficiency of the eighteenth-century press, and to the appetite of the reading public. Voltaire quickly grasped the polemical (and comic) potential of the story of one group of Catholics using, for their own political reasons, trumped-up charges and a faulty judicial process to execute a fellow group of Catholics. Not only was the question of religious faith put into question by these events, so were the due processes of the legal system and civil society: the laws should protect man, even a Jesuit, from injustice, not aid and abet the intolerant and the bigoted. And Voltaire learned something too about the power of the press to sway public opinion. His magnificently ironical *Sermon du rabbin Akib* was an instant success, and the work was widely distributed, even in England, where it appeared many times in the press.[4] Pombal, anxious to project a positive 'Enlightened' image of Portugal in Europe, and concerned about public opinion, published the sentence against Malagrida, and a justification for it, in French translation. But it was too late: Malagrida had achieved fame across Europe as a victim of the Inquisition, and moreover Voltaire's name was linked indissolubly to his cause. From Pombal's point of view, the publicity war was lost in advance; Voltaire was victorious.

The 'Malagrida affair' paved the way for the better remembered Calas affair. The cruel execution of Malagrida had taken place in a foreign country, and it did, in Voltaire's portrayal at least, have a comic side. The Calas affair was closer to home, and it was not amusing at all. The Calas family were Protestant merchants who lived in Toulouse. In October 1761, one of the sons of the family was found dead. The authorities moved quickly and decided on scant evidence that he had been murdered by his father. In March 1762 Jean Calas was tortured and then broken on the wheel in front of a crowd in the place Saint-Georges in Toulouse. From start to finish, proper judicial process was ignored, and there was a strong suspicion that the Catholic judges were motivated by religious prejudice. Voltaire was outraged: he made contact with Jean Calas's widow, and began to publish a series of writings proclaiming the executed man's innocence. This grew into a more general plea for religious toleration, culminating in the publication in 1763 of the *Traité sur la tolérance* (*Treatise on Toleration*). In June 1764—just weeks before the publication of the *Pocket Philosophical Dictionary*—the privy council in Paris overruled completely the judgements of the Toulouse courts; finally in 1765, three years after the death sentence pronounced on Jean Calas, all members of the family were declared innocent. It was an enormous victory for Voltaire, who was remembered thereafter as 'l'homme aux Calas'. Even Diderot, who did not always find Voltaire

---

[4] See Antonio Gurrado's introduction to his critical edition of the *Sermon du rabbin Akib*, OCV 52.

easy to like, was full of praise, writing to his mistress Sophie Volland: 'What a good use of genius! . . . If ever Christ existed, I can assure you that Voltaire would be saved.' Voltaire's campaigns of the 1760s against judicial incompetence and in favour of religious tolerance would continue throughout the 1760s, and would shape definitively the image of Voltaire which has passed to posterity.

To return to 1764: the patriarch Voltaire had attained the biblical 'threescore years and ten' and he was not of a retiring nature. He had published his *Traité sur la tolérance* in which he reaffirmed the importance of toleration, and now he wanted to focus more forcefully on the sources of intolerance: religious bigotry. He was angry. Moreover, thanks to the Malagrida and then the Calas affairs, he had learnt about the power of public opinion, and he was clearly thinking about how he could put this power to use. In 1763, in his *Remarques pour servir de supplément à l'Essai sur les mœurs*, he spoke of the 'power of opinion', and the idea resurfaced in his tragedy *Olympie* (1764): 'L'opinion fait tout; elle t'a condamné' ('Opinion is all-powerful; it has condemned you'). Again in 1764, Voltaire wrote: 'Opinion rules the world, but in the long run it is the philosophers who shape opinion.' It was in these circumstances that Voltaire turned (back) to his *Pocket Philosophical Dictionary*.

A Pocket Philosophical Dictionary

The project for this book was not a new one, it went back to his years at the court of Frederick the Great. In 1752 there had been talk of a collective alphabetical work aimed at fighting prejudice and fanaticism. Frederick was to be the patron of the project, and it seems that Voltaire duly sketched out the first articles in suitably aggressive and anticlerical style. His departure from Berlin brought this work to a sudden halt, and Voltaire then busied himself with other books. But he had clearly returned to the *Dictionary* by early 1760, when he told Mme Du Deffand that he was planning a 'dictionary of ideas': 'I am absorbed in making a reckoning for myself, in alphabetical order, of everything that I must think about this world and the next, all of it for my personal use, and perhaps, after my death, for the use of respectable people' (D8764). Later that year he sent her the article 'Ezekiel', then in 1762 he sent part of 'Moses' to Damilaville and Diderot. We can infer that after publishing his *Traité sur la tolérance* he decided it was time to confront *l'Infâme* head-on. In June 1763, he wrote to the d'Argentals:

The time has come when my blood is boiling, the time has come to do something. I must hurry, age is advancing. There's not a moment to lose. They make me act the big tragic roles to amuse our children and our Genevans. But it's not enough to be an old actor. I am and I must be an old author, for you have to live out your destiny until the last moment. (D11283)

The publication of the *Pocket Philosophical Dictionary* caused a storm as great as Voltaire had feared (and hoped). He wrote much in his letters about fearing for his personal safety, and even if we make allowances for a certain sense of theatre, he undoubtedly felt uncomfortable. Voltaire had attacked the enemy head-on and knew they would be remorseless. But Voltaire was the better writer, and there now ensued the most extraordinary campaign of letter-writing in which Voltaire announced to all the world that, of course, he knew nothing at all about this new book. To Damilaville, his confidential friend in Paris, Voltaire wrote in July 1764: 'God preserve me, my dear brother, from having anything to do with the *Pocket Philosophical Dictionary*! I have read some of it: it reeks horribly of heresy'—and then Voltaire added 'But since you are curious about these irreligious works and keen to refute them, I'll look out a few copies, and send them to you at the first opportunity' (D11978). There, in a nutshell, was Voltaire's publicity campaign. The book was banned in Paris, so Voltaire was promising Damilaville to send him some copies which he could circulate in the capital; and at the same time, there were a few choice sentences of denial which Damilaville could read out on any appropriate occasion. In fact, Voltaire used a range of defensive strategies.

To begin with, he could simply deny. To d'Alembert in Paris, 'I beg you to declare that I have no part in the *Pocket Dictionary*' (D12073). No matter that d'Alembert knew perfectly he was the author: his role was simply to repeat the lie. A second strategy was to suggest that the true author was a certain theology student called 'Dubut'. This tactic was not an unqualified success: Voltaire calls him young in one letter, and old in the next, and he can't quite get the name right, hesitating between Dubut, Dubu, Desbuttes . . . And a third strategy was to suggest that the *Dictionary* was a collective work, thereby minimizing the significance of his own particular contribution. Again to d'Alembert he wrote: 'This collection is the work of several hands as you will have easily noticed. People insist with amazing fury on believing me to be the author' (D12090). Voltaire's desire to invent stories at moments got the better of him: not only was his participation in the *Dictionary* part of a collective enterprise, he suggested, but he became involved merely to help a large family who were in need (D12137)—the pathos was not persuasive and this version was soon dropped. The most effective lies were the simplest, and Voltaire fell back on the notion of a collective work: to any number of correspondents in the autumn of 1764, Voltaire repeated that this work was by several authors, even 'a collection of pieces already known taken from different writers' (D12159). Better still, the work was by 'a society of men of letters', a phrase which echoes the title page of the *Encyclopédie* which had begun to appear in 1751. So he could reassure a correspondent in December 1764: 'It is certain that the *Portatif* is not by me, and that this work is by a society of men of letters who are well known abroad' (D12266). This fiction, in being so often repeated, began to acquire an aura of truth, or at least of familiarity. The first English translation of the *Dictionary* appeared promptly in 1765, and its title is interesting: *The Philosophical Dictionary for the Pocket. Written in French by a society of men of letters, and translated into English [. . .], corrected by the authors.* The English translator seems to have been taken in by Voltaire's protestations; or perhaps he too found the notion of collective authorship a convenient fig leaf when publishing what was a controversial work even in England.

This whole comedy of denial was something of a fixture in Voltaire's comic repertoire—he had stage-managed something similar after the publication of the equally anonymous *Candide* in 1759. But it did have a serious side too. Voltaire had published his book anonymously, and the authorities, in order to prosecute him, would have needed proof that he was the author. Everyone knew that Voltaire was the author, but so long as they had no absolute *proof*, then he was safe from prosecution. Anonymity was a perfectly respectable, and legally sensible, means of publishing a dangerous work. Only Jean-Jacques Rousseau thought it improper to refuse to sign your name on a title page; and needless to say, Voltaire thought Rousseau's scruples ridiculous. But Voltaire's insistent claims that the *Dictionary* was a collective work are intriguing in so far as they contain a tiny grain of truth, to which we will return.

One theme dominates everything else in the *Dictionary*: the critique of the Bible. Beginning with 'Abraham', Voltaire opens *in medias res* with an attack on the whole biblical tradition, as the patriarch of Ferney goes head to head with Abraham the first patriarch of Israel. In the Qur'an, Islam is referred to as 'the religion of Abraham', so to begin with the person seen as a founding figure of not just one but two faiths is a bold opening: from the outset, Christianity's claim to uniqueness is relativized. Voltaire's particular focus is on the Old Testament: he shows that the world view which it presents, far from being inspired by God, derives from earlier pagan structures of myth; it paints a picture of God which is absurd and cruel, and expounds views that are repugnant, even immoral. This is a world view at odds with the findings of modern science, and moreover one which is incoherent and contradictory, a work of fiction in fact. This critique of the Judaeo-Christian tradition was widely shared by the freethinkers of the Enlightenment, but none of the other *philosophes* could rival Voltaire's learning in the subject. He knew the enemy better than anyone else, and writes with a depth of historical knowledge (even if he presents it tendentiously) which cannot fail to impress, at times intimidate, the reader. Voltaire is gentler with the New Testament; he may not have fully shared its spiritual values, but he was in sympathy with its ethical core. Throughout, Voltaire 'desacralizes' religious faith, subjecting it to the pragmatic test of how it helps mankind. So in the article 'Baptism', he considers the sacrament as an image: 'In itself, any sign is immaterial: God attaches his grace to the sign he is pleased to choose'—in other words, claims to transcendence are circular and meaningless. What matters is practical, ethical action: 'Philosophy'—by which he means reasoned reflection—'brings peace to the soul' (article 'Fanaticism'). Alongside the articles on religion, a smaller but important subset deals with philosophy (including 'Good, Sovereign Good', 'All is Good', 'Great Chain of Being', 'Great Chain of Events', 'On Free Will', 'End. Final Causes', 'Sensation'). Politics is touched on (for example 'States, Governments', 'Tyranny', 'War'), the rights of man ('Equality'), and justice ('Civil and Ecclesiastical Laws')—this last theme will acquire more importance in future revisions. And finally, perhaps surprisingly, we find a couple of articles on aesthetic topics ('Beauty', 'Criticism').[5] Taken as a whole, then,

---

[5] See N. Cronk, 'L'Article "Critique" et la présence de la poésie dans le *Dictionnaire philosphique portatif*', *Méthode!*, 14 (2009), 155–60.

Voltaire offers us in parallel a critique of the Judaeo-Christian tradition, and an alternative system of belief grounded in reason. All mankind can acknowledge a Supreme Being, who created the universe and who punishes evil. What more do we need? All that matters for Voltaire is the practical effect of this belief: the happiness of individuals, prospering in a tolerant society. The individual exercise of critical reason is essential to this world view—and this perhaps explains the otherwise puzzling inclusion in the work of articles dealing with beauty and literary criticism. Article after article makes reference to the Supreme Being, and yet there is no article 'Deism'—for the simple reason that Deism is at the core of the whole edifice of the *Dictionary*.

The reader is immediately struck by the form of this work. The eighteenth century was a great age of dictionaries, and two particular models stand out. The first is Pierre Bayle's *Dictionnnaire historique et critique* (1697), a pioneering expression of scepticism that exercised an enormous influence on the thinkers of the French Enlightenment. Some of Voltaire's articles in the *Dictionary*, beginning with the first, 'Abraham', draw much of their material from Bayle. The second model is the great *Encyclopédie* edited by Diderot and d'Alembert, which had as its ambitious purpose to gather together knowledge on all subjects, filtered through a 'philosophical' (Enlightened) viewpoint. Voltaire's response to the *Encyclopédie* is complex. First, there are personal considerations. The earliest volumes had begun to appear from 1751, when Voltaire was with Frederick in Germany, and it was only in 1754 that d'Alembert invited Voltaire to become a collaborator; his first articles appeared in volume 5 (1755), and even then d'Alembert would only entrust him with articles of a safe nature, like 'Taste', 'Genius', or 'History'. Voltaire repeatedly dropped hints that he would like to tackle a meatier philosophical topic, but d'Alembert—or was it Diderot?—was clearly not keen on his closer involvement. Voltaire remained a prominent contributor (author of some forty-five articles in all), but one confined to non-controversial articles, which was not a position that suited him. After the appearance of volume 7 in 1757, the publication of the *Encyclopédie* was halted by the authorities; Diderot was unwilling to accept Voltaire's suggestion that publication could continue abroad, and the project seemed blocked for the foreseeable future; the following year Voltaire decided to cease his collaboration. Secondly, Voltaire was always attuned to questions of readership, and readership was determined by the price of books. The *Encyclopédie* was an enormously costly enterprise, and Voltaire poked fun at the notion that books so expensive could ever be thought dangerous: 'The king justified his confiscation: he had been warned that the twenty-one folio volumes that were to be found on the dressing-table of every lady were the most dangerous thing in the world for the kingdom of France.' Writing to d'Alembert about the *Encyclopédie* in April 1766, Voltaire is trenchant on the relationship between price and readership:

I should really like to know what harm can be caused by a book costing a hundred *écus*. Twenty in-folio volumes will never cause a revolution; it's the little pocket books at thirty *sous* you have to be wary of. If the gospels had cost 1,200 sesterces, the Christian religion would never have got off the ground. (D13235)

Thirdly, Voltaire had misgivings about the intimidating scale of the encyclopedic project. The very drive for completeness implicit in the enterprise inhibited not just the volume's portability but its polemical thrust. Voltaire undoubtedly admired such articles as Deleyre's 'Fanatisme' ('Fanaticism', 1756) or Diderot's 'Intolérance' ('Intolerance'), which would appear in 1765. But they are buried in a mass of other articles less interesting and less well written, and Voltaire was highly critical of certain long, verbose, and sometimes poorly written articles. His own strong preference was always for prose which was brief and incisive.

The *Encyclopédie* came to a halt, as we have seen, in 1757 at the letter 'G', so when Voltaire published his own *Pocket Philosophical Dictionary* in 1764, no one knew when or if the *Encyclopédie* would ever be completed (in the event, the remaining volumes 8–17 were published all together in December 1765). The article 'Idol, idolater, idolatry' Voltaire had written for the *Encyclopédie*, and he redeployed it in the *Dictionary*. In a letter to d'Argental (D12155), Voltaire suggests that other articles ('Love', 'Self-Love', 'Love Called Socratic Love', 'Friendship') had also originally been destined for the *Encyclopédie*, but this does not seem altogether persuasive. What is clearly the case, however, is that in some articles in the *Dictionary*, Voltaire is in dialogue with articles in the *Encyclopédie*. This can be explicit, as when at the end of 'Certain, Certainty', a footnote refers the reader directly to the article on the same subject in the *Encyclopédie*. In other cases, as with the articles 'Good, Sovereign good' or 'Beauty', the reply remains implicit, but nonetheless clear to any reader who knew the corresponding article in the *Encyclopédie*.

The *Encyclopédie* undoubtedly provides a stimulus for some of the topics which Voltaire treats in his own work, but in other respects Voltaire deliberately sets his face against this model. Voltaire's *Dictionary* is more of a spoof dictionary than a real encyclopedia. It is a collection of mostly short articles, arranged apparently at random with no other structure than the arbitrary shape of the alphabet: it is the happy chance of the alphabet—or is it?—that a discussion of 'Christianity' is immediately followed by an equally serious discussion of 'Circumcision'. But behind the serendipity of the alphabet, the recurrent themes are linked. At the end of 'Chain of Events', the narrator announces that he will return to the subject, 'perhaps', when he reaches discussion of fate. And at the end of 'Fate', he invites the reader to move on to 'liberty' ('On Free Will') and the letter L. He talks about friendship, and comes on to homosexuality: 'It's a topic I'll be coming back to later,' he confides. Freed from the obligation to cover everything, Voltaire focuses on what he considers really important—though of course the article titles do not always prepare us for what to expect. Most of all, Voltaire cultivates an aesthetic of brevity. With a few notable exceptions, like 'Christianity', most articles are short, and the writing is concise, pithy, forceful.

Voltaire's Voices

Unlike the *Encyclopédie*, Voltaire's *Pocket Philosophical Dictionary* is focused on one message. But Voltaire presents his message not by means of a solo voice, but with a bravura polyphonic performance. To begin with, the fragmented structure of the *Dictionary* encourages the multiplication of voices: with each article, the reader has the impression of a fresh start. In two articles, moreover, it really is the case that Voltaire is not the (primary) author. As he came under increasing pressure to name the collaborators in his alleged society of men of letters, as we saw above, he began to name Abauzit as the author of 'Apocalypse' and Polier de Bottens as the author of 'Messiah'. This was long thought to be a fiction—one more to add to the list—, and it was only in the course of the twentieth century that it was realized that Voltaire was, confusingly, telling the truth. The article 'Apocalypse' is very largely the text of a clandestine manuscript which he slightly rewrote (the original manuscript was subsequently published in 1770): in taking over an anonymous work, he was not being dishonest, for we can suppose that at least some of his readers might have recognized the borrowing. In the first half of the eighteenth century in France, many scholarly critiques of the Bible had circulated in the form of clandestine manuscripts, and in absorbing one such text into his own *Dictionary*, Voltaire was gesturing towards his own intellectual roots. 'Messiah' poses a different problem. Voltaire had recruited Polier de Bottens, a prominent Swiss pastor, to write articles for the *Encyclopédie*, but the banning of that project had delayed their publication. So Voltaire included the article in abbreviated form in his own *Dictionnaire*, in advance of its full publication in the *Encyclopédie* the following year. It is remarkable how the radical voices of Abauzit and Polier de Bottens merge with Voltaire's, confirmation that much of the *Pocket Philosophical Dictionary*, at the level of the argument at least, is not especially original.

The presence in the *Dictionary* of these two imported voices encourages us to look more carefully at the whole question of voice within this work. Voltaire writes with an 'I' which is disarmingly personal. When we read in 'Love Called Socratic Love' the final sentence, 'I just don't believe there was ever a civilized country that made laws that went counter to morality' (p. 22), we have the feeling that it is Voltaire himself who is speaking, and more than that, that he is speaking directly to us, the readers. In 'Cannibals', the narrator reminisces about a time in 1725 when 'four savages' were brought to the court at Fontainebleau, 'and I had the honour of speaking with them' (p. 26). Can this be true? Voltaire tells the story on several other occasions, and he was at Fontainebleau that year for the marriage of Louis XV, so presumably this is Voltaire speaking in person. Similarly in 'Body', the narrator drops into the conversation that 'I had a few conversations with [Berkeley] a long time ago' (p. 68), and again, since we know that Voltaire did meet the Irish philosopher, we are reassured that we are listening to Voltaire's 'real' voice. But we have to be careful. In 'On Laws', the narrator tells a story heard 'during the last trip I made from India to France' (p. 178): since Voltaire himself never made the journey from India to France, the 'I' who is speaking to us here so confidently is an invented voice, and not Voltaire's own.

The more closely we look, the more dizzying these different

voices become. The article 'Grace' is an eloquent attack on the jargon
of theologians, written in an appealingly informal style. The narrator's
voice appears in quotation marks, a mystery which is resolved only in
the last sentence of the article: 'It's Marcus Aurelius talking, not me'
(p. 153). Needless to add, Marcus Aurelius is not the author of the
article attributed to him, but as a wise ruler, he lends pagan grav-
itas to the discussion of a Christian topic. The article 'Superstition'
presents itself as a 'Chapter taken from Cicero, Seneca, and Plutarch'
(p. 239), which is not strictly true; but those three writers are known
to have written on the subject of superstition, and of course it helps
Voltaire's argument to be able to suggest that his ideas about religious
superstition are independent of the Christian tradition. The whole
of 'Glory' is a speech delivered in the voice of the dervishes' august
leader Ben-al-Betif, and his deistic message is all the more powerful for being expressed through this apparently alien voice. Another
variation is to do away altogether with the single narrator, and several
articles are composed formally as dialogues between two voices (the
three 'Catechisms', 'On Free Will', 'God', 'Fraud'). Voltaire even uses
the hallowed device of the manuscript—a fictional trick as old as *Don
Quixote*—to suggest that he is merely passing on something which he
has found, something for which he is not responsible. In the article
'God', the dialogue between Logomachos and Dondindac 'has been
found in a manuscript in the Constantinople library' (p. 120). The
dialogue of the 'Chinese Catechism' is more ambitious: it postures
as a translation from Chinese via Latin, and Voltaire goes so far as to
identify the number of the manuscript in the Vatican Library. It does
not of course exist, but it is at least a pleasing fantasy that this robust
exposition of deism was readily available to a succession of popes.
This polyphonic effect is further enhanced in subsequent reworkings
of the text, notably in the 1767 revision in which Voltaire introduces
the names of a number of fictive authors.[6]

Different narrating voices speak in different articles, then, but in
addition, each article contains within it traces of other voices. No
reader can fail to notice the large number of quotations found in
the text, sometimes attributed, sometimes not. There are frequent

---

[6] See N. Cronk, 'Qui parle dans le *Dictionnaire philosophique portatif*? Polyvocalité et
posture auctoriale', in L. Macé (ed.), *Lectures du 'Dictionnaire philosophique'* (Rennes,
2008), 177–95.

citations of classical authors (Latin rather than Greek), and Voltaire tends to assume that his reader shares his own Jesuit education: the Latin quotations are rarely glossed. Even in this highly polemical work, Voltaire does not try to conceal the pleasure he takes in poetry: the article 'Idol' refers to Cicero and Horace, then fires off in rapid succession, in the original Latin, extracts from Martial, Ovid, Statius, and Lucan. Other quotations can be unattributed, some are invented: the whole of the article 'Civil and Ecclesiastical Laws' is made up of 'notes, found amongst the papers of a jurist' (p. 182)—a meaningless explanation, but the juxtaposition of fragments which follows is powerful precisely because we cannot pin down with precision the origin of the speaking voice. Voltaire is not above quoting himself, though silently, as when at the end of 'Toleration' the narrator reminds us of something we have been told before: the allusion is to a passage from Voltaire's earlier *Letters concerning the English Nation*.

The effect overall is to create a patchwork of consonant voices, precisely that 'society of men of letters' whom Voltaire claimed had written the work: in a sense, he was not wrong. So we are faced by a whole range of voices rather than one singular voice; and yet by a peculiar trick of mirrors, all the voices seem to be Voltaire's. Even when he quotes Cicero, we have the sensation of an act of ventriloquism, by which Voltaire speaks through him. The voices can be Chinese or Classical, real or fake, living or dead, attributed or anonymous, it all amounts to the same thing: they all believe in a Supreme Being, they all sound like Voltaire. But as the voices shift, so must our stance as readers: this is a text which is immediately appealing to the reader, not least through its humour, but one which also makes the reader work hard. Many articles open with questions addressed directly to the reader: 'What is toleration? It is the prerogative of humanity' ('Toleration', p. 242). And the position of the reader is not always a comfortable one, as in the article 'Grace', where we are addressed from the start as papal advisers: 'You holy papal advisers in post in the Rome of today, you illustrious and infallible theologians, I defer to no one in my respect for your divine decisions' (p.152). In each article, the reader has to ask afresh, 'Who is speaking?', and also, more disarmingly, 'Who is reading?'

This plurality of voices, far from creating discordance (or even a true dialogue), has the effect of magnifying Voltaire's message. It is rare for us to be in any doubt about his true intentions. In 'Messiah',

in discussing the Jewish hatred of Christian doctrine, at moments
the narrator strikes a tone that comes close to sounding anti-Semitic.
Voltaire adopts the voice of a Christian bigot, but we fleetingly wonder
if it might also be Voltaire's own voice—are there limits perhaps to his
own toleration? His basic technique for attacking Christianity is to
attack its historical Judaic roots: this is not in itself anti-Semitic, it is
a form of polemical history, but it cannot be denied that this aggressive style can make twenty-first-century readers uneasy. It is also
true that some of his remarks about Islam can seem uncomfortably
harsh to modern sensibilities, but Voltaire is not generally accused of
being anti-Islamic. In truth, his hatred was focused on the Christian
fanatics of France of his day, it is they who are his prime target. His
attacks on intolerance in other religions are always a way of attacking Christianity by the back door. We live in a different world from
Voltaire's, and the question of religious intolerance has inevitably a
different resonance for us. What cannot be denied is that this question remains as topical now as when Voltaire wrote. His purpose was
to write a hard-hitting book which would make his readers uncomfortable, and in that he succeeded, and continues to succeed.

A unifying and humane effect is created by his confidential tone
of voice, and his cultivation of a pseudo-intimate tone is a striking
characteristic of the book. Voltaire was of course steeped in the poetry
of Horace, much of which he knew by heart, and his debt to Horatian
sermo, the Roman poet's assumption of a colloquial voice, is considerable. Another constant of these disparate (but not different) voices is
of course the mode of irony. In the article 'Flood', modern scientific
evidence is presented which might seem to cast doubt on the biblical
account of the Flood. But the narrator reassures us: 'None of this
casts doubt on the veracity of the account of the universal flood given
in the Pentateuch: quite the reverse. That was a miracle, so must be
believed; and, being a miracle, it's not subject to the laws of physics' (p. 169). Readers must make of this what they will. The narrator
explains the difference between idolaters and those of true faith: 'The
difference between them and us is not that they had images and we
don't: the difference is that their images pictured the fantastic creatures of a false religion whereas ours stand for real people professing a
true faith' (p. 157). So far, so good, and we note the 'us' which assumes
common thinking between narrator and reader. But then comes an
example, and the whole edifice comes crashing down: '[The Greeks]

had Asclepius and his goat and we have St Roch and his dog' (p. 157). The ironic parallel forces us to change perspective. Both Hume and Gibbon, the two greatest ironists of the British eighteenth century, deployed withering irony, notably on the subject of miracles, and both were familiar with (though not always uncritical of) Voltaire.

Irony, it is said, distances the reader, and introduces a caustic or chilly note. True, but it is important to realize that beyond Voltaire's hallmark irony (which is well known), there is also a voice of strong emotion (which is less well known, and less commented on). In the article 'Fanaticism' he describes in forceful language those who are touched by fanaticism as mad and ugly, suffering an infection of the brain, he says, which puts them beyond the reach of reason. At the end of the article 'Falseness of Human Virtues', the narrator speaks of the arrogance of those who would put religious doctrine before virtue, then he breaks off: 'Such arrogance is revolting. I'll say no more, because I'm starting to get angry' (p. 139). This is no affectation: Voltaire writes with passion, and his strength of feeling communicates itself through the labyrinth of different voices. If the book caused such shock waves from the moment of its publication, that is surely because these passionate voices disturb us.

A Work in Progress

The first edition of *A Pocket Philosophical Dictionary* contains seventy-three articles; this is the version which we translate here, as being the edition which created such scandal on its first appearance.[7] But it would be wrong to give an impression of the *Dictionary* as a text which is fixed or stable. Like other of Voltaire's longer prose works, the *Letters concerning the English Nation*, for example, or his universal history, the *Essai sur les mœurs* (*Essay on Manners*), this is a work which is always in movement, not a 'finished' work but a work forever in progress. Critical editions in the past have not understood this essential feature of Voltaire's writing. He always privileges movement over stasis, perhaps on the principle that it is harder to hit a moving target, perhaps because he is more interested in provoking questions than in

---

[7] On the aesthetic integrity of this edition, see S. Menant, 'Composition et effets de lecture dans le *Portatif*', in L. Macé (ed.), *Lectures du 'Dictionnaire philosophique'* (Rennes, 2008), 23–33.

shaping answers, perhaps simply because he dislikes putting a final full stop at the end of any discussion. Whatever the reason, there is a fundamental fluidity about the way in which Voltaire conceives of his longer prose works which makes them seem surprisingly modern.

In successive editions Voltaire continued to add other articles, so that by 1769 the *Dictionary* had reached two volumes and 118 articles: the work was no longer 'portable' (*portatif*), and the word was dropped from the title. The *Dictionary* attracted many critics, and the additions which Voltaire made to his work, either in the form of additions to existing articles or as completely new articles, are often ripostes to these criticisms. The dialogue inaugurated by the book thus continues as a dialogue with its critics, and Voltaire manages, always, to have the last word. These additions thrived on the controversy therefore, but do not fundamentally alter the polemical thrust of the work. It could even be argued that the initial structure of the first edition was gradually lost as the intrusive additions became more numerous.

Perhaps Voltaire himself felt this, because after 1769 he left the *Pocket Philosophical Dictionary* on one side, and concentrated on a new project that was in part a continuation of the *Dictionary*, the *Questions sur l'Encyclopédie* (*Questions about the Encyclopédie*). This is another alphabetical dictionary, and it appeared in seven volumes, between 1770 and 1772. It was a best-seller, and though little studied until now,[8] it was in many respects a continuation of the *Dictionary*. Many of the articles were revised versions of those in the earlier *Dictionary*, but Voltaire now extended the dialogue with the *Encyclopédie* and enlarged the range of topics treated. The anti-biblical critique was no longer so central (the debate had moved on since 1764, and some of the arguments had been won), the treatment of issues concerning law and justice was extended, and in addition to these already familiar topics, Voltaire now introduced new articles on a whole range of topics that interested him. The familiar narrative voice remains, but the range of subjects addressed is now broader and more personal. But Voltaire never, ever, ceased his critique of the Bible which is at the heart of the *Pocket Philosophical Dictionary*. He went on to write *Un chrétien contre six juifs* (*One Christian against Six Jews*, 1776) and

---

[8] The first critical edition began to appear in 2007, ed. N. Cronk and C. Mervaud (*OCV* 38–).

La Bible enfin expliquée (*The Bible Finally explained*, 1776). When he died in 1778, at the age of 84, he was working on a new project, an *Histoire de l'établissement du christianisme* (*History of the Establishment of Christianity*).

In a famous essay, Roland Barthes described Voltaire as 'the last of the happy writers',[9] by which he meant apparently that it was easy for Voltaire to assume a humorous stance because the evils he faced were modest compared to the horrors of our own times. This is to underestimate both Voltaire and the horrors of the eighteenth century. In fact many modern satirists have learned their trade from Voltaire. The caustic black humour of the film *Dr Strangelove* (1964)—full title, *Dr Strangelove, or How I learned to stop worrying and love the bomb*—bears a distinctly Voltairean imprint, not surprisingly since Terry Southern, one of its co-writers, had earlier co-authored the novel *Candy* (1958), a provocative reworking of *Candide*. The *Pocket Philosophical Dictionary* appeared just one year after the end of the Seven Years War, and Voltaire's abhorrence of the stupidity of war, already apparent in *Candide*, is evident again here in the article 'War'. This is a book written in anger, when, as Voltaire himself said, his blood was boiling. The comic verve of this book does not disguise Voltaire's fury, it enhances it. The *Pocket Philosophical Dictionary* caused the controversy that it did, not exactly because of its content, but because of Voltaire's treatment of that content. It was his cheek, his casual impertinence which caused such offence, especially when applied to the sacrosanct subject of the Gospels. In the end, it is Voltaire's voice which is the great outrage of this *Dictionary*. It continues to make us laugh, and to make us uncomfortable.

Voltaire's anger did not let up. In 1765, the year after publishing his *Dictionary*, he published *La Philosophie de l'histoire* (*The Philosophy of History*) which went over much of the same ground already covered, but this time in a more systematic and less fragmented way. And this work was dedicated to Catherine the Great of Russia: Voltaire was determined to force the authorities to face up to what he had to say. His relentlessness shows determination and courage. But the authorities were not of a forgiving mind. In 1765 the French government turned a blind eye to the publication of the remaining volumes of the

---

[9] R. Barthes, 'The Last Happy Writer', in *A Barthes Reader*, ed. S. Sontag (London, 1993), 150–7.

Encyclopédie, which had been blocked since 1757—this was a huge victory for Diderot and for the party of the *philosophes* in general. Yet the following year, 1766, there occurred an incident so appalling that Voltaire's blood would boil all over again.

In Abbeville, in Picardy, a young man, the chevalier de La Barre, was condemned and found guilty, together with other youths, of blasphemy and sacrilege. He was accused of causing damage to a crucifix, of singing anti-religious songs, and of showing disrespect to a religious procession. La Barre's room was searched and a number of compromising books were found, including, it was alleged, the *Pocket Philosophical Dictionary*. At the ensuing trial it was suggested that this book had exercised a corrupting influence on the young man, who was condemned to have his tongue torn out, to be beheaded (a concession, because he was a gentleman), and to have his body burned on a pyre along with a copy of the *Pocket Philosophical Dictionary*. This sentence was confirmed by a court in Paris, and La Barre was executed on 1 July 1766, his body burned along with the copy of Voltaire's book. The trial and punishment exemplified all too clearly the vices and prejudices laid bare in Voltaire's *Dictionary*: the improper judicial procedure, the disproportionate punishment, the cruelty of religious fanatics, the lack of simple charity shown by some believers. The fact that the authorities felt the need to burn publicly the *Pocket Philosophical Dictionary* rather made Voltaire's point: they were burning him in proxy. A few days later, on 7 July, just after hearing the news of La Barre's execution, Voltaire wrote to Damilaville:

My dear brother, my heart is withered, I am crushed. I never imagined that anyone would blame this most silly and unrestrained piece of madness on people who preach only wisdom and purity of morals. I am tempted to go and die in some foreign land where men are less unjust. I am silent, I have too much to say. (D13394)

Voltaire did not remain silent, he wrote furiously and prolifically. He circulated an anonymous letter (D.app.279), allegedly sent from Abbeville, dated 7 July. Then he wrote the *Relation de la mort du chevalier de La Barre* (*Account of the Death of the Chevalier de La Barre*), dated 15 July, a longer piece, ostensibly addressed to the Italian jurist Beccaria, who in 1764 had just published his *Dei delitti e delle pene* (*On Crimes and Punishments*), a landmark in Enlightenment thinking on this subject.

The *Pocket Philosophical Dictionary* was not an end, but a beginning, and the fight would continue throughout the 1760s, and beyond. In 1836, one Abner Kneeland produced an English version of the *Philosophical Dictionary* which advertises itself on the title page as the 'first American stereotype edition'. Kneeland, a former Universalist minister turned 'pantheist', wanted his edition to be used as a family Bible: 'There is scarcely an article in the whole work but what contains something calculated to liberalize the human mind, and to expand the feelings of benevolence and charity. As a Family Book, therefore, it will be highly valuable for this purpose as long as the Bible is in use.' And to this end, his edition included blank pages, with appropriate headings, for the recording of the family's Births, Deaths, and Marriages, in just the way that Bibles had done in the past. How Voltaire would have rejoiced, if he could have known that in the land of the Founding Fathers, his *Pocket Philosophical Dictionary* would one day replace the Bible.

In the article 'Peter', Voltaire's narrator ponders on the powers attributed to the Pope in the West: part of the explanation, he says, is 'public opinion, which reigns supreme among human beings; it's not that they really do have a settled view: words are a sufficient substitute' (p. 212). That is a lesson which Voltaire puts to good use in this book. Voltaire writes to influence public opinion, in France and beyond. *A Pocket Philosophical Dictionary* does not present an entirely coherent 'philosophy', but that is not its prime purpose. Its main aim is to provoke us into thought and into argument, to liberate us from impostors of every sort who would deny us the freedom to use our own reason. The conclusion to the article 'Sensation' can perhaps stand for the whole book (p. 236): 'What can we conclude from all that? You who can read and think, you conclude.'

NOTE ON THE TEXT

THE *Dictionnaire philosophique portatif* (*Pocket Philosophical Dictionary*) was first published in one volume by Grasset in Geneva in 1764. Both the author and the publisher had to remain anonymous. Voltaire repeatedly revised the work over the next few years, extending the existing articles and adding new ones: there were two new editions of the *Portatif* in 1765, and another in 1767. For the final revision, which appeared in two volumes in 1769, Voltaire appended another recently published text, the dialogue *A.B.C*, and gave the work a new title: *La Raison par alphabet* (*Alphabetical Reason*).

By a long-standing, but confusing, convention, editors and critics call this text the *Dictionnaire philosophique*, misleadingly so, since that is not the title of the editions which Voltaire authorized.

For this translation we have chosen the first edition of 1764, and restored its rightful title. It is the version of the text which caused the initial *succès de scandale* and provoked widespread condemnation.

The articles in the original French edition are not always ordered alphabetically: in this translation, the order and structure of the original has been respected, with the result that in English the sequence is no longer strictly alphabetical. The original French title has been inserted at the head of each article, to help clarify the original structure. Asterisks signal an editorial note at the back of the book; footnotes are by Voltaire.

A remarkable feature of this work is its narrative tone: Voltaire often employs a pseudo-colloquial voice in order to speak directly to his reader. Translations often make the mistake of normalizing or levelling out Voltaire's narrative voice, and we have attempted here to be faithful to the sometimes surprising shifts of register in the original.

NOTE ON THE TRANSLATION

THE educated classes of Europe and America, for whom French was the lingua franca of civilized discourse, were the audience that Voltaire was addressing in 1764. They were the sort of people—intelligent but not erudite—who today are regular readers of *The Economist*, *The Times*, *The Guardian*, *The New York Times*, or *The Washington Post*. So the tone and style of the *Dictionary* should not sound very different from the tone and style adopted by leader-writers and columnists in such publications. Indeed I believe that if Voltaire were writing in English today he would sound rather like a good leader-writer: informal—but not colloquial—in register; in style straightforward, uncomplicated, and above all readable. That is the tone I have tried to achieve in my translation.

Voltaire quotes frequently from the Bible. The version he used was the Latin Vulgate, from which he translated (or paraphrased) the passages he needed. I have used (or paraphrased) the Authorized (King James) Version. It might be argued that the tone which I have sought to adopt—that of a good newspaper columnist—sits ill with the magnificent cadences of Jacobean English. It is my view, however, that the contrast between contemporary British and American usage and the language of the King James Bible tends, if anything, to reinforce the polemical point being made.

Voltaire frequently uses the term *philosophe*, which had a wider meaning in eighteenth-century French than 'philosopher' does in contemporary English; indeed, it often meant 'freethinker'. Rather than second-guess Voltaire here, I have translated *philosophe* as 'philosopher' throughout; but in certain contexts the reader may wish to bear in mind the broader definition.

Wherever Voltaire quotes French or Italian poetry I have rendered it into blank (or vaguely rhyming) English verse. He often paraphrases English writers as well as the Vulgate, and where this is the case it is faithfully reflected in the translation.

On gender I have followed current good translation practice in avoiding 'men' in rendering '*les hommes*' by using 'human beings', 'humanity', or 'humankind' instead. On the other hand I have not used the ungrammatical plural 'their' with a singular subject—the device by which some writers try to avoid 'his/her'—but employ instead a word like 'people' which is a gender-neutral plural. In general, my philosophy of translation is the same as that of the translator and publisher Christopher MacLehose, who writes: 'My preference remains to seek the best reflection of the text in English rather than to sacrifice a more felicitous rendering in English for the sake of being its mirror.' I have tried to follow his advice. And, wherever possible, I use simple, mainly Germanic, words rather than those of Romance origin (e.g. 'understanding' rather than 'intelligence', 'brotherhood' rather than 'fraternity', and so on). Translations from the French which sound stilted or rhetorical often do so because the translator has not selected enough words of English derivation; and Voltaire, of all people, should never sound stilted or rhetorical.

John Fletcher

SELECT BIBLIOGRAPHY

Critical Editions

Dictionnaire philosophique, 2 vols., directed by Christiane Mervaud (*OCV* 35–6, Oxford, Voltaire Foundation, 1994). The definitive scholarly edition and an essential tool of reference.

Dictionnaire philosophique, ed. Gerhardt Stenger, Garnier-Flammarion (Paris, 2010). The best paperback edition of the French text.

Electronic Enlightenment: Voltaire's prolific correspondence, ed. Theodore Besterman (51 vols., 1968–77), explains the hinterland to this text. Besterman's monumental edition is searchable online, as part of *Electronic Enlightenment* (distributed by OUP): see <http://www.e-enlightenment.com>.

General Background

Aldridge, A. O., *Voltaire and the Century of Light* (Princeton, 1975).

Barber, W. H., *Leibniz in France from Arnauld to Voltaire: A Study in French Reactions to Leibnizianism, 1670–1760* (Oxford, 1955).

Bien, David D., *The Calas Affair* (Princeton, 1960).

Brumfitt, J. H., *Voltaire Historian* (Oxford, 1958).

Cronk, Nicholas, 'Voltaire and the 1760s: The Rule of the Patriarch', in N. Cronk (ed.), *Voltaire and the 1760s: Essays for John Renwick*, *SVEC* 2008: 10, 9–21.

—— (ed.), *The Cambridge Companion to Voltaire* (Cambridge, 2009).

De Beer, Gavin, and Rousseau, André-Michel, *Voltaire's British Visitors*, *SVEC*, 49 (Oxford, 1967).

Delattre, André, 'Voltaire and the Ministers of Geneva', *Church History*, 13 (1944), 243–54.

Gay, Peter, *Voltaire's Politics: The Poet as Realist*, 2nd edn. (New Haven, 1988).

Gray, John, *Voltaire* (London, 1998).

Hampson, Norman, *The Enlightenment* (Harmondsworth, 1968).

Israel, Jonathan I., *Enlightenment Contested: Philosophy, Modernity, and the Emancipation of Man, 1670–1752* (Oxford, 2006) [ch. 29 treats 'Voltaire's Enlightenment'].

Kors, Alan Charles, *Atheism from the Reformation to the Enlightenment* (Oxford, 1992).

Manuel, Frank E., *The Eighteenth Century Confronts the Gods* (New York, 1967).

Mason, Haydn, *Pierre Bayle and Voltaire* (Oxford University Press, 1963).
Nadler, Steven, *The Best of All Possible Worlds: A Story of philosophers, God, and Evil in the Age of Reason* (Princeton, 2008).
O'Brien, Karen, *Narratives of Enlightenment: Cosmopolitan History from Voltaire to Gibbon* (Cambridge, 1997).
Pearson, Roger, *The Fables of Reason: A Study of Voltaire's 'contes philosophiques'* (Oxford, 1993).
——*Voltaire Almighty: A Life in the Pursuit of Freedom* (London, 2005).
Porter, Roy, *The Enlightenment* (London, 2001).
Rossi, Paolo, *The Dark Abyss of Time: The History of the Earth and the History of Nations from Hooke to Vico* (Chicago, 1984).
Schwarzbach, Bertram Eugene, *Voltaire's Old Testament Criticism* (Geneva, 1971).
Spink, J. S., *French Free-Thought from Gassendi to Voltaire* (London, 1960).

Critical Studies

Gay, Peter, *The Party of Humanity* (New York, 1963), 7–54.
Monty, Jeanne R., 'Voltaire's Rhetoric: The Use of Written Evidence in the Alphabetical Works', *SVEC* 120 (1974), 41–77.
Perkins, Merle L., 'Theme and Form in Voltaire's Alphabetical Works', *SVEC* 120 (1974), 7–40.
Todd, Christopher, *Voltaire: Dictionnaire philosophique* (London, 1980).
Trapnell, W. H., *Voltaire and His Portable Dictionary* (Frankfurt am Main, 1972).

Critical studies in French

Macé, Laurence (ed.), *Lectures du 'Dictionnaire philosophique'* (Rennes, 2008).
Menant, Sylvain, *Littérature par alphabet: Le 'Dictionnaire philosophique' de Voltaire*, rev. edn. (Paris, 2008).
Mervaud, Christiane, *Le 'Dictionnaire philosophique' de Voltaire*, new edn. (Oxford and Paris, 2008) [with extensive further bibliography].
Monty, Jeanne R., *Étude sur le style polémique de Voltaire: Le 'Dictionnaire philosophique'*, *SVEC* 44 (Geneva, 1966).
Moureaux, José-Michel, 'Voltaire apôtre: De la parodie au mimétisme', *Poétique*, 66 (1986), 159–77.

Other Works of Voltaire in English Translation

Candide and Other Stories, trans. Roger Pearson, Oxford World's Classics (Oxford, 1990; new edn., 2006).

Letters concerning the English Nation, ed. Nicholas Cronk, Oxford World's Classics (Oxford, 1994; rev. edn., 2005) [the 1733 English edn. which preceded the 1734 publication of the *Lettres philosophiques*].

Political Writings, trans. David Williams, Cambridge Texts in the History of Political Thought (Cambridge, 1994).

Select Letters of Voltaire, trans. Theodore Besterman (London, 1963).

Treatise on Tolerance and Other Writings, trans. Simon Harvey and Brian Masters, Cambridge Texts in the History of Political Thought (Cambridge, 2000).

Further Reading in Oxford World's Classics

Descartes, René, *A Discourse on the Method*, trans. and ed. Ian Maclean.

Diderot, Denis, *Jacques the Fatalist*, trans. and ed. David Coward.

—— *The Nun*, trans. and ed. Russell Goulbourne.

—— *Rameau's Nephew* and *First Satire*, trans. Margaret Mauldon, ed. Nicholas Cronk.

Graffigny, Françoise de, *Letters of a Peruvian Woman*, trans. and ed. Jonathan Mallinson.

Johnson, Samuel, *The History of Rasselas*, ed. Thomas Keymer.

Montesquieu, *Persian Letters*, trans. Margaret Mauldon, ed. Andrew Kahn.

Rousseau, Jean-Jacques, *Confessions*, trans. Angela Scholar, ed. Patrick Coleman.

—— *Discourse on Political Economy and The Social Contract*, trans. Christopher Betts.

—— *Discourse on the Origin of Inequality*, trans. Franklin Philip, ed. Patrick Coleman.

—— *Reveries of the Solitary Walker*, trans. and ed. Russell Goulbourne.

Swift, Jonathan, *Gulliver's Travels*, ed. Claude Rawson and Ian Higgins.

A CHRONOLOGY OF VOLTAIRE

1694   21 Nov.: officially born as François-Marie Arouet in Paris, the second (surviving) son of a successful notary and tax official. Unofficially Voltaire himself claimed to have been born nine months earlier, on 20 February, the illegitimate son of the chevalier Guérin de Rochebrune (or Roquebrune), a writer of popular songs and scion of an ancient, aristocratic family from the Haute Auvergne.

1701   13 July: death of Voltaire's mother.

1704–11 Educated at the Jesuit college of Louis-le-Grand, the Eton of its day.

1712   Becomes a law student, but spends most of his time writing and mixing in smart, libertine company.

1713   Packed off first to Caen and then to a position in the French embassy in Holland. Brought home swiftly when on the point of eloping with his Protestant first love, Olympe Dunoyer, known as Pimpette.

1715   1 Sept.: death of Louis XIV.

1716   May–Oct.: exiled from Paris to Sully-sur-Loire, suspected of having written a satire against the Regent, Philippe d'Orléans.

1717   16/17 May: arrested and imprisoned without trial in the Bastille on account of a further political satire.

1718   Apr.: released and banished for six months to Chatenay, near Sceaux, about six miles from Paris. June: adopts nearly anagrammatic pseudonym of Voltaire, 18 Nov.: his first tragedy and first major work, *Œdipe*, is staged and is a great and immediate success. The Regent gives him a gold medal and a pension; George I sends a gold medal and a watch.

1718–26 A period of successful financial speculation, social prestige, and literary productiveness: *La Henriade* (1723), an epic poem about Henry IV (1553–1610) on the theme of religious intolerance, is regarded as a masterpiece and establishes his reputation once and for all. Nov. 1723: almost dies of smallpox and saved only, as he commented, by drinking two hundred pints of lemonade.

1726   After responding in kind to a slur on his origins from the worthless but aristocratic Chevalier de Rohan, is beaten up by the latter's servants as the Chevalier watches from a carriage. Subsequently threatens a duel (supposedly an impertinence on the part of a bourgeois). 17/18 Apr.: the Rohan family have him thrown into the Bastille. May: goes into exile in England.

1726–8 Exile in England. Discovers the work of Isaac Newton. Mixes with Bolingbroke, Pope, and Swift.

1729–33 Literary activity in Paris, including further tragedies and his first attempt at writing history (the *Histoire de Charles XII*, 1731).

1733 Publishes his *Letters concerning the English Nation* in London.

1734 His French version of the *Letters* (with the addition of a letter on Pascal) published in Paris as the *Lettres philosophiques*. These are condemned and burnt by the Parlement of Paris. Voltaire leaves the capital to live in a *ménage à trois* with his mistress Mme du Châtelet at her home at Cirey.

1734–43 A period of happiness with Mme du Châtelet, as well as considerable philosophical and literary activity (beginning with the *Traité de métaphysique* written in 1734). Aug. 1736: receives his first letter from Frederick of Prussia. June 1739: sends Frederick of Prussia the *Voyage du baron de Gangan*, a first version of *Micromégas*.

1743 Begins to enjoy a brief period of favour at court, with the support of Mme de Pompadour and despite Louis XV's distrust. Elected a Fellow of the Royal Society in London.

1745 Appointed Historiographer to the King at Versailles.

1746 25 Apr.: elected to the Académie Française.

1747 A first version of *Zadig* published under the title *Memnon*, this being the first of his stories to appear in print.

1748 Sept.: *Zadig* published. Also *The Way Things Are* (*Le Monde comme il va*).

1749 10 Sept.: death of Mme du Châtelet of puerperal fever following the birth of a daughter, who also died after a few days. The father was the soldier and poet Jean-François de Saint-Lambert (1716–1803).

1750 June: departure for the court of Frederick of Prussia.

1752 *Micromégas* published.

1753 March: leaves Frederick's court after relations between the two become impossible. Illegally detained in Frankfurt by Frederick's men. Takes up temporary residence in Colmar.

1755   Settles at Les Délices on the outskirts of Geneva. 1 Nov.: the Lisbon earthquake, of which news reaches him before 24 Nov.

1756   Publishes the *Poème sur le désastre de Lisbonne*; and the first complete official text of his world history, the *Essai sur les mœurs* (*Essay on Manners*), which was to be reprinted sixteen times in the next thirty years.

1759   Jan.–Feb.: publication of *Candide*. Moves into the château at Ferney near Geneva, where he lived for the remainder of his life. He refurbishes the chapel and adorns its façade with the inscription: 'Deo erexit Voltaire' ('a fine word between two great names', as a waggish poet, the abbé Delille, later remarked)—the chapel being thus dedicated to God, rather than to a saint, and having a figure of Christ over the altar but not a crucifix. He arranged that his own tomb should lie half in and half out of the chapel.

1762   Beginning of the campaign to rehabilitate Calas, and later other victims of religious intolerance.

1763   Publishes *Traité sur la tolérance*.

1764   Publishes *Dictionnaire philosophique portatif*.

1765   Publishes *La Philosophie de l'histoire*. First English translation of *Dictionnaire* published in London, *The Philosophical Dictionary for the Pocket*.

1766   Publishes *Commentaire sur le livre Des délits et des peines*.

1767   Publication of *L'Ingénu*.

1769   Publishes *La Raison par alphabet*.

1770–2 Publishes *Questions sur l'Encyclopédie*.

1773–4 Publication of *Le Taureau blanc* (*The White Bull*).

1774   10 May: death of Louis XV.

1778   Returns to Paris for the production of his penultimate tragedy *Irène* and is acclaimed and fêted by the whole capital. He dies on 30 May. To avoid the indignity of his being refused a decent burial by Parisian church authorities, his body is smuggled out of the capital at dead of night and later buried at Scellières in Champagne. His remains are subsequently transferred to the Panthéon in Paris on 11 July 1791.

A POCKET PHILOSOPHICAL
DICTIONARY

CONTENTS

ABRAHAM

ABRAHAM is one of those names famed throughout Asia Minor and Arabia, like Thoth in Egypt, the first Zoroaster in Persia, Hercules in Greece, Orpheus in Thrace, Odin in the northern countries, and many others, all better known for their celebrity status than for a well-attested place in history. Here I am only talking about profane history; in the case of the Jews (our adversaries and teachers, whom we believe in and detest), because their history has obviously been written by the Holy Ghost himself, our feelings about it are those which are proper. I am referring here only to the Arabs; they claim to descend from Abraham through Ishmael, the patriarch who, they believe, built Mecca and died in that city. The fact is that the seed of Ishmael has been infinitely more favoured by God than the seed of Jacob. Both races have in truth produced thieves; but the Arab thieves have been prodigiously superior to the Jewish thieves. Jacob's descendants conquered only a small country which they then lost; and Ishmael's descendants have conquered a part of Asia, a part of Europe, and a part of Africa, founding an empire vaster than the Roman Empire, and have chased the Jews from the caves that they called the Promised Land.

Judging things only from examples found in our modern histories, it would be fairly difficult for Abraham to have been the father of two different nations; we are told that he was born in Chaldea, the son of a poor potter who earned a living making small clay idols. It is hardly plausible that this potter's son crossed impassable deserts and went on to found Mecca nearly a thousand miles away in the tropics. Had he been a conqueror, he would no doubt have turned to the fine land of Assyria; and if he was, as depicted, only an ordinary man, he could not have founded kingdoms outside his own country.

According to the Book of Genesis he was seventy-five when he left the land of Haran after the death of his father Terah the potter, but Genesis also states that Terah begat Abraham at seventy and lived to the age of two hundred and five, and that Abraham only left Haran after his father's death. On this reckoning it is clear from Genesis itself that Abraham was a hundred and thirty-five when he left Mesopotamia. He went from an idolatrous country to another called Shechem, in Palestine. Why did he go there? Why did he leave the fertile banks of the Euphrates for a land as far off and as barren and stony as that of Shechem? The Chaldean language must have been very different from that of Shechem; it was not a trade centre; Shechem is more than two hundred and fifty miles from Chaldea: deserts have to be crossed to get there: but God wished him to make the journey; he wanted to show him the land his descendants would occupy several centuries after him. The human mind finds it difficult to understand the reasons for such a journey.

Hardly had Abraham arrived in the small mountainous country of Shechem when famine forced him to leave. He went to Egypt with his wife in search of food. It is five hundred miles from Shechem to Memphis; is it natural to go that far to beg for corn, in a country where one does not understand the language? That is an odd journey for someone to undertake at the age of nearly a hundred and forty.

He brought his wife Sarah to Memphis. She was extremely young, almost a child compared to him, since she was only sixty-five years old. Because she was very beautiful he decided to take advantage of her good looks. 'Pretend to be my sister', he said, 'so that people will treat me well for your sake.' He ought rather to have told her, 'Pretend to be my daughter.' The king fell in love with Sarah and gave the supposed brother many sheep, oxen, he-asses, she-asses, camels, men-servants, and maidservants, which proves that Egypt at the time was a very refined and very powerful kingdom, therefore very old, and that brothers who handed over their sisters to the kings of Memphis were handsomely rewarded.

According to Scripture the young Sarah was ninety when God promised her that Abraham, who was then a hundred and sixty, would, before the year was out, get her with child.

Abraham, who liked travelling, went into the horrible desert of Kadesh with his pregnant wife, who was still young and pretty. Sure enough, a king in this desert fell in love with Sarah just as the king of Egypt had done. The father of all believers told the same lie as in Egypt: he gave out that his wife was his sister; as a result of this affair, too, he acquired sheep, oxen, menservants, and maid-servants. Thanks to his wife, it can be said, Abraham became very rich. Commentators have written a prodigious number of volumes to justify his conduct and to reconcile discrepancies in the chronology. The reader is referred to these commentaries, all of them compiled by men of subtle and delicate intellect, excellent thinkers, quite devoid of prejudice and not in the least pedantic.

SOUL
(ÂME)

To see one's soul would be a fine thing. *Know thyself* is an excellent precept, but it is God alone who can put it into practice: who but God can know his own essence?

We call 'soul' that which animates. We know hardly anything else about it, thanks to the limitations of our intelligence. Three-quarters of the human race takes it no further and does not bother about the thinking self; the other quarter goes on looking, but no one has found anything and never will.

Poor philosopher, you see a plant growing and you talk of *growth* and even *soul of growth*. You notice that bodies possess and engender motion, and you say *strength*; you watch your hunting dog learning its job under you, and you exclaim, *instinct*, *sentient soul*; you enjoy joined-up thinking, and you call it *mind*.

But, for goodness' sake, what do you understand by the words 'that flower is growing'? Is there a real being called *growth*? This body pushes another, but does it possess within itself a distinct entity called *strength*? That dog retrieves a partridge, but is there a being called *instinct*? Would you not laugh at a thinker (be he Alexander the Great's tutor in person) who said to you 'All animals are living things, so there is in them a being, a substantial form that is life'?

If a tulip could talk and said to you, 'My growth and I are two beings clearly joined together', would you not make fun of the tulip?

Let us first see what you know, what you are sure of: that you use your feet to walk, that you use your stomach to digest, that you use your whole body to feel, and that you use your head to think. Shall we see if your reason alone has given you enough insight to conclude, without supernatural assistance, that you have a soul?

The first philosophers—both Chaldean and Egyptian—said, 'There must be something in us which produces thought; that something must be very subtle: a breath, fire, ether, a quintessence, a faint image, an entelechy, a number, harmony.' According to the divine Plato, it is a composite of the *same* and of *the other*; and Epicurus, following Democritus, said that the soul was made up of atoms thinking within us. But, friend, how does an atom think? Admit you've no idea.

The opinion which should probably be adopted is that the soul is an immaterial being. But you certainly cannot conceive what an immaterial being is, can you? 'No,' the scholars reply, 'but we know that its nature is to think.' So how do you know this? 'We know it because it thinks.' O scholars, you are as ignorant as Epicurus, I fear! The nature of a stone is to fall, because it falls; but my question is, what makes it fall?

'We know', they go on, 'that a stone has no soul'; I agree with that. 'We know that a negation and an affirmation are not divisible, are not parts of matter'; I'm of the same opinion. But matter—something we know nothing about—possesses qualities that are not material, that are not divisible; it gravitates towards a God-given centre. But this gravitation has no parts, it is indivisible. The driving force of bodies is not something made up of parts. The growth of living bodies, their vitality, their instinct, are not separate things, divisible entities, either; you can no more cut in half the flowering of a rose, the life of a horse, or the instinct of a dog, than you can cut in two a sensation, a negation, or an affirmation. So your fine argument based on the indivisibility of thought proves nothing.

What do you call your soul, then? What idea do you have of it? By yourself, without revelation, you cannot allow that you possess anything other than a power, unknown to you, of thinking and feeling.

Now, tell me frankly, this power of thinking and feeling, is it the same as that which enables you to walk and to digest food? You admit that it is not, because your reason cannot tell your stomach to digest if it is dyspeptic, and your immaterial being could not tell your feet to walk if they are suffering from gout.

The Greeks understood well enough that thought often had nothing to do with the activities of our organs; they accepted that these organs have an animal soul, and thinking had a finer, more subtle soul, a *noûs*.

But there is this thinking soul, which on myriad occasions exercises authority over the animal soul. The thinking soul tells its hands to grip, and they grip. It does not tell its heart to beat, its blood to flow, or its chyle to form; that all happens independently, so we have two pretty embarrassed souls, not exactly masters in their own house.

This first (animal) soul certainly does not exist: it is none other than the movement of your organs. Take care, human beings, for you no longer have any proof, through your feeble reason, that the other

soul exists. You can only know it through faith. You were born, you
live, you act, you think, you grow old, without knowing how. God gave
you the faculty of thought as he gave you everything else, and if he
had not come to inform you at the time designated by his Providence
that you have an immaterial and immortal soul, you would have no
proof of the fact.

Let us look at the fine systems about these souls which have been
elaborated by your philosophy.

According to one such, the human soul is part of the substance of
God himself; another claims that it is part of a great whole; a third
asserts that it has existed from all eternity; a fourth maintains that it
is made, not created; others affirm that God makes souls as they are
required, that they arrive at the moment of coitus, that they live in
the seminal animalcules. No, says another, they live in the Fallopian
tubes—only to be contradicted by a Johnny-come-lately who assures
us that the soul waits six weeks for the embryo to take shape and then
takes up residence in the pineal gland, except where it encounters a
damaged foetus, in which case it retreats until a better opportunity
arises. A final view is that the soul lives in the *corpus callosum*. Such
was the opinion of La Peyronie: only someone who was the King
of France's surgeon-general could assign the soul a billet in such a
manner. However, his *corpus callosum* has not enjoyed the same good
fortune as the surgeon did.

In question no. 75 *et seq.* Aquinas says that the soul is a *subsist-*
ent form per se, that it is *all in all*, that its essence differs from its
strength, that there are three *vegetative* souls, namely *the nutritive*, *the*
augmentative, and *the generative*; that the memory of spiritual things
is spiritual, and that the memory of corporeal things is corporeal; and
that the reasoning soul is *immaterial in its operations*, and *material in*
its being. St Thomas has written two thousand pages of this force and
clarity; that's why he is the 'angel' amongst scholars.

Just as many systems have been elaborated concerning the way in
which this soul will continue to enjoy sensation once it has left the
body through which it exercised its sensory faculties, and the manner
in which it will be able to hear without ears, smell without a nose,
and touch without hands; what body it will then reoccupy, if it is to
be the one it inhabited at the age of two or at the age of eighty; how
the *self*—personal identity—will subsist, how the soul of a man succumbing to imbecility at the age of fifteen and dying an imbecile

at seventy will pick up again the train of thought he was pursuing at puberty; by what feat of skill a soul who had a leg amputated in Europe and lost an arm in America will recover that leg and that arm, even though both will in the meantime have decayed into compost on which vegetable matter will have grown and got eaten by animals. If one tried to account for all the extravagant things about itself which this poor human soul has dreamt up, there would be no end to it.

What is really strange is that in the laws of God's own people not a word is said about the spirituality and immortality of the soul: nothing in the Decalogue, nothing in Leviticus, and nothing in Deuteronomy.

It is certain, it is beyond doubt, that nowhere does Moses offer the Jews either rewards or punishments in another life; he never speaks about the immortality of their souls; he holds out no hope of heaven and does not threaten them with hell; the temporal is all.

Before he died he told them in Deuteronomy: 'When ye shall beget children, and children's children, and shall do evil in the sight of the Lord thy God, ye shall soon utterly perish from off the land, and shall be left few in number among the heathen.'

'For I the Lord thy God am a jealous God, visiting the iniquity of the fathers upon the children unto the third and fourth generation.'

'Honour thy father and thy mother, that thy days may be prolonged.'

'Thou shalt eat bread without scarceness; thou shalt not lack anything.'

'If ye serve other gods, and worship them, ye shall perish.'

'If ye love the Lord your God and serve him with all your heart, I will give you the rain of your land in his due season, the first rain and the latter rain, that thou mayest gather in thy corn, and thy wine, and thine oil, and I will send grass in thy fields for thy cattle, that thou mayest eat and be full.'

'Therefore shall ye lay up these my words in your heart and bind them for a sign upon your hand, that they be as frontlets between your eyes, and thou shalt write them upon the doorposts of thine house, that your days may be multiplied.'

'What thing soever I command you, observe to do it; thou shalt not add thereto, nor diminish from it.'

'If there arise among you a prophet, who giveth thee a sign or a wonder, and the sign or the wonder come to pass, and if he say, Let us go after other gods, which thou hast not known . . . thine hand shall be first upon him to put him to death, and afterwards the hand of all the people.'

'Thou shalt consume all the people which the Lord thy God shall deliver thee; thine eye shall have no pity upon them.'

'Ye shall not eat of unclean birds: the eagle, the griffon, or the ixion.'

'Ye shall not eat of beasts that chew the cud and that divide not the hoof, as the camel, the hare, and the porcupine.'

'If thou shalt observe all my commandments, blessed shalt thou be in the city, and in the field; blessed shall be the fruit of thy body, and the fruit of thy ground, and the fruit of thy cattle.'

'If thou wilt not observe to do all my commandments and my statutes, cursed shalt thou be in the city, and in the field; thou shalt suffer hunger and poverty, thou shalt be destitute and die of cold, want, and fever; thou shalt be smitten with mildew, piles, and the mange; the Lord shall smite thee with suppurating sores in the knees, and in the legs.'

'The stranger shall lend to thee usuriously, and thou shalt not lend usuriously to him, because thou hearkenedst not unto the Lord thy God, to keep his commandments.'

'Thou shalt eat the fruit of thine own body, the flesh of thy sons, and the flesh of thy daughters.'

And so on. . .

It is obvious that in all these promises and in all these threats there is nothing but the temporal, with not a word about the immortality of the soul or the afterlife.

Several commentators have thought that Moses was perfectly au fait with these two great dogmata. They prove it through the words of Jacob who, believing that his son had been devoured by wild beasts, cried out in his grief, 'I will go down into *sheol* unto my son', into inferno, into hell; that is, 'I will die, because my son is dead'.

They find further proof in passages from Isaiah and Ezekiel, but the Hebrews to whom Moses spoke could not have read either Ezekiel or Isaiah because they lived several centuries later.

It is pointless to argue about what Moses may or may not secretly have thought: the fact is that in the laws he laid down he never spoke of an afterlife but kept all punishments and all rewards restricted to the present. If he knew about the afterlife, why did he not spell out clearly such an important dogma? And if he didn't know about it, what was the purpose of his mission? It is a question posed by several very grand people, and their answer is that the master of Moses and of all human beings reserved the right to explain to the Jews in his own good time a dogma that while they were in the desert they were not capable of understanding.

If Moses had proclaimed the doctrine of the immortality of the soul, it would never have been attacked—as it always was—by one school of thought within the Jewish community, namely the Sadducees. The state would not have allowed that great school to flourish, and the Sadducees would not have held the highest offices, and the greatest pontiffs would not have been recruited from among their number.

It appears that it was only after the founding of Alexandria that the Jews separated into three sects, the Pharisees, the Sadducees, and the Essenes. The historian Josephus, who was a Pharisee, informs us in book XIII of his *Antiquities of the Jews* that the Pharisees believed in the transmigration of the soul. The Sadducees held that the soul perished with the body. The Essenes, Josephus also tells us, considered the soul immortal; according to them, souls descended in an ethereal manner into bodies from the loftiest part of the heavens, to which they were pulled back by a very strong force, and after death the souls belonging to good people took up residence across the seas in a country which was neither hot nor cold and neither windy nor wet. The souls of the wicked were packed off to a place with a very different climate. Such was the theology of the Jews.

All three sects were condemned by the man who was sent to enlighten all humankind; had it not been for him, we would never have been able to discover anything about our soul, since the philosophers have never come to a settled opinion upon it, and Moses, who until the present time was the world's only true lawgiver, and who spoke to God face-to-face even though he only saw him from behind, left human beings in a state of profound ignorance on this crucial matter. So it is only in the last seventeen hundred years that we have been certain of the existence of the soul and of its immortality.

Cicero had nothing but doubts; his grandson and granddaughter were able to get the truth when the first Galileans arrived in Rome.

But before that, and since then in the rest of the world where our apostles have not yet ventured, everyone had to say to their soul, 'Who are you? Where do you come from? What do you do? Where are you going? You are, I'm not sure what, a thinking and feeling entity?' And were you to think and feel for a hundred thousand million years, you would not through your own insight, without the help of God, be able to find out anything more.

O humankind! You have been given the gift of understanding by this same God to enable you to conduct yourself properly, and not in order to peer into the essence of his creation.

FRIENDSHIP
(AMITIÉ)

IT is the marriage of the soul, a contract between two persons of virtue and sentiment. I say *sentiment*, because a monk or a hermit can be pure of all nastiness and still lack friendship in their lives. I say *virtue*, because the wicked have only accomplices; libertines have only companions in debauchery; those who have regard only for self-interest have partners; politicians gather party hacks around them; ordinary men of leisure have acquaintances; princes have sycophants; but only persons of virtue have friends. Cegethus was Catiline's accomplice, and Maecenas was one of Augustus' courtiers, but Cicero was Atticus' friend.

What does this contract between two persons of good breeding and of affectionate disposition entail? The duties can be slight or they can be considerable, depending on the strength of feeling involved, the number of services rendered, and so on.

For the Greeks and Arabs the cult of friendship had greater significance than it has for us. Their writings on the subject are admirable. We have nothing similar; we're altogether rather a cold lot.

Among the Greeks, friendship was a matter of religious belief and the subject of legislation. The Thebans had a regiment made up of lovers. And what a fine regiment that was! Some people have assumed that it was a regiment of sodomites, but they're wrong, mistaking the inessential for the real point. Among the Greeks friendship was laid down by religion and was subject to the law. Unfortunately it was customary to turn a blind eye to pederasty, but the law cannot be held responsible for such shameful abuses. It's a topic I'll be coming back to later.

LOVE
(AMOUR)

'AMOR omnibus idem' ('Love is the same everywhere'*). Recourse must here be had to the physical; it is the stuff of Nature which has been embroidered upon by the imagination. Do you want to get an idea of what love is? Look at the sparrows in your garden, or the pigeons; watch the bull being taken to your heifer; see this proud horse being led by a couple of stable boys to the tranquil mare awaiting him, moving her tail to receive him, see how his eyes shine, listen to him whinnying, observe his leaps, his curvets, his erect ears, his mouth opening convulsively, his flaring nostrils, his hot breath, the way he tosses his flowing mane, and his mettlesome rush towards the object which his nature has destined for him; but don't be envious, think instead of the advantages which we humans enjoy, and which through love compensate us for all those given to animals by Nature: beauty, strength, lightness, and nimbleness.

There are even some animals to which sexual pleasure is unknown, in particular fish: the female lays millions of eggs in the mud, and the first male to come along swims over them and, without bothering which female they belong to, fertilizes them with his sperm.

Most animals that copulate experience pleasure only through one of their senses, and once their appetite is satisfied, all desire is extinguished. You are the only animal that enjoys hugging and kissing: your whole body responds to it. Above all, delights of which you can never tire are available to your lips; and you may make love whenever you wish to, whereas animals can only do so when in season. If you care to reflect on these pre-eminent advantages, you will concur with the Earl of Rochester that 'in a land of atheists, love would make anyone worship the Almighty'.*

Human beings, gifted as they are with the ability to perfect everything granted them by Nature, have perfected love. Cleanliness and body-care increase the pleasure of touch by making the skin more delicate, and attention paid to sexual hygiene increases the sensitivity of the organs of pleasure.

Just as metals alloy with gold, all other feelings come together in love: friendship and respect make their contribution; the talents of mind and body are additional bonds.

> Nam facit ipsa suis interdum foemina factis,
> Morigerisque modis et mundo corpore cultu
> Ut facile insuescat secum vir degere vitam.

Lucretius, bk. V*

Above all, self-esteem makes every link stronger. People congratulate themselves on their choice, and the whole construct, grounded as it is in Nature, is further adorned with a mass of illusions.

That's the advantage you have over animals; but if you enjoy so many pleasures they know nothing about, you also endure sufferings they have no conception of! What is truly awful for you is the fact that over three-quarters of the earth's surface Nature has infected love's pleasures—and the sources of life—with a frightful disease to which human beings alone are subject, and which affects the reproductive organs only where they are concerned!

It is not the case with this plague, as it is with so many other illnesses, that our excesses are to blame. It was not introduced into the world by debauchery. The Phrinés, the Laïses, the Floras, the Messalinas did not catch it. It was born in islands where people lived in innocence, and it spread from there to the Old World.

If Nature can ever be accused of despising her handiwork, of being at variance with her plan and of acting contrary to her own views, it is in this instance. Is this, then, the best of all possible worlds? And if Caesar, Mark Antony, and Augustus did not catch this illness, is it not feasible that it did not kill François I? No, people say, things worked out for the best. I'd like to think so, but it's sad for those Rabelais dedicated his book to.*

LOVE CALLED SOCRATIC LOVE
(AMOUR NOMMÉ SOCRATIQUE)

THIS is a vice which is a vile attack upon Nature and which, if universally adopted, would lead to the destruction of the human race, so how can we explain the fact that notwithstanding it is so natural? It appears to be the height of deliberate corruption, and yet it is the common experience of people who have not yet had the chance to get corrupted. It creeps into innocent hearts that know nothing yet of ambition, deceit, or the lust for riches; it affects blind youth which, not having worked out where its instincts lie, rushes into this perversion when barely out of short trousers.

The attraction which draws the two sexes together declares itself early on, but whatever has been said about women in Africa and southern Asia, this attraction is generally much more marked in men than in the opposite sex. It's a law laid down by Nature for all animals: the male always attacks the female.

The young males of our species, being brought up together, experiencing the force being built up in their bodies by Nature, and not encountering the natural object of their desires, fall back on what resembles it. For two or three years a boy often looks as pretty as a girl, thanks to the freshness of his complexion, the colour in his cheeks, and the softness of his eyes. If other youths fall in love with him, it is because Nature has made a mistake; by latching on to the boy who possesses its beauty they are paying homage to the opposite sex, and when the resemblance fades with age, the misunderstanding comes to an end.*

> Citraque juventam
> Aetatis breve ver et primos carpere flores.*

It is well known that Nature's error is much more widespread in warmer countries than in the icy north, because blood is hotter there and opportunities are more frequent; thus what appears as no more than a weakness in Alcibiades is a revolting abomination in a Dutch sailor or a Russian victualler.

I cannot stand the way people claim that the Greeks authorized this licence, quoting Solon the lawgiver because he said, in this bit of doggerel,

Thou shalt cherish a lovely boy,
So long as no stubble darkens his chin.*

But, let's be honest, was Solon a lawgiver when he penned these fatuous lines? He was young then, and once the debauchee attained wisdom, he put no such loathsomeness into the laws of his republic. It would be like accusing Théodore de Bèze of advocating pederasty from the pulpit just because in his youth he wrote lines for the young Candide, in which he said:

Amplector hunc et illam.*

One of Plutarch's texts has been similarly misunderstood. In his table talk, on the subject of love, he has one speaker say that women are not worthy of true love, but another contributor supports the women's cause, as well he ought.*

It is as certain as anything can be in our knowledge of the ancient world that Socratic love was not a disgusting form of love. It is the word 'love' that has given rise to the misunderstanding. What were called the 'lovers' of a young man were just like the companions of our princes: children of honour, young people assigned to the education of a noble youth, sharing the same studies and the same military exercises; a warlike, saintly institution which was abused in orgies, night-time parties, and the like.

The lovers' troop established by Laius was an invincible company of young warriors who had sworn an oath to lay down their lives for each other. It was the finest example of discipline in the ancient world.

It is all very well for Sextus Empiricus and others to say that the laws of Persia advocated pederasty; let them quote the text of the law in question, let them show us the code of the Persians; and even if they are able to produce it, I will still not believe it, I will say that it is not true, for the very good reason that it is impossible. No, it is not in human nature to make a law that goes contrary to Nature and indeed constitutes an outrage to it, a law that would wipe out the human race if it were obeyed to the letter; how many people have assumed that shameful practices tolerated in a country are prescribed by its laws! A sceptic in everything, Sextus Empiricus must have been dubious about this piece of jurisprudence. If he lived today and saw two or three young Jesuits sexually abusing schoolboys, would he be right in saying that such activities were permitted under the rules of their order laid down by Ignatius Loyola?

The love of boys was so common in Rome that no one would have dreamt of punishing such a trifle when everyone indulged in it so freely. The Emperor Augustus, a debauched and cowardly murderer who did not shrink from sending Ovid into exile, thought it perfectly acceptable that Virgil should sing the praises of Alexis and that Horace should write odes to Ligurinus. But the ancient *Lex Scantinia* banning pederasty was still on the statute book. The Emperor Philippus revived it and drove the rent-boys from Rome. I just don't believe there was ever a civilized country that made laws that went counter to morality.

SELF-LOVE
(AMOUR-PROPRE)

NOT far from Madrid a beggar with a dignified air was asking for money. A passer-by said to him: 'Aren't you ashamed to be plying this vile trade when you could be working?' 'Sir,' replied the beggar, 'what I want from you is charity, not advice' and, with his Castilian dignity intact, he turned his back on the person. He was a proud beggar, that fellow, taking umbrage at a trivial slight. He was demanding alms through one form of self-love, and was refusing to accept a rebuke through another form of self-love.

A missionary travelling in India met a fakir who was chained up and lying completely naked on his stomach; he was having himself flogged for the sins of his compatriots, who were giving him a few farthings in the local currency. 'What self-sacrifice!' exclaimed one of the bystanders. 'Self-sacrifice?' said the fakir: 'Don't you see that I'm getting a spanking in this world so that in the next I can return the favour, when you'll all be horses and I'll be the rider?'

So in India, in Spain, and throughout the habitable world those who have claimed that self-love is the basis of all our feelings and all our actions have been quite correct, and just as no one takes up the pen to prove to anyone that they have a face, there is no need to convince people that they love themselves. For us self-love is a form of self-preservation; it's similar to the way the species is perpetuated; it's necessary, it's precious to us, it gives us pleasure, and it needs to be concealed.

ANGEL

(ANGE)

ANGEL (from the Greek for 'messenger'): you will not be much the wiser on learning that the Persians had their Peris, the Hebrews their Malakim, and the Greeks their Daimonoi.

But what is perhaps more instructive is the fact that one of human-kind's earliest ideas was always to place intermediary beings between God and ourselves; they are the demons, the genii invented by the Ancients: humans never made gods other than in their own image. People saw princes using messengers to convey their orders, so the deity also dispatched his couriers, Mercury and Iris.

The Hebrews—the only people led by God in person—did not at first give names to the angels whom the Lord was good enough to send them; during the Babylonian captivity they borrowed names from the Chaldeans; Michael and Gabriel were named for the first time by Daniel, a slave in Nebuchadnezzar's palace. The Jew Tobias, who lived in Nineveh, knew the angel Raphael who travelled with his son to help him withdraw the money owed him by the Jew Gabael.

Jewish law, as enshrined in Leviticus and Deuteronomy, makes no mention of angels or their cult, so the Sadducees did not believe in angels.

But much is said about them in histories of the Jews. They had bodies, and on their backs they had wings, just as, according to the Gentiles, Mercury had on his heels; sometimes they hid their wings under their clothes. How could they not have had bodies, since they ate and drank, and since the inhabitants of Sodom tried to commit the sin of pederasty with the angels visiting Lot?

The ancient Jewish tradition, according to Maimonides, distinguishes ten orders of angels: 1, the Chaios Acodesh, pure, holy; 2, the Ofamin, swift; 3, the Oralim, the strong; 4, the Chasmalim, the flames; 5, the Seraphim, sparks; 6, the Malakim, angels, messengers, deputies; 7, the Eloim, the gods or judges; 8, the Ben Eloim, sons of the gods; 9, Cherubim, images; 10, Ychim, the animated.

The story of the fallen angels is not found in the books of Moses; the first account of it is that given by the prophet Isaiah, who in haranguing the King of Babylon cries out 'What has become of the collector of tribute! The firs and the cedars rejoice in his fall! How fell'st thou from heaven, O Helel, star of the morning?' 'Helel' was translated by the Latin word 'Lucifer'; then an allegorical meaning attached itself to the name of Lucifer; it was given to the prince of the angels who waged war on heaven; and thereafter Lucifer, which signifies Phosphor and the dawn, was adopted as the name of the devil.

The Christian religion is grounded in the fall of the angels. From the spheres which they inhabited those who rebelled were hurled down into hell, in the centre of the earth, and became devils. In the shape of a serpent one of them tempted Eve and thus damned the human race. Jesus came to redeem humanity and vanquish the devil who tempts us still. However, this basic tradition is to be found only in the apocryphal Book of Noah, and even there in a quite different way than in the received version.

In Letter 109 St Augustine makes no bones about giving nimble and agile bodies to both the good and the wicked angels. Pope Gregory II reduced the ten choirs of angels recognized by the Jews to nine choirs, nine hierarchies or orders,* to wit: seraphim, cherubim, thrones, dominions, virtues, powers, archangels, and lastly the angels whose name is given to the eight other hierarchies.

In the temple the Jews had two cherubim; each had two heads, one of an eagle with six wings and the other of an ox. These are depicted nowadays as flying heads with two small wings beneath their ears, and the angels and archangels appear as young people with two wings on their backs. As for thrones and dominions, no one so far has ventured to depict them.

In Question 108, article 2, Thomas Aquinas says that thrones are as close to God as the seraphim and cherubim, because it is upon them that God is seated. Duns Scotus counted a thousand million angels. In ancient mythology there were good and bad genii, and these passed from the East to Greece and Rome; we confirmed that view by accepting that all human beings have a good and a bad angel, the first coming to their assistance, and the other doing them harm, from the moment of their birth to the hour of their death; but we don't yet know if the good and bad angels move continually from one post to another, or if they are relieved by others. (See Aquinas's *Summa Theologica* on the subject.)

We do not know precisely where the angels abide, that is whether it be in the air, the void, or the planets; God has not deigned to inform us.

CANNIBALS
(ANTHROPOPHAGES)

I'VE been talking about love, so it is a bit difficult going from people who kiss each other to those who eat each other. It is only too true that cannibals have existed; we found them in the Americas, and probably some are there still. And in the ancient world the Cyclops were not alone in occasionally feeding on human flesh. Juvenal reports that among the Egyptians—so wise a people, so renowned for their laws, such pious worshippers of crocodiles and onions—the people of Tentyra ate one of the enemy soldiers they captured. In recording this he does not rely on hearsay: he was in Egypt, a short distance from Tentyra, and the crime was committed before his very eyes. He also cites the Vascones and the citizens of Sagunto, both of whom once ate the flesh of their compatriots.*

In 1725 four savages were brought from the Mississippi to Fontainebleau, and I had the honour of speaking with them. One was a lady of that country, and when I asked her if she had eaten men, she replied in all innocence that she had. I appeared somewhat shocked, but her excuse was that it was better to eat your dead enemy than to let him be devoured by wild beasts, and that the victors deserved the privilege.* In skirmishes and in pitched battles we kill our neighbours, and for the basest of rewards we strive to feed the crows and the worms. That is the real horror, the true crime: what is the difference between being eaten by a soldier, a crow, or a dog?

We respect the dead more than the living. We should respect both. Nations we call civilized are right not to spit-roast their enemies; because if we were allowed to eat our neighbours, we would soon be eating our fellow countrymen, and that would have very serious implications for social morality. But civilized peoples have not always been so; for a long while many were savages; and in the course of the infinite number of rotations our planet has known, the human race has sometimes been numerous and sometimes very sparse. What happened to human beings is what happens now to elephants, lions, and tigers, whose numbers have greatly declined. During the times when a country had few inhabitants they had few arts; people were hunters. The habit of eating what they had killed meant that they could easily treat their enemies as they did their stags and wild boars. It was superstition that gave rise to human sacrifice, but necessity that led to cannibalism.

What is the greater crime, to assemble in a mood of piety to worship a deity by plunging a knife in the heart of a girl wearing an infula on her forehead, or to eat a nasty person whom one has killed in self-defence?

There are, for all that, many more examples of girls and boys being sacrificed than of girls and boys being eaten; nearly all nations have sacrificed boys and girls. The Hebrews did. It was called an 'anatheme', meaning an offering; it was a true sacrifice, and in chapter 29 of Leviticus it is commanded not to spare living souls dedicated for that purpose; but it is nowhere prescribed that they be eaten, merely threatened with being eaten; and Moses, as we have seen, told the Jews that if they did not observe his rites, not only would they be smitten with the itch, mothers would devour their children. It is true that in Ezekiel's time the Jews must have been in the habit of eating human flesh, because in chapter 39 he prophesied that God would make them eat not only the horses of their enemies, but the riders too, and other warriors. That's positive. And why indeed wouldn't the Jews have been cannibals? It would have been the only thing lacking to make God's people the most loathed on earth.

In a book of tales from English history I read that in Cromwell's time a chandleress in Dublin sold excellent candles made from the fat of dead Englishmen. Some time later one of her customers complained that her candles were no longer of such good quality. 'Alas,' she said, 'it's because Englishmen have been in rather short supply lately.' I wonder who was the more to blame, the people who killed the Englishmen, or the woman who made candles from their tallow?*

APIS

IN Memphis, was the bull Apis worshipped as a god, as a symbol, or as a bull? Fanatics probably considered him a god, wise people saw him as a mere symbol, and the ignorant worshipped the bull. After conquering Egypt, was Cambyses right to kill this bull with his own hands? Why ever not? He showed fools that their god could be spit-roasted without Nature taking up arms to avenge such an act of sacrilege. The Egyptians have been much praised, but I know of no more contemptible a people; there must always have been a fundamental flaw in their character and in their system of government to have made them into such base slaves. I accept that in distant ages largely unknown they conquered the earth, but in historical times they have been subjugated by whoever took the trouble, the Assyrians, the Greeks, the Romans, the Arabs, the Mamluks, and the Turks, in fact by everybody except our Crusaders, but that's because they were as clueless as the Egyptians were cowardly. It was the Mamluk army that beat the French. There are perhaps just two things that are acceptable about the Egyptians: the first is that those who worshipped a bull never tried to force those who bowed down to a monkey to change religion; and the second is that they always used ovens to hatch their chicks.

Their pyramids are highly praised, but they are the monuments of a slave people. The entire nation must have been made to work on them, otherwise such monstrosities would never have got built. What purpose did they serve? To keep in a tiny chamber the mummy of some prince, governor, or intendant whose soul would bring it back to life a thousand years later. But if they were hoping for the resurrection of the body, why remove the brain before embalming it? Without a brain, how were the Egyptians expected to rise from the dead?

APOCALYPSE

JUSTIN MARTYR, writing around AD 170, was the first to discuss the Apocalypse, or Book of Revelation; in the *Dialogue with Trypho* he attributes it to the apostle John the Evangelist. The Jew Trypho asks him whether he believes that Jerusalem will one day be restored. Justin replies that in common with all right-thinking Christians he does believe it. 'There has been dwelling amongst us', he says, 'a certain person called John, one of the twelve apostles of Jesus; he has prophesied that the faithful will spend a thousand years in Jerusalem.'

Christians long held a belief in this thousand-year reign. It enjoyed great credit too among the Gentiles. The souls of the Egyptians re-entered their bodies after a thousand years; in Virgil's *Aeneid* the souls in Purgatory were tested for the same length of time, 'et mille per annos'. The new thousand-year Jerusalem was to have twelve gates, in memory of the twelve apostles; it was to be square in shape; it was to be twelve thousand stadia, that is five hundred leagues, in length, width, and height, so that the houses too were to be five hundred leagues high. It cannot have been very pleasant to live on the top floor, but that is what Revelation, chapter 21, says.

If Justin is the first to attribute the Book of Revelation to St John, some people have challenged his testimony, because in the same *Dialogue with Trypho* he says that according to the account given by the apostles, when Jesus went into the Jordan, he made the waters boil and set them alight, something that is not found in any of the apostles' writings.

The same Justin Martyr cites with confidence the oracles of the Sibyls; what is more, he claims to have seen the remains of the madhouses at Pharos in Egypt in which the seventy-two interpreters were held during Herod's reign. The testimony of a man who had the misfortune of seeing those houses seems to indicate that he should have been locked up there himself.

St Irenaeus, who came later and who also believed in the thousand-year reign, said that he had been told by an old man that St John was the author of the Book of Revelation. But Irenaeus has been criticized for writing that there can only be four Gospels because the world has only four parts, there are only four cardinal winds, and Ezekiel saw only four animals. This line of reasoning he calls solid proof. It has to be confessed that the way Irenaeus establishes proof is on a par with Justin's propensity for seeing things.

In his *Electa* Clement of Alexandria speaks only of an Apocalypse of St Peter, which was highly thought of. Tertullian, one of the leading advocates of the reign of a thousand years, not only affirms that St John foretold this resurrection and the thousand-year kingdom in Jerusalem, but also claims that this Jerusalem was already taking shape in the sky, and that all the Christians in Palestine, and even non-believers, had seen it before dawn for a full forty days; unfortunately, though, at sunrise the city vanished.

In his preface to the Gospel of John, and in his homilies, Origen cites the oracles of the Book of Revelation, but he also mentions the oracles of the Sibyls. However, St Denis of Alexandria, writing about the middle of the third century, says in one of the fragments preserved by Eusebius that almost every scholar rejected Revelation as a book devoid of sense; that it was not written by St John, but by a certain Cerinthus who used a big name to lend credence to his delusions.

The Council of Laodicea, held in AD 360, excluded Revelation from the canonical books. It was strange that Laodicea, a church to which the work was addressed, rejected a treasure intended for it, and that the bishop of Ephesus, who attended the council, also rejected this book by St John, who is buried there.

It was clear to every eye that St John kept turning in his grave and making the earth heave above him. However, the same people who were certain that St John was not dead were equally sure that he was not the author of the Book of Revelation. But those who believed in the reign of a thousand years were unshakeable in their convictions. In book 9 of his *Historia Sacra* Sulpicius Severus calls mad and ungodly those who do not accept Revelation. The matter has now been cleared up: the Church has decided that Revelation is incontestably the work of St John, so there is no appeal.

Every community in Christendom has applied the book's prophesies to itself: the English have found in it the revolutions that have plagued their country, the Lutherans the upheavals in Germany, the French Protestants the reign of Charles IX and the regency of Catherine de' Medici. They are all equally right. Bossuet and Newton have both written commentaries on the Book of Revelation;* but, all in all, the eloquent sermons of the former, and the sublime discoveries of the latter, do them more honour than those commentaries.

ATHEIST, ATHEISM
(ATHÉE, ATHÉISME)

ONCE upon a time anyone who had a secret skill ran the risk of being taken for a sorcerer; every new sect was accused of child sacrifice in the conduct of its mysteries; and philosophers who departed from the jargon of their school were charged with atheism by fanatics and scoundrels, and condemned by fools.

When Anaxagoras had the temerity to claim that the sun is not driven by Apollo mounted on a chariot he was called an atheist, and had to flee.

Aristotle was accused by a priest of atheism, and being unable to punish his accuser he retired to Chalcis. But the most shameful event in Greek history was the death of Socrates.

Aristophanes—someone admired because he was Greek by commentators who forget that Socrates was Greek too—was the first to get the Athenians used to the idea that Socrates was an atheist.

This comic poet, who was neither comic nor a poet, would not be allowed today to put on his farces at the St Laurent Fair; he seems to me much baser and more contemptible than Plutarch describes him. Here's what Plutarch says about this joker: 'Aristophanes' language reeks of the wretched mountebank; his witticisms are about as mean and revolting as they get; the lower orders don't think him funny and people of taste and judgement find him insufferable; his arrogance is not to be tolerated, and decent folk hate his malevolence.'*

Let it be said in passing that he is the clown so admired by Mme Dacier, even though she held Socrates in high esteem too. He is the man who prepared from afar the poison with which the judges put to death the most virtuous man in all Greece.

A farce in which Socrates was shown being hoisted up in the air in a basket, declaring that there was no God and boasting of having stolen a coat while teaching philosophy, was greeted with loud applause by the tanners, shoemakers, and seamstresses of Athens. A people whose evil government allowed such shameful things to happen fully deserved what has since happened to it: enslavement by the Romans, and today by the Turks.

Let us journey through the ages between the Roman Empire and our own time. The Romans were much more sensible than the Greeks and never persecuted a philosopher for his beliefs. The same was not the case with the barbarians who succeeded the Romans. As soon as the Emperor Frederick II quarrelled with the popes he was accused of being an atheist and being the author, together with his chancellor Pierre des Vignes, of the book about the three impostors.

When our own great Michel de l'Hôpital came out against religious persecution he was immediately accused of atheism.* 'Homo doctus, sed verus atheos.'*[1] The Jesuit François Garasse, a man as far beneath Aristophanes as Aristophanes is beneath Homer, a man whose name excites ridicule even among fanatics, everywhere finds 'atheisters': that's his word for all those he thunders against. He calls Théodore de Bèze an atheist, and it was he who misled the public about Lucilio Vanini.*

Vanini's sad end does not move us to pity and anger in the same way as Socrates' does, because Vanini was only a foreign pedant without merit; but still, Vanini was no atheist, in fact he was precisely the opposite.

He was a penniless Neapolitan priest, a preacher and theologian by profession, a disputer to excess about quiddities and universals; 'et utrum chimera bombinans in vacuo possit comedere secundas intentiones'. But for all that there was not an atheistic bone in his body. His concept of God was the soundest and most widely accepted: 'God is his principle and his end, father of both and in need of neither; eternal without being in time; omnipresent without being anywhere. For him there is neither past nor future; he is everywhere and outside everything; governing all things, having created them; unchangeable, infinite without parts; his power is his will'; and so on.

Vanini prided himself on breathing new life into Plato's fine sentiment, also embraced by Averroes, that God had created a chain of beings from the smallest to the largest, the last link of which is attached to his eternal throne; a notion that is, to be frank, more sublime than true, but also one as far removed from atheism as being is from nothingness.

He travelled widely to make his fortune and to engage in disputation, but sadly disputation does not lead to riches; you make as

---

[1] *Commentarium Rerum Gallicarum*, bk. 28.

many sworn enemies as you find scholars or pedants with whom you argue. That was the sole cause of Vanini's misfortunes; his ardour and coarseness in disputation earned him the hatred of a few theologians; and after he had had an argument with someone called Francon or Franconi, this Francon, a friend of his enemies, did not fail to accuse him of being an atheist teaching atheism.

This Francon, or Franconi, aided and abetted by a few witnesses, had the barbarity to maintain at the confrontation what he had advanced. Vanini, in the hot seat, being asked what he thought about the existence of God, replied that he was at one with the Church in worshipping a God in three persons. Picking up a straw, he said, 'This wisp is enough to prove that there is a creator.' He then made a fine speech on vegetation and movement, and on the necessity for a Supreme Being, without whom nothing would move and nothing would grow.

This speech is quoted by Barthélemy de Gramond, then president at the Toulouse *parlement*, in his now sadly neglected *Historiarum Galliae*; he shows extraordinary bias when he claims that Vanini said all that 'through vanity, or fear, rather than from conviction'.

What can be the basis of President Gramond's dreadfully rash judgement? It's obvious that Vanini's response absolves him of any accusation of atheism. So what happened? This unfortunate foreign priest also dabbled in medicine; in his house a big live toad was found, kept in a bowl of water. And sure enough, he was accused of witchcraft: it was claimed that this toad was the god he worshipped; in a practice that is widespread and easily done, blasphemous meanings were given to several passages in his books, by taking objections for answers, by interpreting maliciously a rather dubious sentence, or by poisoning an innocent expression. Finally the faction that was gunning for him leaned on the judges, and the hapless fellow was condemned to death.

To justify his execution they had to accuse the poor wretch of the most appalling crime in the book. The insignificant—very insignificant—Marin Mersenne was mad enough to declare in print that Vanini set out from Naples with twelve of his disciples to convert all the nations to atheism. Pitiful! How could a penniless priest have kept twelve men on his payroll? How could he have persuaded twelve Neapolitans to travel at great cost to spread this abominable, revolting doctrine everywhere, and risk their lives in the process? Would any king be sufficiently powerful to fund twelve men to proselytize atheism? Before Fr. Mersenne no one had propounded such an enormous absurdity, but after him it was endlessly repeated, infecting periodicals and historical dictionaries, and people who adore anything outlandish believed the story without further consideration.

Pierre Bayle* himself, in his *Pensées diverses*, speaks of Vanini as an atheist, and uses him as an example to prove his point that 'a society of atheists can survive'. He assures us that Vanini was a man of the strictest morals, martyred for his philosophical opinions. He is wrong on both counts. Vanini the priest tells us in his dialogues (modelled on those of Erasmus) that he had a mistress called Isabelle. He was as free a spirit in his conduct as he was in his writings; but he was no atheist.

A century after his death the scholar Veyssière de la Croze, and another author writing under the name Philalethes, attempted to vindicate him, but since no one is interested in the life of a luckless Neapolitan—and very bad writer—hardly anyone reads their apologias.

In his book *Athei Detecti* the Jesuit Hardouin, better read than Garasse but just as foolhardy, accuses people like Descartes, Pascal, Nicole, and Malebranche of atheism; fortunately they avoided Vanini's fate.

From the above facts I now pass to the question of morality raised by Bayle, namely, whether a society of atheists could survive. Let us first note here the huge contradiction that lies at the heart of this dispute: those who have attacked Bayle's view with the greatest venom, who have deployed the worst of insults to deny the possibility of a society of atheists, have been the boldest advocates of the theory that atheism is the religion of the government of China.

They have definitely got that wrong: they had only to read the edicts of the emperors of that vast country to see that such documents are sermons, and that everywhere the emphasis is laid on the Supreme Being, at once governor, avenger, and rewarder.

But at the same time they were not wrong about the impossibility of a society of atheists; I don't know how M. Bayle came to overlook a striking example that could have offered conclusive proof of his argument.

In what way does a society of atheists seem impossible? It's because it's considered that human beings would have no restraints, could never live together, that laws can do nothing against secret crimes, so that a vengeful God is needed to punish in this world or in the next the evildoers who have evaded human justice.

It's true that the laws of Moses never spoke of a life to come, never threatened people with punishment after death, never taught the first Jews about the immortality of the soul; but the Jews, far from being atheists, far from thinking they were exempt from divine retribution, were the most religious of human beings. Not only did they believe in the existence of an eternal God, they considered him to be continually present among them; they trembled at the prospect of being punished in their own person, in their wives, and in their children, unto the fourth generation; and this belief acted as a very powerful curb.

But amongst the Gentiles, many sects knew no constraint; sceptics cast doubt on everything; academicians suspended judgement on everything; the Epicureans were convinced that God could not interfere in the affairs of humankind; at bottom, they acknowledged no divinity. They were convinced that the soul is not a substance but a faculty that is born and dies with the body, so they had no yoke other than morality and honour. The senators and knights of Rome were true atheists because the gods did not exist for men who feared nothing and expected nothing from them. So in the time of Caesar and Cicero the Roman senate was, in truth, an assembly of atheists.

In *Pro Cluentio* the great orator declared before the whole senate, 'What harm can death do to Cluentio? We reject all the stupid fables about hell, so what does death rob him of?' Only the feeling of pain.

Caesar was Cataline's friend and, wishing to save his life, put forward to Cicero the argument that executing a criminal is no punishment, that death *is nothing*, merely the end of our troubles, therefore more a happy event than a fatal one. Cicero and the whole senate accepted this argument. So the conquerors and lawgivers of the known universe formed a society of people who, fearing nothing from the gods, were true atheists.

Bayle next looks at the question whether idolatry is more dangerous than atheism, and whether it is a greater crime not to believe in the Divinity than to have unworthy opinions about him. He agrees with Plutarch that it is better to have no opinion than a bad one. But, with all due respect to Plutarch, it is obvious that it was much better for the Greeks to fear Ceres, Neptune, and Jupiter than to fear nothing at all. It's clear that the sanctity of the oath is necessary, and that one must have more trust in those who think that a false oath will be punished than in those who think they can swear falsely with impunity. There is no doubt whatever that in a civilized society it is much more useful to have a religion (even a bad one) than to have no religion at all.

So it seems that Bayle should rather have examined which is the more dangerous, fanaticism or atheism. Fanaticism is certainly a thousand times more harmful, because atheism does not give rise to bloodthirsty passions, whereas fanaticism does; atheism does not prevent crimes, whereas fanaticism commits them. Let us, like the author of *Commentarium Rerum Gallicarum*, suppose that Chancellor de l'Hôpital was an atheist, he made only wise laws and always counselled moderation and harmony. The fanatics carried out the massacres of St Bartholomew. Hobbes was considered an atheist, but he led a peaceful and blameless life. The fanatics of his time drenched England, Scotland, and Ireland in blood. Spinoza was not merely an atheist, he taught atheism; but it was certainly not he who played any part in the judicial murder of Barneveldt, nor was it he who tore the De Witt brothers to pieces and had them roasted alive.

Atheists are for the most part bold but mistaken scholars who reason badly and who, being incapable of understanding the creation, original sin, and other difficulties, fall back on the hypothesis of the eternity of things and of necessity.

Ambitious and licentious people have little time for reasoning and for embracing a bad system: they have better things to do than compare Lucretius and Socrates. That's the way things are with us.

It was not the same with the Roman senate, which was almost entirely made up of people who embraced atheism, both in theory and in practice; that is to say people who believed neither in Providence nor in the afterlife; that senate was an assembly of philosophers, voluptuaries, and ambitious people, all very dangerous, who were the ruin of the republic.

I would not care to have to deal with an atheistic prince who might find it suited him to have me ground in a pestle and mortar; I'm pretty sure I would be pounded. If I were a ruler I would not wish to have to deal with atheistic courtiers who might find it suited them to have me poisoned; I would have to take an antidote every day, just in case. So, for princes and their subjects it is absolutely essential that the notion of a Supreme Being—creator, governor, rewarder, and avenger—is deeply engraved on everyone's mind.*

There are atheistic peoples, says Bayle in his *Pensées sur les comètes*. The Kaffirs, Hottentots, Tupinamba, and many other small peoples have no God; they neither deny nor affirm him, they have never heard of him; tell them that there is a God, they will readily believe it; tell them that everything happens off its own bat, they will believe that too. To claim that they are atheists is much the same as saying that they are anti-Cartesians; they are neither for nor against Descartes. They are just children; children are born neither atheists nor deists, they are nothing.

What conclusions are we to draw from all this? That atheism is very pernicious in those who govern, but also in the learned even where their lives are innocent, because from their study they can exert influence on those in authority; that if atheism is not as harmful as fanaticism it almost always proves deadly for virtue. Let me add above all that there are now fewer atheists than ever, since the day when philosophers acknowledged that there is no growing thing without seed, no seed without design, and so on, and that wheat does not spring from putrefaction.

Geometers who are not philosophers have rejected final causes, but true philosophers have accepted them; and as a well-known author has said,* a catechist declares God to children, and Newton shows him to the wise.

BAPTISM
(BAPTÊME)

BAPTISM, a Greek word meaning immersion. For human beings who are always led by their senses, it was easy to imagine that what washed the body also washed the soul. There were big tanks in the basements of the temples of Egypt for the priests and initiates. From time immemorial people in India have purified themselves in the waters of the Ganges, and this ceremony is still very much in vogue. It passed to the Hebrews, who baptized all foreigners who embraced Jewish law but did not wish to be circumcised. Women in particular were baptized: they were not made to undergo circumcision, except in Ethiopia. It was a form of regeneration; it gave one a new soul, as in Egypt. See Epiphanes, Maimonides, and the Gemara.

John baptized people in the River Jordan; he even baptized Jesus, who however never baptized anyone, but who was happy to endorse this ancient ceremony. In itself, any sign is immaterial: God attaches his grace to the sign he is pleased to choose. Baptism soon became the first rite and the seal of the Christian religion. However, the first fifteen bishops of Jerusalem were all circumcised; it is not certain whether they were baptized.

People overdid this sacrament in the early centuries of Christianity; it was not at all unusual to be baptized on your deathbed. The example of the Emperor Constantine is fairly convincing proof of this. This was his reasoning: 'Baptism purifies everything, so I can kill my wife, my son, and all my relations, then get baptized, and I'll go to heaven'—as indeed happened. It set a dangerous precedent, so the custom of waiting until one was at death's door before taking a dip in the holy bathtub was gradually abolished.

The Greeks still kept up the practice of baptism by immersion, but towards the end of the eighth century the Latins, having extended their religion's reach as far as Gaul and Germany and seeing that immersion could kill children in cold countries, adopted simple aspersion instead, much to the disapproval of the Greek church.

The bishop of Carthage, St Cyprian, was asked whether people who had only had water sprayed over them were truly baptized. He replied in Letter 76 that while several churches did not accept that sprinkling was enough to make you a Christian, he thought that it was, but it conferred an infinitely lesser grace on them than on those who in line with common practice had been pushed three times under the water.

You were initiated into the Christian community as soon as you had been immersed: until then you were only a catechumen. To be initiated you needed servers, or sponsors, what we nowadays call godparents, so that the Church could be sure that the new Christians were trustworthy and that the sacred mysteries would not be divulged. That's why in the early centuries of our era the Gentiles were as ill-informed generally about the Christian mysteries as the Christians were about the Eleusinian ceremonies or the cult of Isis.

In his attack on the Emperor Julian, Cyril of Alexandria says this: 'I would write about baptism if I weren't afraid this document might fall into the hands of the uninitiated.'

From the second century onwards infant baptism started to be carried out: it was natural that Christians wanted their children to benefit from this sacrament, since without it they would be damned. It was eventually decided that it should be administered one week after their birth, because the Jews circumcised their sons at that age. That is still the custom in the Greek church. However, in the third century it became the dominant practice to get oneself baptized only on one's deathbed.

According to the strictest of the church fathers, those who died in their first week on earth were damned. But in the fifth century Peter Chrysologus came up with the concept of limbo, a kind of semi-hell, more precisely the edge of hell, or a suburb of hell, to which were sent little children who had died before they could be christened and where the patriarchs dwelt before Christ's descent into hell. Since then, therefore, the view has prevailed that Jesus descended into limbo and not into hell.

There has been much debate as to whether a Christian in the deserts of Arabia could be baptized with sand; the answer is no. Or whether one can be baptized with rose water; it was decided that it had to be pure water, but muddy water would do. So it is easy to see that the whole issue has depended on the wisdom of the pastors who first raised it.

BEAUTIFUL, BEAUTY
(BEAU, BEAUTÉ)

Ask a toad what makes for beauty, the supremely beautiful, the *to kalon*, and he'll tell you it's a female with two big round bulging eyes, a small head, a wide, flat mouth, a yellow belly, and a brown back. Ask a Guinean and he'll say that for him beauty is an oily black skin, sunken eyes, and a flat nose.

Ask the devil and he'll tell you that beauty is a pair of horns, four claws, and a tail. Consult the philosophers, finally, and you'll get a load of twaddle: they need something in keeping with the archetype of the beautiful in essence, with *to kalon*.

I was at the theatre one day with a philosopher: 'How beautiful this tragedy is!' he said. 'What's so beautiful about it?' I asked. 'It's that the dramatist has achieved his aim,' he replied. The next day he took some medicine that did him good. 'It achieved its aim,' I said; 'what beautiful medicine!' He realized that a remedy cannot be said to be beautiful, and that to apply the word 'beauty' to something, it must arouse our admiration and give us pleasure. He agreed that this tragedy had inspired both feelings in him, and that was *to kalon*, the beautiful.

We travelled to England, and saw the same play, expertly translated: it made the whole audience yawn. 'Ah,' he said, '*to kalon* is not the same for the English as for the French.' After a great deal of thought he concluded that beauty is very often a relative thing, in much the same way as what is decent in Japan is indecent in Rome, and what is fashionable in Paris is passé in Peking. So he saved himself the trouble of writing a long treatise on the beautiful.

ANIMALS
(BÊTES)

How pitiful, how mean, to say that animals are machines without feeling or consciousness, who always do things the same way, never learn anything, never perfect anything, and so on.

What, this bird that builds its nest in a semicircle when attaching it to a wall, or in a quarter-circle when building it in a corner, or in a full circle up a tree: does this bird always do things the same way? This gun dog you've been training for three months, does it not know a lot more at the end of that period than it did before you started? The canary you've been teaching a tune to, can it repeat it at the first attempt? Don't you spend hours getting it to learn the song? Don't you see that it makes mistakes but manages to correct them?

Is it because I'm talking to you that you consider that I have feelings, memory, and ideas? Well, I won't talk to you; watch me coming in with a worried air, looking anxiously for a document, opening the bureau where I remember putting it, finding it, and reading it with delight. You consider that I've experienced feelings of affliction and pleasure and that I possess memory and consciousness.

Grant the same to a dog that's lost its master and looked for him, moaning pitifully, in the highways and byways, entering the house all agitated and worried, rushing up and down stairs and from room to room, and at last in the study finds the master it loves, and shows its delight by yelping, jumping about, and licking his face.

Cruel persons grab this dog that shows prodigiously more affection than most human beings, pin it to a table, and dissect it alive to show you its mesaraic veins. You find in the dog the same organs of feeling as you have. So tell me, mechanist, has Nature arranged all the springs of feeling in this animal so that it will not feel anything? Has it got nerves that make it impassive? Do not suppose Nature capable of such an impertinent contradiction.

But do not the schoolmen ask 'What is the soul of animals?' I don't understand the question. A tree has the ability to gather in its fibres the circulating sap and develop buds, leaves, and fruit: will you ask what is the soul of this tree? It has received these gifts, and the animal those of feeling, of memory, and of a few ideas. Who made all these gifts? Who gave all these faculties? He who makes the grass grow and the earth turn towards the sun.

The souls of animals are substantial forms, said Aristotle, and after Aristotle the Arab school, and after the Arab school, the school of the Angelic Doctor,* and after his school, the Sorbonne, and after the Sorbonne no else anywhere.

'The souls of animals are material', say other philosophers,* but they have not had any greater impact than the rest. They have been asked in vain, 'What is a material soul?' They have to admit that it consists of matter that has sensation; but who gave it that sensation? It is a material soul, that is, it is matter which gives sensation to matter. There is no way out of this circular argument.

Listen to other animals reasoning about animals; their soul is a spiritual being that dies with the body; but what proof do you have of this? What idea do you have of this spiritual being which, in truth, has feeling, memory, and a measure of ideas and combinations, but which can never know as much as a child of six. On what basis do you imagine that this being that is not body dies with the body? The greatest animals are those which have argued that this soul is neither body nor spirit. What a fine system! By spirit we can understand only something unknown which is not body. Thus the system of these gentlemen boils down to this, that the soul of animals is a substance that is neither body nor something that is not body.

Where can so many contradictory ideas have emanated from? From the human habit of always examining something before being sure that it even exists. The tongue of a pair of bellows is its valve, so it gets called the soul of the bellows. What is this soul? It's a name I've given to the valve which, when I work the bellows, sinks, lets in air, rises, and then drives the air through a tube.

Here there is no soul distinct from the machine. But who works the bellows in animals? I've already told you, he who guides the motion of the stars. The philosopher was right who said, 'Deus est anima brutorum',* but he should have gone further.

GOOD, SOVEREIGN GOOD
(BIEN, SOUVERAIN-BIEN)

THE Ancients argued a lot about the sovereign good. They might just as well have asked what is the sovereign blue, or the sovereign casserole, or the sovereign read, or the sovereign stroll, and so on.

People put their 'good' where they can, and have as much of it as possible, each in their own way.

> Quid dem, quid non dem, renuis tu quod jubet alter.*
> Castor gaudet equis, ovo prognatus eodem
> Pugnis.*

The greatest good is that which delights you with such force that it leaves you powerless to feel anything else, just as the greatest evil is that which is going to rob you of all feeling. Those are the two extremes of the human condition, and they are short-lived.

Extreme delights, like extreme torments, cannot last a lifetime: the sovereign good and the sovereign are pipe dreams.

There is a lovely fable by Crantor:* he summoned to the Olympic games Riches, Pleasure, Health, and Virtue. Each claimed the apple. Riches said, 'I am the sovereign good, because with me everything can be purchased.' Pleasure said, 'The apple is mine, because people only want riches to get me.' Health declared that without her pleasure was impossible and riches useless. Finally, Virtue stated that she was above the other three because with money, pleasures, and good health one can make oneself very miserable if one behaves badly. The apple was awarded to Virtue.

It's a most ingenious fable, but it fails to deal with the absurd question of the sovereign good. Virtue is not a 'good', it's a duty; it's in a different genre and of a superior order. It has nothing to do with painful sensations, or with pleasurable ones. The virtuous person with gout and the stone, without friends or support, deprived of all essentials, persecuted, imprisoned by a tyrant in the pink of health, is very unhappy, whereas his insolent tormentor, fondling a new mistress on his purple couch, is very happy. You can say that the persecuted sage is better than his insolent persecutor, you can say that you love the one and hate the other; but you have to admit that the sage in chains is livid. If the sage doesn't agree, he's deceiving you, he's just a charlatan.

ALL IS GOOD
(BIEN, TOUT EST)

IT really set the cat among the pigeons in the Schools, and even among thinking people, when Leibniz, paraphrasing Plato, erected the edifice known as 'the best of all possible worlds' and imagined that everything was just fine. From his post in northern Germany he asserted that God could have made only one world. Plato had at least allowed him the possibility of making five: reason dictates that there are only five solid bodies, the tetrahedron or triangular pyramid with equal base, the cube, the hexahedron, the dodecahedron, and the icosahedron. But since our world is not shaped like any of Plato's five bodies, he had to allow God a sixth.

Let's not dwell on the divine Plato. Leibniz, who was certainly a better geometer and profounder metaphysician, rendered human beings a service by showing us that we must be very happy, that God could not have done more for us, and that he had been bound to choose from among all possible worlds the best; of that there can be no doubt.

'So what happens to original sin?' people asked. 'It will become whatever it can,' said Leibniz and his friends; but in public he wrote that original sin necessarily had its place in the best of all possible worlds.

What? Get yourself thrown out of a land of delights where you could have lived for ever if you hadn't eaten an apple? What? Give birth in poverty to wretched children who will suffer everything and make others suffer everything too? What? Catch every disease, feel every sorrow, die in pain, and, to cap it all, burn for ever and ever? Was that really the best hand you could have been dealt? That is not too 'good' for us; so how can it be good for God?

Leibniz realized that he couldn't answer that one, so he wrote fat books which he didn't understand himself.

A Lucullus, enjoying sound health and a good dinner with his friends and his mistress in the salon of Apollo, can laughingly deny that there is such a thing as evil, but he has only to look out of the window to see wretched people, and he has only to run a temperature to feel wretched himself.

I don't like quoting people. It can be quite a ticklish job; you tend to take things out of context and risk getting into all sorts of scrapes. But I must quote Lactantius, a church father; in chapter 13 of his book *On the Wrath of God* he puts these words into the mouth of Epicurus: 'Either God wishes to remove evil from the world, but cannot; or he can, but does not wish to; or he cannot and does not wish to; or he can, and wishes to. If he wishes to but cannot, that is impotence, and contrary to God's nature; if he can but does not wish to, that is wickedness, and equally contrary to his nature; if he cannot and does not wish to, that is both wickedness and impotence; if he can and wishes to (which, of all the possibilities, is the only one that matches our idea of God), what is evil doing in this world?'

It's a pressing question, and Lactantius' response is very weak: God, he says, does want evil, but has given us wisdom so that we can acquire goodness. Given the strength of the objection, one must admit this rebuttal is pretty feeble, because it presupposes that God could only grant wisdom by producing evil. Rather laughable, that kind of wisdom!

The origin of evil is an abyss; no one has been able to see to the bottom of it. It is what reduced so many ancient philosophers and lawgivers having recourse to two principles, one good and the other bad. Typhon was the bad principle among the Egyptians, and Arimane among the Persians. As we know, the Manichaeans adopted this theology; but as they had never spoken to either the good principle or the bad one, we can't take their word for it.

Of all the silly things that people have believed and that must be numbered among our misfortunes is something that is no trivial instance of stupidity: the belief in two all-powerful beings who battle it out to establish which can exert the greater influence in the world, making a pact like the two doctors in Molière: 'Pass me the emetic and I'll pass you the bleeding-knife.'

After the Platonists, Basilides, in the first century AD, claimed that God had given his worst angels the job of making our world; they were not skilled, so they made things as we see them. This theological fable crumbled to dust in the face of the terrible objection that it is not in the nature of an all-powerful and all-wise God to have the world built by incompetent architects.

Simon was aware of this objection and forestalled it by saying that the angel who ran the workshop was damned for doing his job so badly; but the roasting of this angel isn't of much help to us.

The business of the Greek woman Pandora is no better at dealing with the objection. That box containing all our ills, at the bottom of which hope remains, is a truly charming allegory; but Pandora was made by Vulcan solely in order to get at Prometheus, who had made a man out of mud.

The Indians have not had much more success: God, having created a man, gave him medicine that would keep him healthy for ever; the man loaded it on to his donkey, the donkey got thirsty, the serpent pointed it towards a spring, and while the donkey was drinking the serpent grabbed the medicine for itself.

The Syrians imagined that man and woman were created in the fourth heaven, and that they took it into their heads to eat cake instead of their usual food, ambrosia. Ambrosia was excreted through the pores, but after eating cake they had to go to the stool. So the man and the woman asked an angel to show them the way to the bathroom. 'Well, you see,' said the angel, 'that tiny little planet, about sixty million leagues from here, is the privy for the entire universe; go there quickly.' They went there and never came back; and since then the world has been the way it is.

People will always ask the Syrians why God allowed the man and the woman to eat cake and bring upon us a host of such terrible evils.

Moving hurriedly on—so as not to get bored—from the fourth heaven, I come to Lord Bolingbroke. This man, who was without doubt a great genius, gave the famous Alexander Pope his plan 'all is good', which can be found word-for-word in Bolingbroke's posthumous works and which Lord Shaftesbury included in his *Characteristics*. Read the chapter on moralists in Shaftesbury and you will see these words:

'Much is alleged in answer to show why Nature errs, and how she came thus impotent and erring from an unerring hand. But I deny she errs . . . 'Tis from this order of inferior and superior things that we admire the world's beauty, founded thus on contrarieties, whilst from such various and disagreeing principles a universal concord is established . . . In the several orders of terrestrial forms a resignation is required, a sacrifice and mutual yielding of natures one to another. The vegetables by their death sustain the animals, and animal bodies dissolved enrich the earth, and raise again the vegetable world . . .

The central powers, which hold the lasting orbs in their just poise and movement, must not be controlled to save a fleeting form, and rescue from the precipice a puny animal, whose brittle frame, however protected, must of itself so soon dissolve.'*

Bolingbroke, Shaftesbury, and Pope their popularizer offer no better answer to the question than anyone else: their 'all is good' boils down to 'everything is governed by immutable laws'. Who doesn't know that? We learn nothing new when people tell us, as any child could, that flies are born to be eaten by spiders, spiders by swallows, swallows by shrikes, shrikes by eagles, and that eagles are born to be killed by men, men to kill each other and be eaten by worms, and then, except for one in a thousand, by devils.

How's that for a clear, consistent arrangement among animals of all kinds? Everywhere there is order. An admirable example is the way a stone forms in my bladder: mineral juices gradually enter my bloodstream, filter into my kidneys, pass through the urethra, end up in my bladder and, in an excellent illustration of Newtonian mechanics, amalgamate there; a stone takes shape, grows bigger, and through the finest arrangement in the world the pains that I suffer are a thousand times worse than death. A surgeon, expert in the arts invented by Tubal-Cain, sticks a sharp, pointed instrument into my perineum, grabs my stone with his tweezers and breaks it up by a necessary mechanism and, by the same mechanism, I die a horrible death; *all that is good*, the obvious consequence of unchanging physical laws, I quite agree, I knew so too.

If we were bereft of feeling there would be nothing wrong with the physics here. But that's not the point. We're asking you whether or not there are sensory evils and where they derive from. 'God sends not ill,' says Pope in his fourth epistle on the *all-is-good*, 'for partial Ill is universal Good.'* That's a rather strange universal good, made up of kidney stones, gout, crimes of every kind, suffering of every variety, death and damnation.

Humanity's fall is the plaster which we stick on the various maladies afflicting body and mind and which you call general health; but Shaftesbury and Bolingbroke have no time for original sin, and Pope does not mention it. It's clear that their system saps the very foundations of Christianity but explains nothing.

But their system has, for all that, been granted a seal of

approval recently by several theologians, who cheerfully accept its contradictions. Fine! No one should envy people the consolation of reasoning as best they can about the evils that cascade down on us. It is only right to allow the desperately ill to eat what they like, and even to go so far as to claim that this system is consolatory. As Pope writes:

> Who sees with equal eye, as God of all,
> A hero perish, or a sparrow fall,
> Atoms or systems into ruin hurled,
> And now a bubble burst, and now a world.*

That, I grant you, is an amusing sort of consolation; don't you find something rather comforting in Lord Shaftesbury's opinion that God is not going to overturn his eternal laws just to please a puny animal like us? But it has to be admitted that this puny animal has the right to cry out humbly and to try and understand as it cries out. Why are these eternal laws not made for the well-being of every individual?

This system of *all is good* represents the creator of all things merely as a powerful and wicked monarch who as long as his designs are realized isn't bothered that four or five hundred thousand people lose their lives and the rest drag out their days in dearth and tears.

So far from being consoled by the opinion that this is the best of all possible worlds, philosophers who embrace it find it depressing. The question of good and evil remains an unravellable mess for those who seek in good faith; it's just a mental exercise for those who engage in debate: they are like convicts playing with their chains. For non-thinking people it is rather like a fish being transported from a river to a pond: they have no idea that it's so that they can be eaten during Lent; likewise we know nothing ourselves of the causes of our destiny.

Let's put at the end of almost every chapter on metaphysics the two letters that Roman judges used when confronted with a case they could not understand: *N.L.* (*non liquet*), 'that is unclear'.

LIMITS OF HUMAN INTELLIGENCE
(BORNES DE L'ESPRIT HUMAIN)

THE limits are everywhere, my poor learned friend. You want to know how your arms and feet obey your wishes but your liver doesn't? You desire to find out how thought develops in your feeble mind, and the child in this woman's womb? Take your time before answering. What is matter? You and your like have written thousands of books on the subject and discovered a few attributes of this substance; children know them as well as you do, but what precisely is this substance? And what is it that, for want of a better term, you've called 'intelligence', *esprit*, from the Latin *spiritus* ('breath')? You haven't a clue, have you?

Look at the seed I toss on the soil, and show me how it sprouts and produces a stalk bearing an ear of corn. Tell me how, on the same piece of ground, an apple grows at the top of that tree and a chestnut on the tree next to it. I could fill a whole book with questions to which your answer would be restricted to these four words: 'I do not know.'

And yet you've taken your degrees: you've put on your mortar board and fur-lined hood and been dubbed 'master'. And that cheeky fellow who bought the post he occupies thinks he's also purchased the right to pronounce on things he knows nothing about.

Montaigne's motto was 'What do I know?'* Yours is 'What do I *not* know?'

CHARACTER
(CARACTÈRE)

FROM the Greek word for 'impression', 'engraving'; it's what Nature has engraved in us. Can we rub it out? Big question. If my nose is crooked and I have cat's eyes, I can hide them behind a mask. Can I do that with the character Nature's given me? A man who was born violent and quick-tempered appeared before François I, king of France, to complain about someone getting preferential treatment; the royal visage, the courtiers' respectful bearing, the room in which the audience took place, all made a powerful impression on the man; his harsh voice softened, he presented his petition humbly, you'd have thought he'd been born as mild a person as were (at that moment at least) the courtiers among whom he felt a degree of agitation. But François I, being skilled at reading people's faces, soon noticed that the man's eyes, though lowered, were burning with a dark flame, and that the tense muscles in his face and his tightly compressed lips betokened someone who was not as mild as he was made to seem. The man followed the king to Pavia; after the battle they were both taken prisoner and transferred to Madrid, where the king's majesty no longer made the same impression on the man; familiarity soon bred contempt, and one day, pulling the royal boots off rather clumsily, he hurt the king and made him angry, at which point the man threw the boots out of the window and told the king to get lost.

Pope Sixtus V was born with an obstinate, haughty, impetuous, arrogant, vindictive, and exuberant disposition; the trials of the noviciate seemed to have had a mellowing effect on his character, but just as he was beginning to enjoy a good reputation within his order he lost his temper with a guard and beat him senseless with his bare fists. After he was appointed inquisitor in Venice he displayed great arrogance in the conduct of his duties. On being made a cardinal he was so possessed with the *rabbia papale* ('papal rage') that it prevailed over his hot temper: he feigned a death-like humility and was elected pope. Then, at a stroke, the coiled spring which had been long compressed by political expediency regained all its former elasticity and he became one of the most arrogant and despotic of rulers.

Naturam expellas furca tamen ipse redibit.*

Religion and morality may put a damper on a person's natural inclinations but cannot suppress them altogether. The drunkard in a cloister, restricted to half a sester of cider at every meal, will not get inebriated, but will always hanker after wine.

Age weakens the character: it's a tree that produces only a few defective fruits, but their nature is unaltered; it's covered with knots and moss, it's worm-eaten, but it's still an oak or a pear tree. If people could change its character they would acquire one, and become the masters of Nature. Can one acquire anything? Do we not receive everything? If you tried to urge a lazy person to take up a regular job, or if you sought to douse in the cold water of apathy the feverish soul of a hothead, or if you undertook to inspire a love of music and poetry in someone with cloth ears and without taste, you would have no more success than if you attempted to restore the sight of someone born blind. We perfect, we soften, we conceal what Nature had put in us, but we don't put in anything ourselves.

A farmer is told, 'You've got too many fish in this pond, they won't thrive; there are too many animals in your field, there's not enough grass, they'll lose weight.' It turns out after this exhortation that the pike have eaten most of the man's carp, and the wolves half his sheep, while the remainder gain weight. Will he pat himself on the back for his management style? You are that countryman: one of your passions devours the others, and you think you've got control over yourself. Are we not all rather like that old general of ninety who comes across a group of young officers behaving badly with ladies of easy virtue and shouts out in a rage: 'Gentlemen, is that the example I've given you?'

CERTAIN, CERTAINTY
(CERTAIN, CERTITUDE)

'How old's your friend Christopher?' I ask. 'Twenty-eight: I've seen his marriage contract, his baptismal certificate, I've known him since he was a child, he's twenty-eight, I'm certain of it, sure of it.'

Hardly have I heard this reply to my question from a man so certain of what he's saying, and from twenty others who confirm it, than I discover how, for reasons kept secret, a very strange ploy was used to pre-date Christopher's baptismal certificate. Those I'd been speaking to know nothing about it yet, but they're still certain about something that's not true.

If before Copernicus' time you'd asked everyone on earth 'Has the sun risen?' and 'Has it set today?' you'd have been told 'We're quite sure of it'. They were certain, but they were wrong.

For a long time soothsaying, witchcraft, and demonic possession were in everyone's eyes the most certain things in the world. What a vast number of people observed these wonderful phenomena and entertained no doubts whatever about them! Now they're no longer quite so sure.

A young man embarking on the study of geometry has come to see me. He's still only at the stage of the definition of triangles. 'Aren't you certain', I ask him, 'that the three angles of a triangle are equal to two right angles?' He replies that not only is he not sure, but that he hasn't even got a clear grasp of the proposition. I demonstrate it to him; then he becomes quite certain about it, and will remain so for the rest of his life.

That's a certainty quite different from the others; they were merely probabilities which, on examination, turned out to be mistaken; mathematical certainty, however, is unchanging and eternal.

I exist, I think, I feel pain.* Is all that as certain as a truth of geometry? Yes. Why? Because these truths are proven by the same principle that a thing cannot exist and not exist at the same time. I can't, at one and the same time, exist and not exist, feel and not feel. A triangle cannot, at one and the same time, have a hundred and eighty degrees—the sum of two right angles—and not have them.

So the physical certainty of my existence and of my feeling, and mathematical certainty, have the same value, even though they're different in kind.

It's not the same with certainty based on appearances or on unanimous reports made by human beings.

'But', you ask, 'aren't you sure Peking exists? Don't you have Peking cloth at home? Haven't the people from different countries, of varying points of view, who've written violently against each other while preaching the true gospel in Peking, made you certain of the city's existence?' My answer is that I find it extremely likely that there's a place called Peking, but that I wouldn't bet my life on it as I'd bet my life on the fact that the three angles of a triangle are equal to two right angles.

In the *Encyclopédie* we find this rather droll point being made: a person should be as sure and certain that the Maréchal de Saxe has risen from the dead if all Paris says so, as they'd be that the Maréchal won the battle of Fontenoy because all Paris says he did. Don't you see what a peculiar argument that is? I believe all Paris when I'm told something morally possible, so I have to believe all Paris when I'm told something morally and physically impossible.

It appears that the author of this article was pulling our leg, and that the other writer* who waxes lyrical in the article's conclusion, written in self-refutation, was pulling our leg too.[1]

---

[1] See the article 'Certitude' in the *Encyclopédie*.

CHAIN OF EVENTS
(CHAÎNE DES ÉVÉNEMENTS)

It's been claimed for a long time that all events are linked together by an invincible destiny; it's called fate, and according to Homer it's a higher authority than Zeus himself. The lord of all the gods and of all humankind openly admitted that he couldn't prevent his son Sarpedon dying at the appointed time. Sarpedon was born at the moment he had to be born, and he couldn't have been born at any other; he couldn't meet his death anywhere but at Troy; he couldn't be buried anywhere but in Lycia; at the appointed time his body had to produce vegetables which had to metamorphose into the substance of several Lycians; his heirs had to establish a new order in his states; this new order had to influence that of neighbouring kingdoms; there resulted new arrangements over war and peace with the neighbours of Lycia's neighbours: and so, with one thing leading to another, the destiny of the whole earth depended on Sarpedon's death, which in turn depended on another event, which was linked to others right back to the origin of things.

If only one of these events had been arranged differently, another universe would have resulted. Now, it wasn't possible for the present universe not to exist, so it wasn't possible for Zeus, Zeus though he may have been, to save his son's life.

In our day Leibniz—so he says—invented, under the name 'sufficient reason',* this system of necessity and fatality. But it's very ancient; for a while now there's been 'no effect without cause', and the tiniest cause often produces the greatest effects.

Lord Bolingbroke admits that the petty squabbles between the Duchess of Marlborough and Lady Masham gave him the opportunity to bring about the special pact between Queen Anne and Louis XIV that led to the Peace of Utrecht; that treaty strengthened Philip V's hold on the throne of Spain; he took Naples and Sicily from the house of Austria; the Spanish prince who is now king of Naples obviously owes his title to Lady Masham, and he wouldn't be in possession of it, perhaps wouldn't even have been born, if the Duchess of Marlborough had been more accommodating towards the Queen of England; his existence in Naples depended upon an act of folly, one more or one less, at the court in London. Look at the situation in which all the world's peoples find themselves: it's based on a sequence of events that appear to stem from nowhere but depend on everything. In this huge machine everything is cog, spring, rope, and pulley.

It's the same in the physical universe. A wind blowing from deep within the African continent and from the southern seas brings us part of Africa's atmosphere, which falls as rain in the Alpine valleys; that rain fertilizes our soils; our north wind in turn blows our vapours into Africa; so we do Guinea good, and it repays the compliment. The chain stretches from one end of the universe to the other.

But it seems to me that the truth of this principle is strangely abused. People are inclined to think that there is no atom too small for its movement not to have influenced the present arrangement of the whole world; and that there's no accident, be it among human beings or within the animal kingdom, that's too insignificant to serve as an essential link in the great chain of destiny.

Let's get this straight: every effect obviously has its cause, going back from cause to cause in the abyss of eternity, but not every cause has its effect, down to the very end of time. I freely admit that each event is produced by the next, and that if the present is born of the past, the present in turn gives birth to the future; all things have progenitors, but all things do not necessarily have progeny. Here it's just the same as in genealogy: every family tree goes back to Adam, as we know, but in every family there are always people who die without issue.

There's a family tree of the events of this world. It's well-known fact that the inhabitants of Gaul and Iberia descend from Gomer, and the Russians from his younger brother Magog; this genealogy is found in so many fat tomes! On that basis it can't be denied that it's Magog we have to thank for the sixty thousand Russians now under arms in the Pomeranian area and the sixty thousand Frenchmen near Frankfurt; but as for whether Magog spat to right or left near Mount Caucasus, or made two ripples or three in a well, or slept on his left side or his right, I don't see how that could have had much influence on the decision of Empress Elizabeth of Russia to send an army in support of the Holy Roman Empress Maria Theresa. I can't see what a really important issue—whether my dog dreams in his sleep or not—might have to do with the affairs of the Grand Mogul.

We need to remember that Nature isn't full up and that not every movement leads to another until it encircles the globe. If you throw a solid object into water you can easily work out that the movement of the body, and the ripples it makes in the water, are soon reduced to nothing; the motion is dissipated and the status quo ante restored. Thus any movement Magog could have produced by spitting in a well can have had no impact on what is going on in Russia and Prussia now. Current events, therefore, are not the children of all past events; they have a direct lineage, but a thousand little collateral lines are of no use to them. So, once again: every being has a father, but not every being has children. I'll have more to say about this later, perhaps, when I talk about fate (*destin*).

GREAT CHAIN OF BEING
(CHAÎNE DES ÊTRES CRÉÉS)

THE first time I read Plato and saw the gradation of beings that goes from the tiniest atom to the Supreme Being I was deeply impressed, but on closer examination the great spectacle disappeared, as all apparitions once vanished in the morning at cockcrow.

The imagination is fascinated at first to see the imperceptible progression from brute matter to organized matter, from plants to zoophytes, from these zoophytes to animals and from them to human beings, from human beings to spirits, from these spirits clothed in a small aerial body to immaterial substances; and finally to see the thousand different orders of these substances who go from beauty to perfection, rising to the godhead itself. Pious souls delight in this hierarchy; in it they see the Pope and his cardinals followed by the archbishops and bishops, after which come the parish priests, curates, lesser priests, deacons and subdeacons, and then the monks, with the capuchins bringing up the rear.

But there is a bit more distance between God and his most perfect creatures than between the Holy Father and the dean of the Sacred College. This dean can become pope, but the most perfect of the spirits created by the Supreme Being cannot become God; there is infinity between it and God.

This chain or supposed gradation no longer exists in plants and animals, as is proved by the fact that there are plant and animal species which have been destroyed. There are no more murexes. Eating griffon and ixion is forbidden; these two species have disappeared from the face of the earth, whatever Bochart says, so where's the chain?

Even where some species haven't been lost, it's obvious they can be destroyed. Lions and rhinoceroses are close to extinction.

It's highly probable that there were human races that can no longer be found, but I want them all to have survived, like the whites, the blacks, the Kaffirs whom nature has endowed with an apron of skin hanging from belly to mid-thigh, the Samoyeds whose wives have black nipples, and so on.

Isn't there an obvious gap between a man and an ape? It's not difficult to imagine a two-footed featherless creature, endowed with intelligence but not the gift of speech or a face like ours, that could be tamed, taught to obey signs, and made to serve us. And between this new species and humankind one could well imagine others.

Beyond human beings, divine Plato, you place a string of celestial substances in the sky; instructed by faith, we believe in some of these substances. But what reason do you have to believe in them? It seems you haven't spoken to Socrates' spirit. And that chap Heres, who rose from the dead just to teach you the secrets of the other world, told you nothing about those substances.

The so-called chain is not broken in the visible universe either.

What gradation, I ask you, is there between your planets? The moon is forty times smaller than our globe. After travelling from the moon into the void you find Venus; it's about the same size as the earth. From there you go to Mercury; it turns in an ellipse that is very different from the circle described by Venus; it's twenty-seven times smaller than us, the sun is a million times greater, and Mars five times less. The rotation of Mars takes two years, its neighbour Jupiter's twelve, and Saturn's thirty. Saturn, the furthest from us, is not as big as Jupiter. So where's the gradation claimed?

And then, how do you expect there to be a chain linking everything in such huge empty spaces? If there is such a chain, it's definitely the one discovered by Newton which makes all the globes in the planetary universe gravitate towards each other within the immense void.

Oh Plato, you who were so greatly admired! Everything you told us has turned out to be a fairy story. But a philosopher has emerged in the Cassiterides,* where people in your day went about naked, and he's taught the world truths that are as monumental as your imaginings were puerile.

HEAVEN IN ANTIQUITY
(LE CIEL DES ANCIENS)

IF a silkworm gave the name 'heaven' to the tiny covering of down that's spun around its cocoon, its reasoning would be similar to that of all the ancients, who called 'heaven' the atmosphere which, as M. de Fontenelle puts it so well in *Conversations on the Plurality of Worlds*,* is the down surrounding our cocoon.

The vapours arising from our earth and seas to form clouds, meteors, and thunder were taken at first to be the dwelling place of the gods. In Homer the gods always descend in golden clouds, which is why painters even nowadays depict them seated on a cloud; but since it was only proper for the ruler of the gods to enjoy greater comfort than the others he was given an eagle to ride upon, because the eagle flies higher than all the other birds.

Seeing that city rulers lived in citadels, the ancient Greeks thought the gods probably had a citadel too, and placed it on Mount Olympus in Thessaly. Its summit is sometimes hidden in the clouds, so their palace was on a level with their heaven.

Then the stars and planets that appear to be attached to the blue canopy of our atmosphere became the dwellings of the gods, seven of whom had a planet all to themselves while the rest lodged wherever they could; the general council of the gods met in a large room (to which the Milky Way gave access) because, since human beings had town halls on earth, the gods needed a room up in the air.

When the Titans—a kind of creature halfway between man and the gods—declared war on those gods with some justice, in order to reclaim part of their inheritance on their father's side (being sons of the sky and the earth), they merely piled two or three mountains one on top of the other, reckoning that that would amply suffice to make themselves masters of heaven and the castle of Olympus.

> Neve foret terris securior arduus aether;
> Affectasse ferunt regnum coeleste gigantes,
> Altaque congestos struxisse ad sidera montes,

which, roughly translated, means: 'so that lofty heaven should offer no more security than earth, the giants are said to have tried to seize the kingdom of the immortals by piling mountains up as high as the starry skies'.*

This child's and old wives' take on astrophysics was prodigiously ancient; it's certain, however, that the Chaldeans held views as sane as ours about what is called heaven: they placed the sun at the centre of our planetary system, at about the same distance from earth as we do; they made our globe and all the planets revolve around the sun; that's what Aristarchus of Samos teaches us; it's the true world-system into which Copernicus has since breathed new life; but the philosophers kept the secret to themselves so as to be held in greater respect by the people and their rulers, or rather so as to stay out of trouble.

Human beings are so in thrall to the language of error that we still call the clouds and the gap between the earth and the moon 'heaven'; we say 'go up to heaven' just as we say 'the sun turns', although we're well aware that it doesn't; in the eyes of the inhabitants of the moon we're probably 'heaven', and each planet locates its 'heaven' in the planet next door.

If Homer had been asked which heaven the soul of Sarpedon had gone to, or where Hercules' heaven was, he would have been quite at a loss to say but would have responded with some harmonious verses.

What certainty did people have that the ethereal soul of Hercules was more at home on Venus or Saturn than on earth? Would it have felt more comfortable on the sun? In such a furnace that's not very likely. What did 'heaven' mean to the ancients anyway? They knew nothing about it, but kept going on about 'heaven and earth' as if they were talking about an atom and the infinite. There's no such thing as heaven, strictly speaking; there are a prodigious number of globes rolling around in the emptiness of space, and our earth rolls around just like the others.

The ancients believed that going to heaven meant 'going up', but you don't 'go up' from one globe to another; the heavenly bodies are sometimes above our horizon and sometimes below it. So let's suppose that Venus, having visited Paphos, went back to her planet after it had set: Venus would not be 'going up' in relation to our horizon, she would be going down, in which case we ought to say 'descending to heaven'. But the ancients were unable to understand anything as subtle as that; they had vague, uncertain, and contradictory notions about everything that had to do with physics. Many fat tomes have been written in an attempt to discover what they thought about questions of that sort. A few words would have sufficed: 'They didn't think anything.'

A small number of wise men were the exception to this, but they came late on the scene, and few people set out to explain their thinking, and when they did, the charlatans of this world sent them packing heavenwards by the most direct route.

CIRCUMCISION
(CIRCONCISION)

LIKE most of today's explorers, Herodotus talks a lot of nonsense when he passes on what he learned from the barbarians he travelled amongst. So we can't be expected to believe him when he tells the stories of Gyges and Candaules, or of Arion riding a dolphin, or of the oracle, asked what Croesus was doing, answering that he was just then cooking a turtle in a lidded stewpot, or of Darius getting himself proclaimed king thanks to his horse being the first to whinny, or a hundred other fables written for the amusement of children and for the compilations of rhetoricians. But when Herodotus recounts what he's seen and talks about the native customs he's investigated and the foreign antiquities he's examined, then it's grown-ups he's addressing.

In the book *Euterpe* he writes: 'It seems to me—I'm using my own judgement here and not relying on hearsay—that the inhabitants of Colchis originally came from Egypt, because I've found that the Colchians remembered the ancient Egyptians far more than the Egyptians remembered the ancient customs of Colchis.

'These inhabitants of the Black Sea coast claimed to be a colony established by Sesostris; I would make the same conjecture myself, not merely because they are dark-skinned and have curly hair, but because the peoples of Colchis, Egypt, and Ethiopia are the only ones on earth to have practised circumcision from time immemorial. The Phoenicians and Palestinians acknowledge that they adopted the custom from the Egyptians, and the Syrians who now occupy the banks of the Thermodon and Parthenius, and the Macronians their neighbours, admit that it was only recently that they began conforming to this Egyptian practice. That's chiefly the reason why they're recognized as being of Egyptian origin.

'Since the ceremony is a very ancient one in both countries, I couldn't say, with respect to Ethiopia and Egypt, in which of the two male circumcision originated, but it's likely that the Ethiopians took it from the Egyptians. Conversely, now that they're trading more extensively with the Greeks, the Phoenicians have stopped circumcising the newborn.'

From this passage in Herodotus* it's evident that several populations took circumcision from the Egyptians, but no country has ever
claimed to get it from the Jews. So to whom can we attribute the origin
of the custom? To the country that five or six others acknowledge getting it from? Or to another less powerful, less commercially active,
less warlike nation, stuck in a corner of Arabia Petraea, that has never
passed any of its practices on to anyone else?

The Jews say that out of charity they were once invited to Egypt.
So isn't it rather likely that the smaller of the two peoples imitated a
custom belonging to the larger one, and that the Jews adopted some
of the usages of their masters?

Clement of Alexandria reports that when Pythagoras went to Egypt
he had to get himself circumcised before he could be admitted to their
mysteries; that's because, for anyone aspiring to join the priesthood
in Egypt, it was imperative to be circumcised. Such priests already
existed when Joseph arrived in the country; its government was a very
old institution, and the ancient Egyptian ceremonies were observed
with scrupulous exactitude.

The Jews acknowledge that they stayed two hundred and five years
in Egypt and during that period they did not get themselves circumcised, so it's clear that during those two hundred and five years it was
not from the Jews that the Egyptians took the practice of circumcision. And would they have done so once the Jews had—according to
their own account—stolen all the vessels they'd been lent and gone
into hiding in the desert with their spoils? Is a master likely to adopt
the cardinal tenet of the religion professed by his thieving runaway
slave? That's just not human nature.

The Book of Joshua says that the Jews were circumcised in the
desert: in chapter 5, verse 9, we read that 'I have rolled away the
reproach of Egypt from off you'. Now, for a population that found
itself between the Phoenicians, the Arabs, and the Egyptians, what
could this 'reproach' be, if it wasn't something which made it contemptible in the eyes of these peoples? How could this 'reproach' be
lifted from its shoulders? By removing a bit of foreskin? Isn't that the
clear meaning of this passage?

In Genesis it's said that Abraham had been circumcised before-
hand, but he went to Egypt, which for long had been a flourishing
kingdom governed by a powerful ruler, so there's no reason why in
an ancient realm like that circumcision hadn't been practised long

before the Jewish nation was established. What's more, there was no
follow-up to Abraham's circumcision: his progeny were circumcised
only in Joshua's time.

Now, before Joshua, the Israelites had—by their own admission—
adopted many of the Egyptians' customs and copied several of their
sacrifices and ceremonies, such as the fasts observed on the eve of
festivals of Isis, ablutions, the shaving of priests' heads, incense, the
candelabrum, the sacrifice of a red heifer, purification with hyssop,
refraining from pig-meat, and horror of foreigners' cooking utensils:
all this attests to the fact that the tiny Hebrew people—despite their
loathing for the great Egyptian nation—had retained a great many of
their former masters' customs. The sending of the goat Azazel into
the desert, laden with the sins of the people, was obviously copied
from an Egyptian practice; the rabbis even accept that Azazel is not
a Hebrew word. So there was nothing to prevent the Jews imitating
the Egyptian practice of circumcision, just as their neighbours the
Arabs did.

There's nothing extraordinary about the fact that God, who sanctified the very ancient Asian rite of baptism, should have sanctified too
the no less ancient African practice of circumcision. We've already
seen that he is master when it comes to attaching his graces to the
signs which he deigns to choose.

What's more, the Jewish people, having adopted circumcision in
Joshua's time, have kept up the practice to this day; the Arabs too
have remained faithful to it; but the Egyptians, who at first circumcised both boys and girls, eventually stopped doing it to girls and
reserved it for priests, astrologers, and prophets. That's what Clement
of Alexandria and Origen tell us. Indeed, it doesn't appear that the
Ptolomies were ever circumcised.

The Latin authors, who treat the Jews with such contempt that
they call them mockingly 'curtus Appella' and say 'credat Judaeus
Apella, curti Judaei',* don't apply the same terms to the Egyptians.
Today the entire population of Egypt is circumcised, but that's for
another reason: it's because Islam adopted the ancient Arab custom
of circumcision.

It was this Arabic circumcision that passed to the Ethiopians, who
still circumcise boys and girls.

It has to be admitted that the ceremony of circumcision seems pretty
odd at first sight, but it's noteworthy that from time immemorial in

the East the priests consecrated themselves to their deities by marking their bodies in particular ways, and that an ivy leaf was tattooed on priests' wrists. Lucian tells us that the devotees of the goddess Isis had characters printed on their wrists and necks. The priests of Cybele became eunuchs by self-castration.

It seems highly likely that the Egyptians, who venerated the phallus and carried its image in their processions with much pomp, thought up the idea of offering to Isis and Osiris, who were responsible for all earthly creation, a snippet from the member chosen by those gods to perpetuate the human race. The ancient customs of the East differ so radically from ours that to any reasonably well-read person nothing must seem especially odd. When told that the Hottentots remove one testicle from each of their male children a Parisian is quite taken aback. The Hottentots are perhaps surprised that Parisians hang on to both of theirs.

BODY
(CORPS)

JUST as we don't know what a spirit is, we've no idea what a body is: we observe a few properties, but what is the thing in which these properties reside? There are only bodies, say Democritus and Epicurus; there are no bodies, say the followers of Zeno of Elea.

Bishop Berkeley of Cloyne was the most recent philosopher to claim, on the basis of numerous sophisms, to have demonstrated that bodies do not exist: they are, he says, without colour, smell, or warmth; these modalities are in your sensations and do not reside in objects. He could have saved himself the trouble of proving such a well-known fact, but from there he proceeds to extension and solidity, which are corporeal essences, and he thinks he's proved that a piece of green cloth has no extension because the cloth isn't in fact green; the sensation of greenness is only in you, so the sensation of extension is also only in you. And having demolished extension in this way, he concludes that solidity, to which it is attached, itself falls, so that there's nothing in the world but our ideas. In this way, ten thousand men killed by ten thousand cannonballs are at bottom—according to this learned man—merely ten thousand apprehensions of our soul.

It oughtn't to have been difficult for My Lord Bishop of Cloyne to avoid falling into this ridiculous excess. He believes he's shown that there is no such thing as extension, because a body seen through his telescope seems four times larger than when viewed with the naked eye, and four times smaller when looked at through another lens. From this he concludes that since a body cannot, at one and the same time, be four feet and six feet and only one foot in length, that length does not exist, so there's nothing there at all. He merely needed to take a measure and say, 'however long a body appears to me, it is so many measures long'.

It was quite easy for him to see that it's not the same with extension and solidity as it is with sounds, colours, tastes, smells, and so on. It's obvious that there are feelings in us aroused by the configuration of parts; but extension is not a feeling. When this burning log goes out, I'm not warm any longer; when these notes are no longer struck, I don't hear the tune; when this rose fades, I can't smell it any more;

but the log, the tune, and the rose have extension independently of me. Berkeley's paradox isn't worth refuting.*

It's interesting to know what led him to this paradox. I had a few conversations with him a long time ago;* he said he'd got the idea from the fact that extension's recipient subject cannot be conceived. And indeed, in his book, he wins the argument when he asks Hylas what this subject, this substratum, this substance is: 'It's the extended body,' replies Hylas, whereupon the bishop, alias Philonous, pokes fun at him, and poor Hylas, realizing that he's said a silly thing—that extension is the subject of extension—is embarrassed and admits he just doesn't get it, that there's no such thing as body, that the material world doesn't exist, and that there's only an intellectual world.*

All Hylas had to say to Philonous was: 'We know nothing, really, about this subject, this extended, solid, divisible, mobile, figured (etc.) substance; I know it no more than I know the willing, thinking, and feeling subject; but the subject exists nonetheless, since it has essential properties which can't be taken away from it.'

We're all like most of the women in Paris: they tuck in heartily without knowing what goes into the stew; so we enjoy bodies, without knowing their make-up. What is the body made of? Of parts, and these parts turn into other parts. What are these last parts? Bodies, still; you can go on dividing endlessly, and get nowhere.

In fine, a subtle philosopher,* noting that a picture is made up of ingredients none of which is a picture, and a house of materials none of which is a house, imagined (somewhat differently) that bodies are constructed of an infinity of tiny beings that are not bodies: he called them 'monads'. This system is not without its good points and, were it revealed, I would think it very possible; all these little beings would be mathematical points, kinds of souls waiting only for a habit to inhabit. It would be never-ending metempsychosis: a monad would enter a whale now, a tree next, and then a juggler. It's a system as good as any other; I've as much liking for it as the declension of atoms, the grace versatile,* and Dom Calmet's vampires.

ON CHINA
(DE LA CHINE)

WE go to China and bring back clay, as if we didn't have any ourselves; cloth, as if we were short of the stuff; a tiny herb to infuse in water, as if we didn't have simple plants in our part of the world. In return we want to convert the Chinese, but we shouldn't question the ancientness of their civilization or tell them they're idolaters. How would we like it, indeed, if a Capuchin, after being well received in a Montmorency château, tried to convince them that they were, like the king's secretaries, new-minted nobility, and accused them of idolatry because in the château he'd found two or three statues of constables held in great respect?

Wolff, the famous professor of mathematics at the university of Halle, delivered a very fine speech in praise of Chinese philosophy; he lauded this ancient people, so different from us in ways of thinking, in facial hair, and in the shape of their ears, eyes, and noses; he praised, as I say, their love of virtue and worship of a supreme God; he gave full credit to the emperors, mandarins, writers, and law courts of China; less so to the country's bonzes.*

Now, this Wolff drew hundreds of students of all nationalities to Halle. In the same university there was a professor of theology called Lange who couldn't inspire anybody to attend his lectures; in despair at freezing to death all alone in his auditorium he sought, as one might expect, to destroy the professor of mathematics; and as is the way with such people, he did not shrink from accusing him of not believing in God.

Some European writers who'd never been to China had claimed that the Peking authorities were atheists. Wolff praised the philosophers of Peking, so Wolff was an atheist; envy and hatred never manage to construct a better syllogism than this. That argument of Lange's, supported by a cabal and a protector, was felt to be conclusive by the king of the country,* who offered the mathematician a difficult choice: either leave Halle within twenty-four hours, or face the gallows. Wolff was a man of sound reasoning, so he didn't fail to make a speedy exit. His departure robbed the king of the two to three thousand crowns which the philosopher brought into the kingdom every year through the influx of his students. This example ought to make rulers understand that they shouldn't always listen to calumny and sacrifice a great man to the fury of an imbecile.

So let's get back to China. Stuck as we are in the western corner of the globe, what were we thinking of, getting involved in furious arguments and in hurling insults at each other, all over whether or not there were fourteen princes before the Chinese Emperor Fu Xi, and whether this Fu Xi lived three thousand or two thousand nine hundred years before our common era? I don't mind two Irishmen taking it into their heads to have an argy-bargy in Dublin about who in the twelfth century was the owner of the land I now occupy, but isn't it obvious that they ought to ask me, the person who has the archives in his hands? It's the same in my view with the first emperors of China; people should address the question to the country's law courts.

You can talk the hind legs off a donkey about the fourteen princes who reigned before Fu Xi, but all your wrangling will serve to prove is that China was densely populated in those days and that the rule of law held sway there. Now, I ask you, does a united people, governed by princes under the law, not presuppose great antiquity? Just think how much time is needed for a particular combination of circumstances to lead to the development of iron mining, to the use of that metal in agriculture, and to the invention of the flying shuttle loom and of all other arts and crafts.

Those who create children with a stroke of the pen have made a rather comical calculation. According to Fr. Petau's elegant hypothesis, two hundred and eighty-five years after the Flood the earth had a hundred times more inhabitants than anyone would dare claim today, and the Cumberlands and the Whistons* have made equally amusing calculations. If all these good people had only consulted the registers in our American colonies, they would have learned how slow population growth is, and that it can even go into reverse, diminishing rather than increasing.

So we, people of recent origin, descendants of the Celts, we who only yesterday were clearing the forests that covered our savage lands, should leave the Chinese and the Indians to enjoy their fine climate and their great antiquity in peace. Above all let's stop calling the Emperor of China and the Peshwa of Deccan idolaters. There's no need to get fanatical about the merits of the Chinese: their empire's constitution is truly the best in the world, the only one based on paternal authority (which doesn't stop the mandarins beating their children black and blue), the only one where a provincial governor is punished if he's not acclaimed on leaving office by the populace; the only one to have instituted rewards for virtue whereas everywhere else the law is restricted to punishing crime; the only one to have got its conquerors to adopt its laws, whereas we are still subject to the customs of the Burgundians, Franks, and Goths who conquered us. But it has to be admitted that the lower orders, ruled by the bonzes, are as rascally as our own; that foreigners are always grossly overcharged there as they are here; that in the sciences the Chinese are still stuck at the point we were at two hundred years ago; that like us they have a thousand ridiculous prejudices; that they believe in charms and in judicial astrology, as we've done for ages.

Let's admit, too, that they are still astounded by our thermometers, by the way we freeze liquids with saltpetre, and by all the experiments of Torricelli and Otto von Guericke, just as we were when we saw these marvels of physics for the first time; and let's add that their doctors are no better at curing fatal illnesses than ours are, and that in China, just as here, it's nature that cures minor illnesses; but none of this can obscure the fact that four thousand years ago, when we were still illiterate, the Chinese knew all the essential and useful things on which we pride ourselves today.

CHINESE CATECHISM
(CATÉCHISME CHINOIS)

*Or, conversations between Ku-su, a disciple of Confucius,
and Prince Koo, son of the King of Loo, tributary of the Chinese
Emperor Gnen-van, 417 years before our common era.*

Translated into Latin by Fr Fouquet, erstwhile ex-Jesuit. The MS is in the
Vatican Library, no. 42759.

KOO: People tell me to 'worship heaven' (*Chang-ti*); what am I supposed to understand by that?

KU-SU: It's not the heaven you can see, because the sky above is only
air—air made up of all the earth's exhalations. It would be pretty
silly to worship vapours.

KOO: But it wouldn't surprise me. People have fallen for things that
are a lot stupider than that, it seems to me.

KU-SU: True. But you must be wise, seeing that you're going to be
a ruler.

KOO: There are so many people who worship heaven and the
planets!

KU-SU: The planets are just like our earth. The moon, for instance,
could worship our sand and our mud with about as much justification as we would have in kneeling before the sand and the mud of
the moon.

KOO: What do people mean when they say 'the heaven and the earth',
'to ascend into heaven', 'being worthy of heaven'?

KU-SU: What they're saying is very stupid. There's no such thing
as heaven.[1] Each planet is surrounded by its atmosphere, which is
like a shell, and it revolves around its sun in space. Each sun stands
at the centre of several planets which rotate continually around it.
There's no zenith and no nadir, no rise or fall. You can see that if
people on the moon said they were 'ascending to earth', that they
had to make themselves 'worthy of earth', they'd be barking mad.
So are we, when we say something meaningless like 'we must make
ourselves worthy of heaven'. It's as if we were saying 'we must

---

[1] See the article 'Heaven in Antiquity' [pp. 60–2].

make ourselves worthy of air', 'worthy of the Draco constellation', or 'worthy of space'.

KOO: I think I get it: we should worship only the God that made heaven and earth.

KU-SU: Yes. God alone should be worshipped. But when we say he made heaven and earth, that's a huge pious banality. Because if we understand by 'heaven' the prodigious space in which God lit so many suns and set so many worlds rotating, it's much more ridiculous to say 'heaven and earth' than to say 'the mountains and a grain of sand'. Our globe is infinitely smaller than a grain of sand compared with the million billion universes among which we disappear altogether. All we can do is to add our feeble voice here to that of the innumerable beings who praise God throughout the vast stretches of space.

KOO: So we were thoroughly misled when we were told that the Buddha descended from the fourth heaven in the form of a white elephant.

KU-SU: That's just an old wives' tale spun to children by the bonzes. Our sole duty is to worship the eternal author of all beings.

KOO: But how could one being have created the others?

KU-SU: Look at that star: it's fifteen hundred thousand million *lis* from our tiny planet. It projects rays that will make two angles, equal at the apex, in your eyes; they make the same angles in the eyes of all animals. Isn't that evidence of a fixed design? Isn't that an admirable law? And who creates a work, if not a worker? Who makes laws, if not a lawgiver? So isn't there a worker, an eternal lawgiver?

KOO: But who made this worker? And how was he made?

KU-SU: Your highness, I was strolling yesterday beside the vast palace your father's built. I heard two crickets talking. One said to the other, 'That's a terrific building.' 'Yes,' said the other, 'proud as I am to be a cricket, I have to admit that someone more powerful than a cricket created this marvel; but I've no idea who that someone is; I can see that he exists, but I don't know what he is.'

KOO: I say, you're a more learned cricket than I am! That's what I like about you: you don't claim to know things you don't.

SECOND CONVERSATION

KU-SU: So you agree that there is an independently existing, all-powerful being who is the supreme artisan of all things?

KOO: Yes. But if he enjoys an independent existence, he cannot be confined; so is he everywhere? So does he exist in all matter, in every part of me?

KU-SU: Why not?

KOO: So does that make me a part of the divinity?

KU-SU: That doesn't necessarily follow. This piece of glass is filled throughout with light, but is it—itself—light? It's only sand, nothing else. All things are in God, no doubt; that which animates everything must be everywhere. God isn't like the emperor of China, living in a palace and sending mandarins to carry out his orders. Since God exists, his existence necessarily fills the whole of space and all his works; and since he is in you, it behoves you to do nothing in his presence that you would be ashamed of.

KOO: What does one have to do, to dare look at oneself without repugnance or shame before the Supreme Being?

KU-SU: To be just.

KOO: What else?

KU-SU: To be just.

KOO: But the Taoists say that there is no such thing as being just or unjust, and that there is neither vice nor virtue.

KU-SU: But do they say that there is no such thing as health or sickness?

KOO: No, because that would be quite mistaken.

KU-SU: The mistake in thinking that there is no such thing as sickness or health of the soul, and no such thing as vice and virtue, is just as great, and it's more pernicious. It's monstrous to say that it's all the same: is it all the same whether you feed your son, or crush him to death? Is it all the same whether you give succour to your mother, or stab her through the heart?

KOO: You're giving me the shivers. I loathe the Taoists, but there are so many nuances in the notion of just and unjust that one is often at a loss. Who can know precisely what is allowed and what is forbidden? Who can with complete assurance set the boundaries between good and evil? What rule can you give me so that I know the difference?

KU-SU: The rule of my master Confucius: 'Live in such a way that, when you're at the point of death, you would wish to have lived; treat your neighbour as you'd wish others to treat you.'

KOO: Such precepts, I agree, should be the code of all humanity.

But what will it matter to me, as I lie dying, that I've lived well? What good will it do me? When it's broken, will the clock be happy to have struck every hour on the hour?

KU-SU: The clock has no feeling and it can't think. It can't feel remorse as you do when you feel guilty.

KOO: But what if after committing several crimes I manage to feel no remorse any longer?

KU-SU: Well, you'd have to be smothered. You can be sure that among those who don't like to be oppressed there will be found people who will make sure you're unable to commit any more crimes.

KOO: So God, who is in them, will let them be wicked after allowing me to be?

KU-SU: God has given you reason. Don't abuse it yourself, and don't let them abuse it. Not only will you be wretched in this life, but who's to say you won't be equally unhappy in another?

KOO: And who says there is another life?

KU-SU: If in doubt, you should behave as if there were one.

KOO: But what if I'm sure there isn't?

KU-SU: I defy you to think that.

THIRD CONVERSATION

KOO: You're egging me on, Ku-su. So that I can be rewarded or punished when I no longer exist, there will have to be something in me that feels, and that thinks, after I'm gone. Now, since before my birth nothing of me had feeling or thought, why should it have after my death? What could this incomprehensible part of me be? Will the buzzing of this bee still be heard after the bee is no more? Will the leaves of this plant live on after the plant is uprooted? Aren't leaves a term used to signify the inexplicable way the Supreme Being wanted the plant to draw its sap from the earth? Likewise, the soul is a word invented to express, in an obscure and feeble manner, what makes life tick. All animals have motion, and this ability to move is called 'active force'; but this force is not a distinct being. We have passions, memory, and reason; but these passions, this memory, this reason, are probably not separate entities, they're not beings existing within us, they're not little people that have a special existence; they're generic terms invented to fix our ideas. So the soul that signifies our memory, our reason, our passions, is itself a mere word. What makes things move in Nature? God. What makes every plant grow? God again. What makes animals move? God, once more. What makes people think? God, yet again.

If the human soul[2] were a little person trapped in our body directing its movements and ideas, wouldn't that indicate, in the eternal artisan of the world, an impotence and a sleight of hand quite unworthy of him? Wouldn't it show that he was incapable of creating automata that contained within themselves the gift of movement and thought? You taught me Greek, you got me to read *The Iliad*, where I find Vulcan depicted as a divine blacksmith for making golden tripods that moved to the council of the gods of their own accord: but this same Vulcan would seem a pathetic charlatan to me if he'd hidden in the body of those tripods a small boy who moved them without anyone noticing.

There are cool dreamers who've considered it a very imaginative notion to have planets rotated by genii who push them continually along; but God has not been reduced to such a pitiful expedient: in a word, why use two means of driving a machine when one will suffice? You wouldn't dare deny that God has the power to animate the little-known being we call matter, so why would he use another agent to animate it?

More to the point, what might the soul be, that you give so freely to our body? Where might it come from? When might it arrive? Would the creator of the universe have to be constantly on the alert when couples are making love, noting carefully the moment when sperm leaves the man's body and enters the woman's, so as to be able to despatch a soul to the sperm? And if the sperm dies, what will happen to the soul? Either it will have been created needlessly, or it will have to wait for another opportunity.

That, I admit, is an odd business for the master of the universe to be engaged in. And not only would he have to keep a constant eye on human coupling, he would have to do the same with all the animals, because like us they have memory, ideas, and passions; and if a soul is needed for these feelings, this memory, these ideas, and these passions to be formed, God would have to work continually

---

[2] See the article 'Soul' [pp. 10–16].

to forge souls for the elephants, the fleas, the owls, the fish, and the bonzes.

What idea would that give of the architect of so many millions of worlds if he had to tinker constantly with his creation to keep it working properly?

That's a small taster of the reasons that incline me to doubt the existence of the soul.

KU-SU: You argue in good faith, and this virtuous sentiment, even if it's misguided, would appeal to the Supreme Being. You may be mistaken, but you don't aim to get things wrong, so you can be forgiven. But just think: you've only raised doubts, and these doubts are sad. Consider other, more consoling possibilities: it's hard to be snuffed out; have the hope to live on. You know that thought is not matter; you know that it has no connection with matter, so why is it so difficult for you to believe that God has put a divine principle into you that cannot be dissolved and cannot be terminated by death? Would you go so far as to say that it's impossible for you to have a soul? Probably not. So if it's possible, isn't it very likely that you've got one? Could you reject for the human race such a beautiful and necessary system? Will you let a few difficulties put you off?

KOO: I'd like to embrace this system, but I'd like to see it proved. I can't make myself believe something for which I have no evidence. I'm always struck by the great idea that God is the creator of all things, is everywhere and within everything, and that he gives life and motion to everything; and if he is in all the parts of my being as he is in all parts of nature, I don't see what need I have of a soul. What would I do with this tiny subordinate being when my driving force is God himself? What purpose would a soul serve me? It is not we who give ourselves our ideas because we have them nearly always despite ourselves; we even have them when we're asleep; everything happens in ourselves without our having to lift a finger. It'd be no use the soul telling the blood and animal spirits 'I'd be grateful if, to please me, you'd flow in this fashion'; they'll always circulate in the manner God prescribes. I prefer being the machine of a God who's been demonstrated to me than the machine of a soul whose existence I doubt.

KU-SU: Well, if God himself is your driving force don't ever sully with criminal activity the God that is within you; and if he has given you a soul, don't let it ever cause him offence. In both systems you have free will; you're a free person, that is, you can do just as you please; so use this freedom to serve the God who gave it to you. It's a good thing you're a philosopher, but it's essential you're a just person. You'll be all the more so once you believe you've got an immortal soul.

Tell me: is it not the case that God is sovereign justice?

KOO: No doubt. And if it were possible for God to cease to exist (which would be a blasphemous thing to say), I would wish, myself, to act with fairness.

KU-SU: Is it not the case that when you're on the throne it'll be your duty to reward virtue and punish criminal activity? Would you wish God not to do what you're required to? You're well aware that in this life there are, and always will be, virtuous people who suffer misfortune and criminals who go scot-free, so it's necessary for good and evil to be judged in another existence. It's this idea—so simple, so natural, and so widespread—that has led so many peoples to embrace the belief in the immortality of the soul and in a divine justice that weighs them in the balance after their death. Is there any other system more reasonable, more compatible with Divinity, and more useful to the human race?

KOO: So why have several nations failed to embrace this system? You are aware that we have in our province about two hundred families of former Sinoos who once lived in part of Arabia Petraea; neither they nor their ancestors have ever believed in the immortality of the soul; just as we have the five *Jing*,* they have the Pentateuch. I've read it in translation. Their laws are, of necessity, similar to those of all other peoples: they command people to respect their parents and never steal, lie, kill, or commit adultery; but these same laws make no mention of rewards or punishments in an afterlife.

KU-SU: If these poor people haven't yet developed the idea of an afterlife, no doubt they will one day. But what do we care about a tiny wretched people when the Babylonians, Egyptians, Indians, and every other civilized nation have embraced this healthy doctrine? If you were ill, would you reject a remedy that has earned the approval of every person in China on the grounds that a group of uncouth hillbillies have refused to have anything to do with it? God has given you reason: it has told you that the soul must be immortal; so it's God himself who's telling you this.

KOO: But how can I be rewarded, or punished, when I won't be myself any more, when I won't have anything that has made me what I am? It's only through memory that I remain myself. Once my last illness begins I'll lose that memory, so it'll need a miracle to get it back and restore me to the existence I'll have lost, won't it?

KU-SU: So, were a prince to have murdered his family in order to gain the throne, and were he to have tyrannized his subjects, would he be free to say to God, 'It's not me, I've lost my memory, you've got it wrong, I'm no longer the same person'? Do you think that sophism would wash with God?

KOO: All right, all right, I give up. I wished to do the right thing for my own satisfaction, and now I'll do it to please the Supreme Being too. I thought it was sufficient for my soul to be just in this life, and now I'll hope it'll be happy in the next. I can see that this opinion is a good one for peoples and princes to hold, but I'm troubled by the idea that God should be worshipped.

FOURTH CONVERSATION

KU-SU: What is it in our first canonical book, the *Shi-Jing** so highly respected by all Chinese emperors, that you find offensive? You plough a field with your own princely hands to set an example to the people, and you offer up the first-fruits to the Chang-ti, to the Tien, to the Supreme Being; you make a sacrifice four times a year; you are ruler and pontiff; you promise God to do all the good that lies within your power; is there anything distasteful about that?

KOO: Far be it from me to object to any of that. I know God doesn't need our sacrifices or our prayers, but *we* need to offer them up to him; the act of worship wasn't set up for his sake, but for ours. I love saying my prayers, but I don't want them to sound ridiculous, because when I've said 'the mountain of the Chang-ti is a fertile mountain, and you mustn't look at fertile mountains',* and when I've made the sun flee and the moon dry up, will this twaddle please the Supreme Being and be of use to myself and my subjects?

Above all, I can't stand the madness of the sects around us: on the one hand I see Lao-tse whose mother conceived him through the union of earth and sky and endured a pregnancy lasting eighty years. I no more give credence to his doctrine of suppressing and stripping everything away than I believe in the white hair with which he was born or the black cow on which he rode out to spread his teachings.

The god Fo doesn't impress me either, even though he was sired by a white elephant and holds out the promise of eternal life.

What I dislike, above all, is that such delusions are constantly being peddled by bonzes who seduce the people in order to rule over them. They make themselves respectable through acts of mortification which are an affront to nature: some, for as long as they live, renounce the most healthy foods, as if the only way they can please God is by eating a poor diet; others wear an iron collar that they sometimes make themselves fully worthy of, or drive nails into their thighs as if they were wooden planks, and the people follow them blindly. If a king issues a proclamation they don't like, they coolly announce that the edict is not in Fo's commentary and that it is better to obey God than men. How can you cure such a crazy, dangerous, and widespread illness? The principle of toleration, as you know, is the basis of government in China and throughout Asia, but isn't this indulgent attitude rather harmful if it exposes the empire to the risk of being overthrown by fanatics?

KU-SU: May the Chang-ti preserve me from any wish to suppress the spirit of toleration in you: it's such a respectable virtue, one that's as essential to the soul as nourishment is to the body. Natural law allows everyone to believe what they like, just as they can eat what they wish. No doctor has the right to kill his patients because they haven't been following the diet he's prescribed. No ruler has the right to hang those of his subjects who don't think the way he does, but he does have the right to prevent disorder, and if he's a wise man it's quite easy for him to uproot superstition. You know what happened to Daon, sixth king of Chaldea, some four thousand years ago?

KOO: No idea. Do tell me.

KU-SU: The Chaldean priests took it into their heads to worship the pike-fish in the River Euphrates. They claimed that a famous pike called Oannes had once taught them theology, and that this pike was immortal, three feet long, with a small crescent on its tail. Out of respect for Oannes eating pike was forbidden. A big argument blew up among the theologians as to whether the pike Oannes had a hard roe or a soft one. Each side excommunicated the other, and it frequently led to fisticuffs. Here's how King Daon set about restoring order.

He commanded both parties to observe a strict fast for three days, after which he summoned the tenants of the hard-roe theory to be present at his dinner. He had his servants bring in a three-foot pike whose tail had a little crescent attached to it. 'Is this your god?' he asked the learned men. 'Yes, Your Majesty,' they replied, 'because it has a crescent on its tail, so it will certainly have a hard roe.' The king ordered the pike to be slit open, and the finest soft roe in the world was found inside. 'As you see,' he said, 'this pike is not your god, because it has a soft roe.' The pike was eaten by the king and his satraps to the great delight of the hard-roe theologians who'd watched the god of their opponents being deep-fried.

The learned men of the opposite persuasion were sent for at once, and were shown a god with eggs in its body and a crescent on its tail. They declared that it was the god Oannes and had a soft roe. It was fried too, and found to have a hard roe. Thereupon, as both parties were equally foolish and equally hungry, and since good King Daon indicated that pike was all he could offer them for supper, they fell greedily upon the fish, both the hard-roed and the soft. The civil war came to an end and everyone blessed the good King Daon. After that people were able to order as much pike as they liked for dinner.

KOO: I like King Daon a lot, and I promise to imitate him at the first opportunity. So far as I'm able, and short of using force, I'll always stop people worshipping the likes of Fo and pike-fish.

I'm aware that in Pegu and Tonkin there are small gods and little talapoins* who cause the moon to wane and who predict the future clearly; that's to say they see clearly that which is not, since the future has no existence. So far as I'm able I'll stop the talapoins coming here, claiming the future is the present and causing the moon to wane.

What a pity it is that there are sects going from one town to another, peddling their delusional ideas like mountebanks selling quack medicines! How shaming it is for the human mind that little nations think they have the monopoly of truth and that the vast empire of China is mired in error! Is the Supreme Being the god of Formosa or Borneo only? Has the rest of the universe been abandoned by him? My dear Ku-su, he is the father of all humankind; he lets everyone eat pike; the worthiest homage we can pay him is to live a virtuous life; and as the great emperor Yao used to say, a pure heart is the most beautiful of all God's temples.

FIFTH CONVERSATION

KU-SU: Since you love virtue, how will you practise it when you're king?

KOO: By not being unjust to my neighbours or my peoples.

KU-SU: It's not sufficient to do no evil: you will do good; you will feed the poor, not by rewarding idleness, but by giving them useful things to do. You will upgrade the highways, dig canals, erect public buildings, encourage all the arts, ensure that merit in every field is recompensed, and pardon honest mistakes.

KOO: That's what I call not being unjust; that's a good list of duties.

KU-SU: You think like a true monarch; but there's the king and there's the man, there's public life and there's private life. You're getting married soon; how many wives do you intend to have?

KOO: I think a dozen will suffice; any more than that would take up time needed for affairs of state. I don't like kings who have three hundred wives and seven hundred concubines and thousands of eunuchs to wait on them. Above all the craze for eunuchs seems to me too great an outrage to human nature. I can just about forgive the castration of cockerels, they taste all the better to eat for it, but no one has yet skewered eunuchs on a roasting spit. What purpose does their humiliation serve? The Dalai Lama has fifty-odd singing in his pagoda. I'd love to know if the Chang-ti derives much pleasure from hearing the clear voices of those fifty geldings.

I find it even more ridiculous that there are bonzes who do not marry; they boast of being wiser than the rest of the Chinese people: fine, so let them beget wise children. It's a funny way of honouring the Chang-ti, to deprive him of worshippers! It's a strange way of serving the human race, to offer it such an example of self-destruction! The nice little lama called *Stelca isant Erepi* argued that 'every priest should have as many children as he could'; he practised what he preached, and was very useful in his time. As for me, I'll marry off all the lamas and the bonzes, and all the lamesses and the bonzesses, who have a vocation for this sacred work; they'll certainly be better citizens for it, and I'll hope to be doing a great service for the kingdom of Loo.

KU-SU: Oh, what a good prince we'll have in you! You make me weep for joy. You won't be content to have wives and subjects; after all, one can't spend the whole day issuing edicts and making babies, you'll no doubt have friends too.

KOO: I already have several, and good friends they are; they alert me to my faults, and I take the liberty to point out theirs; they console me and I console them; friendship is the balm of life, better than the chemist Erueil's, and better even than the great Ranoud's sachets. I'm surprised that friendship has not been made a religious precept; I'd like to see it included in our ritual.

KU-SU: Take good care you don't! Friendship is by nature sacred; don't you ever try to command it; the heart has to be free. In any case, if you make friendship a precept, a mystery, a rite, or a ceremony, there'll soon be a thousand bonzes preaching it and writing delusional things about it, and that'll make friendship an object of ridicule, so don't expose it to such profanation.

But how will you treat your enemies? Confucius says in many places that one ought to love them. Doesn't that strike you as being rather difficult?

KOO: Love thine enemy? Good heavens, it's dead easy.

KU-SU: That means what?

KOO: What it's meant to mean. I learnt warfare under Prince Décon. When in our campaign against Prince Visbrunk one of the enemy was wounded and fell into our hands, we took care of him like a brother; we frequently offered our own beds to enemy casualties and lay down alongside them on tiger-skins stretched out on the ground; we served them their meals ourselves: what more could be asked? That we love them as we love our mistresses?

KU-SU: I find everything you tell me very edifying, and I'd like all nations to take heed of what you're saying, for I'm reliably informed that there are peoples who have the cheek to say that we don't know what true virtue is, that our good deeds are merely splendid sins, and that we need the teachings of their talapoins to inculcate sound principles in us. Alas, poor souls! It was only yesterday that they learnt to read and write, and now they claim to be able to educate their masters!

SIXTH CONVERSATION

KU-SU: I won't rehash all the platitudes about virtue which people have been peddling here for the last five thousand years or so. There are some that only concern individuals, such as prudence in the guidance of the soul and temperance in the government of the body: they're political and sanitary precepts. The true virtues are those that are useful to society, such as fidelity, magnanimity, benevolence, tolerance, and so on. In China, thank goodness, every old woman instructs her grandchildren in those virtues; for young people it's the basis of all knowledge, in the country and in town. But there's one major virtue that's beginning to disappear, and I'm not too pleased about it.

KOO: What would that be, then? Tell me quickly what it is, and I'll try to see if I can breathe new life into it.

KU-SU: It's hospitality. It's an eminently social virtue, but this sacred bond between human beings is beginning to loosen now that we have taverns. This pernicious institution has, it's said, been brought to us by savages from the West. Those wretched people have apparently no home of their own to welcome visitors into. What a pleasure for me it is to invite into my house, Ki, in beautiful Hon-chan Square in the great city of Loo, a generous foreigner from Samarkand, in whose eyes I become in that instant a sacred person and who is obliged by all laws, human and divine, to be my close friend and welcome me into his home whenever I'm travelling in Tartary.

The savages I'm talking about only put up strangers for money, in disgusting taverns; they charge a lot for this vile hospitality, and I'm told those pathetic creatures believe themselves to be superior to us and boast that their morals are purer than ours. They claim that their clerics are better preachers than Confucius, and that it's their job to teach us justice because they sell bad wine on the high road and their wives strut the streets like mad women while ours breed silkworms.

KOO: I find that hospitality is a very good thing, and it gives me pleasure to practise it, but I am worried about possible abuses. There are people on the borders of Tibet who are very badly housed, who enjoy getting about and would like to travel for nothing from one end of the world to the other; but when you go to Tibet to enjoy their hospitality you'll find neither bed nor board. That rather puts you off being civil.

KU-SU: That's not a big problem. It's easy to put it right by only inviting people who are well recommended. Every virtue carries risks; it's because doing the right thing can be risky that it's nice to embrace it.

How wise and saintly our Confucius is! There's no virtue he doesn't inspire; the happiness of mankind is linked to every single utterance of his. Here's one that's just come back to me; it's number 53:

'Return acts of kindness with kindness, and never avenge insults.'

In the face of such pure morality, what maxim or what law could people in the West put forward in lieu? In how many places does Confucius recommend humility? If people practised his virtue there would never be any arguments on this earth.

KOO: I've read everything Confucius and the wise men of earlier centuries have written about humility, but it seems to me they've never offered a sufficiently precise definition of it; it's perhaps a little big-headed of me daring to take them up on it, but at least I'm humble enough to confess I've not heard them mention it. Tell me what you think.

KU-SU: I'll humbly obey. I think humility is the modesty of the soul, because external modesty is only politeness. Humility can't consist in refusing to admit to oneself the superiority that one may have gained over someone else. A good doctor can't hide the fact that he is more knowledgeable than his delirious patient. The teacher of astronomy has to admit that he is more learned than his students; he can't help thinking it, but he must not be taken in by it. Humility is not abjection; it's a corrective to self-love, as modesty is the corrective to pride.

KOO: So: it's in the exercise of all the virtues and the worship of a simple, universal God that I wish to spend my life, far from the wild fancies of the sophists and the illusions of false prophets. The love of my neighbour will be my virtue on the throne, and the love of God my religion. I'll despise the god Fo, and Lao-tse, and Vishnu who's been reincarnated so many times in India, and Samana-Gotama who descended from heaven to fly kites among the Siamese, and the Kami who arrived in Japan from the moon.

Woe to a people barbarous and stupid enough to believe that there exists a God for them alone: that's blasphemous. What? The sun's rays give illumination to every eye, so how could God's light shine only upon one small, insignificant nation in a remote corner of the globe? How awful! How silly! The divinity speaks to the heart of all human beings, and the bonds of charity should unite them from one end of the universe to the other.

KU-SU: O wise Koo! You've spoken like a man inspired by the Chang-ti in person; you'll be a worthy prince. I've been your teacher, and you've become mine.

THE JAPANESE'S CATECHISM
(CATÉCHISME DU JAPONAIS)

THE INDIAN: Is it true that once upon a time the Japanese didn't
know how to cook, so you subjected your kingdom to the authority
of the Grand Lama, who exercised sovereign control over what you
ate and drank, and from time to time sent a junior lama to collect
your dues and give in return a sign of protection made with his
thumb and first two fingers?*

THE JAPANESE: All too true, I'm afraid. Believe it or not, all appoint-
ments of *canusi*, the master chefs on our island, are made by the
Lama, and not for the love of God. What's more, each of our
lay houses paid an ounce of silver every year to this grand chef
of Tibet. All they got in return were tiny dishes, called 'relics',
that didn't taste too good. And whenever he got some new idea
into his head, like declaring war on the Tangut people, he levied
new taxes on us. We often complained, but to no avail, even
ending up paying a bit more each time we did so. Finally love,
which always brings about the right outcome, delivered us
from this servitude. One of our emperors quarrelled with the
Grand Lama over a woman,* but it has to be confessed that those
who helped us most in this business were our *canusi*, or hopsbis.
It's thanks to them that we shook off the yoke, and here's how we
did it.

The Grand Lama had an amusing trait: he always felt he was
right. Our *dairi* and *canusi* liked to be right sometimes too. The
Grand Lama considered the idea absurd, but our *canusi* wouldn't
back down, and broke off all contact with him.

THE INDIAN: So, since that time, you've no doubt all been enjoying
happiness and tranquillity?

THE JAPANESE: Not a bit of it! We began persecuting and devour-
ing each other, tearing ourselves to pieces, and that went on for
nearly two centuries.* Our *canusi* sought in vain to be right about
everything; they've only begun to see sense within the last hundred
years or so, since when we can boldly claim to be one of the happi-
est nations on earth.

THE INDIAN: How can you enjoy such happiness, if it's true—or so I hear—that you have a dozen cookery factions in your empire? You must have twelve civil wars every year.

THE JAPANESE: How so? Just because you have a dozen chefs all producing different recipes, they don't have to be at each other's throats instead of getting on with dinner. Quite the reverse: everyone will eat well, as they see it, with the chef they like best.*

THE INDIAN: It's true that one shouldn't argue about taste, and all that, but people do argue about taste, and things can get pretty heated.

THE JAPANESE: After a great deal of argy-bargy everyone comes to see that such quarrelling only leads to people getting hurt, so they decide to put up with each other, and there's no doubt whatever it's the best thing they can do.

THE INDIAN: And so who are they, these chefs who share out the skills of wining and dining in your country?

THE JAPANESE: First of all there are the Brew-hes, who will never offer you bacon or black pudding; they cling to old-style cuisine, and wouldn't be seen dead larding a chicken. They're terrific at sums, too; if there's an ounce of silver to be shared with the other eleven chefs they first of all take half of it for themselves and then hand over the rest to those who are best at counting.

THE INDIAN: I bet you don't often eat with that lot.

THE JAPANESE: No. Then there are the Pispats, who on some days of the week and even during a large part of the year would much rather eat twenty guineas' worth of turbot, trout, sole, salmon, and sturgeon than a veal stew costing a few pence.

We *canusi* love beef and a sort of pastry called 'pudding' in Japanese. What's more everyone agrees that our chefs are much more learned than those of the Pispats. No one has explored further the garum of the Romans or become better acquainted with the onions of ancient Egypt, the locust paste of the earliest Arabs, or the horsemeat of the Tartars; there's always something to learn from the books of the *canusi*, commonly known as hopsbis.

I won't go into those who only eat according to the precepts of Therlu, or those who swear by the diet of Vincal, or the Baptistanas, or the others; but the Quekars merit a closer look. They're the only dinner guests I've never seen swearing and getting drunk. It's very hard to cheat them, because they'll never cheat you. It seems that the commandment to love one's neighbour as oneself was invented just for them, because in truth how can a Japanese boast of loving his neighbour as himself when for a bit of cash he'll put a bullet in the man's head, or slit his throat with a kris as broad as your hand, all the while with battle-flags on display? As he's just as likely to cop a bullet or have his throat cut, it can far more truthfully be said that he hates his neighbour as himself. The Quekars have never behaved frenziedly like that: they say that poor human beings are clay pots not meant to last and so it's not worth their while setting out gaily to smash into each other.*

I can tell you that if I weren't a *canusi* I wouldn't mind being a Quekar. You must admit there's no way one can pick a fight with such peace-loving chefs. There are many others, called Diests. They invite all and sundry to dinner, and you're free at their place to eat whatever you like, larded or barded, unlarded or unbarded, with eggs, or with oil; partridge, salmon; red wine or rosé; it's all the same to them, so long as you're good people and say grace before or after dinner, or even only before lunch; they'll join in your jokes about the Grand Lama, who won't be hurt by it one bit, and about Therlu, and Vincal, and Memnon, and everyone else. It's all perfectly OK so long as our Diests accept that our *canusi* are great chefs, and above all if they never mention reducing our earnings; that way we'll all live together in peace.

THE INDIAN: But there has to be one dominant cuisine: the king's.

THE JAPANESE: True. But when the King of Japan eats well he must be in good humour, and he mustn't give his loyal subjects indigestion.

THE INDIAN: But what if pig-headed individuals try to eat under the king's nose sausages he can't stand, and four or five thousand of them come together armed with grills to barbecue those sausages, and insult people who won't touch them?

THE JAPANESE: They must be punished like drunks who cause a disturbance of the peace. We've catered for that. Only those who follow the royal diet can aspire to the dignities of state. Everyone else can eat as they please, but they can't hold public office. Gatherings are completely banned, and are summarily punished without remission. All dinner-table squabbles are carefully put a stop to in accordance with the precept of our great Japanese chef, who writes in the sacred language 'Suti raho, cus flac, natis in usum laetitiae sciphis pugnare Tracum est', which means 'Dinner is meant to be a decent, contemplative pleasure, so don't throw your wine-glasses at each other'.

With these maxims we live happily here; under our Taicosama our liberties are strengthened; our wealth is increasing; we have two hundred junks of the line and we strike fear into our neighbours' hearts.

THE INDIAN: So I wonder why the good versifier Recina (son of the Indian poet Recina who was so delicate, precise, harmonious, and eloquent) chose to write in a didactic work in verse entitled *Grace* (and not *The Graces*),

> Japan, where once such light blazed
> Now's just a heap of people crazed.*

THE JAPANESE: The Recina you mention is pretty crazy himself. Doesn't the poor chap realize that we taught him what light was all about, and that if in India today people know a planet's true trajectory, it's us he has to thank? And that we alone taught humankind the calculus and the basic laws of Nature?* And that if we get down to more common-and-garden matters, the people in his country learned from us, and from no one else, how to design junks according to mathematical principles? And they even have us to thank for a kind of fine hose, known as loom-weave stockings, that they cover their legs with? Is it likely that having invented so many wonderful and useful things we're a bunch of nitwits, and that a man who's turned the delusions of others into rhyming couplets is the only wise person around? Let him leave us to get on with our cooking, and let him pen verses on more poetic subjects to his heart's content.[1]

THE INDIAN: What do you expect? On top of his own, he's got all the prejudices of the country he comes from and the coterie he belongs to.

THE JAPANESE: That makes for an awful lot of prejudices!

---

[1] NB. This Indian, Recina, on the strength of the crazy views of some of his fellow countrymen, believed that good sauces could only be made when Brahma made a special point of teaching his favourites the recipe himself, and that there were an infinite number of chefs who, try as they might, could never make a decent stew because out of sheer malice Brahma stopped them from doing so. No one in Japan believes such nonsense; this Japanese saying is seen as being true beyond contest:

'God never acts by partial will, but by general laws.'*

THE PRIEST'S CATECHISM
(CATÉCHISME DU CURÉ)

ARISTON: So, my dear Theotimus, you're going to be a village priest?

THEOTIMUS: Yes. I'm being given a small parish, which I prefer to a big one. Not being over-burdened with brains or energy, I certainly couldn't act as spiritual guide to seventy thousand souls, seeing that I've only got one myself. I've always been full of admiration for those with the self-confidence to take on large parishes, but I don't feel capable of shouldering such a burden myself. A big flock scares me, but I could do some good with a little one. I've studied jurisprudence sufficiently to stop my poor parishioners, as far as possible, from losing everything at law; I've enough medical knowledge to indicate a few simple remedies to them when they fall ill; and I know enough about husbandry to give them the occasional bit of helpful advice. The local squire and his lady are decent people who are not pious and who'll help me do some good. I flatter myself that I'll live quite a happy life and not make anyone else unhappy.

ARISTON: Don't you regret not being able to get married? It would be very comforting, after a hard day's preaching, chanting, confessing, communing, baptizing, and burying, to go home to a nice, decent, gentle wife who'd see to the laundry and generally take care of you, who'd nurse you in sickness, add sparkle to your life in health, and who'd give you pretty, well-brought-up children for the general benefit of society. I feel for you, serving humankind as you do, having to forgo what other men find so comforting.

THEOTIMUS: The Greek Church takes good care to encourage its clergy to marry; the Church of England and other Protestant bodies are just as wise; the Church of Rome sees things differently; I'll just have to put up with it. Perhaps now that the philosophical spirit has made such progress a council will legislate in a manner more favourable to humanity than the Council of Trent did, but until then I must obey the law as it stands. It'll be hard, I know, but so many people better than me have agreed to abide by it that I mustn't complain.

ARISTON: You're a learned man, and a wise and eloquent one. How do you intend to preach to country people?

THEOTIMUS: As I would to kings; I'll always talk about morality and never about religious controversy; God keep me from probing concomitant grace, efficacious grace which can be resisted, and sufficient grace which doesn't suffice, and from examining whether the angels who dined with Abraham and Lot were embodied creatures or were just pretending to eat. There are a thousand things my audience wouldn't understand, any more than I do. I'll try to make people good and I'll strive to be good myself, but I won't turn them into theologians, and I'll be as little theological as possible.

ARISTON: What a good priest you'll make! I'd like to buy a country house in your parish. Tell me, please, how you'll deal with confession.

THEOTIMUS: Confession is an excellent thing, a curb on crime that was invented way back in the mists of time. People went in for confession when celebrating all the ancient mysteries; we've copied and sanctified this wise practice; it's very good at persuading hearts poisoned by hatred to forgive and forget, and for making petty thieves give back their ill-gotten gains. But there is a downside. There are many indiscreet confessors, monks in particular, who sometimes fill girls' heads with more foolish ideas than the village lads ever could. Confession shouldn't be about details; it's not a cross-examination in a court of law, it's admitting your faults to the Supreme Being, as one sinner in the hands of another sinner, who'll then accuse himself in turn. This salutary way of owning up isn't meant to satisfy the prurient curiosity of anyone else.

ARISTON: And how will you handle excommunication?

THEOTIMUS: I won't. There are rituals for excommunicating grasshoppers, sorcerers, and actors. I won't ban grasshoppers from my church, seeing that they never go in there. I won't excommunicate sorcerers, because there's no such thing as witchcraft; and as far as actors are concerned, seeing that they are authorized by the magistrate and awarded a pension by the king, I'll take care not to defame them. I'll even admit to you as a friend that I like the theatre so long as it doesn't offend against morality. I'm passionate about Molière's *Misanthrope*, Racine's *Athalie*,* and other plays which seem to me to inculcate virtue and propriety. In my village the local squire puts on some of these in his house with the help of young actors of talent; these productions instil virtue through pleasure, shape people's taste, and teach them to speak properly and enunciate clearly. There I see something that's not only totally innocent but also very useful; I have every intention of going to see these plays for my own enlightenment, but from within a closed box so as not to scandalize the weaker brethren.

ARISTON: The more you tell me about your ideas the more I'd like to become a parishioner of yours. There's a quite important point that's bothering me, though. How would you stop the peasants getting drunk on feast days, as it's their favourite way of celebrating? You see some of them overcome by liquid poison, their heads drooping, their arms dangling, seeing nothing, hearing nothing, reduced to a state well below that of brute beasts, led staggering home by their tearful wives, unfit for work the next day, often ill and brain-damaged for the rest of their lives. You see others driven mad by wine, provoking bloody fights, hitting and getting hit, and often ending up killing someone in appalling scenes that shame the human race; it has to be admitted the state loses more people through excessive drinking than on the battlefield; so how will you be able to cut down on such terrible abuses in your parish?

THEOTIMUS: This is what I'll do: on saints' days I'll allow them, even urge them, to work in the fields after divine service, which I'll hold very early in the morning. What draws people into the tavern is having nothing else to do on feast days. Working days are not times of debauchery and murder. Moderate labour contributes to the health of the body and the soul; what's more, the state needs people to work. At a very conservative estimate five million men can each earn tenpence a day on average, and if on thirty days in every year you let these five million men do nothing, that adds up to a loss to the state of thirty times five million tenpennyworth of labour. And it's certain God never sanctioned a deficit on this scale, or drunkenness either.

ARISTON: In that way you'll be able to reconcile work and prayer. God requires both, so you'll be serving him and your neighbour. But what line will you take in ecclesiastical disputes?

THEOTIMUS: None. No one argues about virtue, since that comes from God. Opinions are what people quarrel about, and they're man-made.

ARISTON: What a fine priest you'll make, to be sure!

CHRISTIANITY
(CHRISTIANISME)

Historical research into Christianity

SEVERAL scholars have been surprised at finding in the works of the historian Josephus no mention of Jesus Christ, since nowadays everybody is agreed that the tiny passage referring to him in the *History* is a later interpolation. But Josephus' father must have been amongst those who witnessed all of Jesus' miracles. Josephus came from a priestly family, and was related to Herod's wife Mariamne; he goes into great detail about everything that the king did, but he makes no mention of the life and death of Jesus; he conceals none of the king's acts of cruelty, but says nothing about the Massacre of the Innocents, carried out on Herod's orders after he'd been told that a future King of the Jews had just been born. According to the Greek calendar, fourteen thousand children were slaughtered on that occasion. It was the most horrific of all acts of wickedness perpetrated by tyrants of every stripe: in the entire history of the world, no other atrocity comes close.

However, the greatest writer the Jewish people have ever produced, the only one the Greeks and Romans held in respect, makes no mention of an event as strange as it was awful. He says nothing about the new star that appeared in the east after the birth of the Saviour, a striking phenomenon that could not have escaped the attention of a historian as knowledgeable as Josephus. He is silent too about the darkness that covered the whole land for three hours in the middle of the day when the Saviour died, and about the large number of graves that opened at that moment and the many bodies of the saints that rose from the dead.

Scholars never cease showing their surprise at the fact that no Roman historian recorded these astonishing events, which took place during Tiberius' reign under the very eyes of a Roman garrison and a Roman governor, who must have sent the emperor and senate a detailed account of the most miraculous thing to have occurred in living memory. The imperial capital itself must have been plunged in thick darkness for three hours; such an extraordinary event would have been noted in the annals of Rome and all other nations. So God can't have liked the idea of profane hands recording such divine happenings.

The same scholars also find a few thorny problems in the Gospel narratives. They note that in St Matthew Jesus told the scribes and Pharisees that upon them may come all the righteous blood shed upon the earth, from the blood of righteous Abel unto the blood of Zacharias son of Barachias, whom they slew between the temple and the altar.

There is no mention in the history of the Hebrews, they point out, of Zacharias being killed in the temple, either before the advent of the Messiah or during his lifetime; but in Josephus' history of the siege of Jerusalem one Zacharias son of Barachias is mentioned as having been killed in the middle of the temple by the zealots' faction. It's in book 4, chapter 19. This leads them to suspect that the Gospel according to St Matthew was written after the sack of Jerusalem by Titus. But all doubts and objections of this kind evaporate when we consider the difference between the infinite distance that there must be between books inspired by God and books written by human beings. God wished to wrap a cloud, as worthy of respect as it is impenetrable, around the circumstances of his birth, life, and death. His ways are completely different from our ways.

Scholars have also become greatly troubled over the difference between the two genealogies of Jesus. St Matthew gives Jacob as Joseph's father; Mathan as Jacob's; and Eleazar as Mathan's. St Luke on the other hand says that Joseph was the son of Heli, Heli of Matthat, Matthat of Levi, Levi of Janna, and so on.

They also have difficulties with the fact that Jesus is not Joseph's son, but Mary's, and they raise some doubts about our Saviour's miracles, citing St Augustine, St Hilaire, and others who have given a mystical, allegorical meaning to the miracle narratives, such as the fig-tree that was cursed and made to wither away for not bearing fruit when figs weren't in season; or the demons cast out and allowed to enter the bodies of a herd of swine in a country where nobody kept pigs; or water changed into wine at the end of a meal where the guests were already quite well lit. But faith confounds all these scholarly quibbles and becomes all the purer for it. The aim of this article is solely to follow the historical thread and give the reader a precise idea of the facts that no one disputes.

First of all, Jesus was born under the law of Moses; he was circumcised in accordance with that law and fulfilled all its precepts; he observed all its feasts and only ever preached morality; he was blessed by John the Baptist in the waters of the River Jordan in a ceremony several Jews underwent but never baptized anyone himself; he never spoke of the seven sacraments; no ecclesiastical hierarchy was set up by him during his lifetime. He concealed from his contemporaries that he was the son of God, engendered consubstantial with God from all eternity, and that the Holy Spirit proceeded from the Father and the Son. He never mentioned that his person was made up of two natures and two wills: he wanted these great mysteries to be announced to humankind in the fullness of time by those enlightened by the Holy Spirit. As long as he lived he departed not a jot from the law of his forefathers; all he revealed to others was a just man pleasing in God's eyes who was persecuted by people racked with envy and condemned to death by prejudiced judges. He wished the Holy Church he'd founded to do the rest.

In chapter 12 of his *History* Josephus mentions a rigorist Jewish sect recently established by someone called Judas the Galilean. 'They despise the evils of the world,' he writes; 'through their constancy they triumph over torments; where death is an honourable one they prefer it to going on living. Rather than utter the slightest word against their lawgiver, or eat forbidden meats, they have suffered from fire and iron and had their bones broken.'

It seems that Josephus is here describing the Judaites and not the Essenes, for here are Josephus' words: 'Judas was the founder of a new sect, quite different from the three others, i.e. the Sadducees, the Pharisees, and the Essenes.' He goes on: 'They are ethnic Jews; they keep themselves to themselves and consider sexual pleasure a vice'; the plain meaning of that sentence indicates that Josephus is talking about the Judaites.

However that may be, people knew about the Judaites before Christ's disciples began to constitute a significant world movement.

The Therapeuts were different from the Essenes and the Judaites; they were more like the Gymnosophists and the Brahmans of India. 'They are', writes Philo, 'proponents of celestial love, which induces in them the exuberance we associate with the Bacchantes and the Corybants, and enables them to enter the state of contemplation they aspire to. This sect arose in Alexandria, a city full of Jews, and spread widely within Egypt.'*

John the Baptist's disciples also spread within Egypt to some extent, but they chiefly moved into Syria and Arabia, while some went on into Asia Minor. In the Acts of the Apostles (ch. 19), we read that Paul met several of them at Ephesus, and asked them 'Have you received the Holy Ghost?' They replied, 'We have not so much as heard that there be any Holy Ghost.' He then asked 'Unto what then were you baptized?' and they answered, 'Unto John's baptism'.

In the early years following Jesus' death there were seven different societies or sects with Judaism, the Pharisees, the Sadducees, the Essenes, the Judaites, the Therapeuts, John the Baptist's disciples, and lastly Christ's disciples, the small flock of whom God led by unknown ways to human wisdom.

In Antioch around AD 60 the faithful were known as Christians, but in the Roman Empire they were known by other names, as we shall see later. Before that they were called brothers, saints, or the faithful. God, having descended to earth to serve as an example of humility and poverty, gave his church the weakest possible start and led it in the same spirit of humility as that in which he'd chosen to be born. The early faithful were all humble people who worked with their hands. The apostle Paul says that he was a tentmaker by trade. St Peter resurrected Dorcas, the seamstress who made the brothers' garments. As can be seen in the Acts of the Apostles (ch. 9), the assembly of the faithful was held at Joppa, in the house of a tanner called Simon.

The faithful spread secretly within Greece, and some went from there to Rome to join the Jews whom the Romans allowed to have a synagogue. They did not at first set themselves apart from the Jews: they kept up the practice of circumcision, and as I've already mentioned, the first fifteen bishops of Jerusalem were circumcised.

When the apostle Paul took with him Timothy, whose father was a Gentile, he circumcised the disciple himself in the little town of Lystra. But his other disciple, Titus, did not wish to be circumcised. The brethren who were disciples of Jesus remained united with the Jews until Paul suffered persecution in Jerusalem for having brought foreigners into the temple. The Jews accused him of trying, through Jesus Christ, to destroy the law of Moses. To clear him of the charge the apostle James suggested to the apostle Paul that he shave his head and go and purify himself in the temple with four Jews who had made a vow to shave their heads: 'Take them with you,' said James (Acts, ch. 21), 'and purify yourself with them, so that all may know that those things whereof they were informed concerning you are nothing, and that you walk orderly and keep the law of Moses.'

Paul was nevertheless charged with impiety and heresy, and his criminal trial lasted a long time, but it can obviously be seen, from the very nature of the accusations levelled at him, that he had come to Jerusalem to observe the Judaic rites.

These were the very words he said to Festus: 'Neither against the law of the Jews, nor against the temple, have I offended any thing at all' (Acts, ch. 25).

The apostles presented Jesus as a Jew, an observer of Jewish law, sent by God to see that it was observed.

'There is profit in circumcision,' says the apostle Paul (Romans, ch. 2), 'if you keep the law; but if you break the law, your circumcision is made uncircumcision. If an uncircumcised man keeps the law, his uncircumcision will be counted for circumcision. For he is a Jew who is one inwardly.'

When in the epistles Paul speaks about Jesus Christ, he does not reveal the ineffable mystery of his consubstantiality with God; we are delivered by him, Paul says (Romans, ch. 5) from the wrath of God, and God's gift has spread among us through the grace given to one man, who is Christ Jesus . . . Death reigned through the sin of one man, and righteousness shall reign in life by one man, Jesus Christ.

In chapter 8, 'We are the heirs of God, and joint-heirs with Christ.' In chapter 16, 'To God only wise, glory and honour through Jesus Christ.' 'You are Christ's, and Christ is God's' (1 Corinthians, ch. 3).

And 'he has put all things under his feet', excepting no doubt God, 'who did put all things under him' (1 Corinthians, ch. 15, v. 27).

People have some difficulty explaining this passage in the Epistle to the Philippians: 'Let nothing be done through vainglory; in lowliness of mind let each esteem others better than themselves; let this mind be in you, which was also in Christ Jesus: who, being in the form of God, thought it not robbery to be equal with God.' This passage seems to have been gone into thoroughly, and completely explained, in a letter, a precious relic of antiquity that has come down to us, written in AD 117* by the churches of Vienna and Lyons. Having suffered only minor vexations 'they do not aspire to the grand title of martyrs,' the letter says, 'thereby following the example of Christ who, though marked by God, did not think he had acquired the status of God's equal'. In his commentary on St John's Gospel Origen too says that the grandeur of Jesus shone forth more when he was humiliated 'than if he had claimed to be God's equal'. The opposite explanation is indeed obvious nonsense. What could this mean: 'Believe that others are superior to you; imitate Jesus, who did not believe that it was robbery or usurpation to be God's equal'? It would be a manifest contradiction; it would be holding up an example of grandeur as an example of modesty; in other words, it would be flying in the face of common sense.

The wisdom of the apostles was the bedrock of the newborn church, a wisdom unaffected by the dispute which arose at Antioch between the apostles Peter, James, and John on the one hand and Paul on the other. When the apostle Peter, otherwise known as Cephas or Simon Bar-Yonah, ate with converted Gentiles, he observed neither the ceremonies of the law, nor the distinction between meats; he, Barnabas, and other disciples ate pork, braised meats, and the flesh of cloven-hoofed and non-ruminant animals; but when several Christian Jews turned up, St Peter reverted to the ceremonies of the Mosaic law and abstained from eating forbidden meats.

This quarrel seems all the more extraordinary on St Paul's part because, having been a persecutor at the outset, he ought to have been more moderate, and also because he'd gone and sacrificed in the temple in Jerusalem, circumcised his disciple Timothy, and carried out the Jewish rites he then reproached Cephas with. St Jerome claims that Paul and Cephas were just pretending to disagree: in his first Homily (vol. 3) he says that they were acting like two barristers getting heated and angry at the bar just to impress their clients; he adds that since Simon Peter was destined to preach to the Jews and Paul to the Gentiles, they pretended to quarrel, Paul so that he could win over the Gentiles, and Peter the Jews. But St Augustine doesn't agree with this at all. 'It annoys me', he says in the Letter to Jerome, 'that such a great man became the patron of mendacity, *patrocinium mendacii*.'

What's more, if Peter was marked out for the observant Jews and Paul for the foreigners, it's highly probable that Peter never went to Rome. There is no mention of Peter travelling to Italy in the Acts of the Apostles.

However that may be, around AD 60 the Christians began separating from the Jewish community and thereby causing much invective and persecution to be directed at them by synagogues stretching from Rome and Greece to Egypt and Asia Minor. Their Jewish brethren accused them of atheism and ungodliness and on Sabbath days excommunicated them three times in their synagogues. But in the midst of these persecutions they always enjoyed God's support.

Bit by bit several churches were formed, and by the end of the first century AD Christians and Jews had become totally separate. The Roman government took no notice of this. Neither the emperors nor the senate cared to go into the quarrels of a small sect which up till then God had guided in obscurity and which he was gradually raising by degrees.

We need to look at what state religion was in under the Roman Empire. Nearly everywhere people believed in sacrifices and mysteries. It's true that the emperors, the grandees, and the philosophers had no faith in these mysteries; but the common herd that, where religion is concerned, lay down the law to the great and the good, imposed on them the necessity of outwardly conforming to the cult. To keep people in bondage it's necessary to wear the same chains as they do. Even Cicero was initiated into the Eleusinian mysteries. The knowledge of one God was the leading dogma announced at those mysterious and magnificent festivals. It must be admitted that the prayers and hymns that have survived from those mysteries are among the most admirable and devout things in paganism.

As a result the Christians, who also worshipped only one God, found it easier to convert many Gentiles. A few philosophers in Plato's circle became Christians. That's why the church fathers of the first three centuries AD were all Platonists.

The intemperate zeal of a few did the fundamental verities no harm. St Justin, one of the early fathers, was taxed with saying in his commentary on Isaiah that the saints would reign on earth for a thousand years and enjoy every sensual pleasure. He was attacked for claiming in his Apology of Christianity that God, having created the earth, handed it over to the care of the angels; they fell in love with women and fathered children; these became the demons.

Lactantius, together with other church fathers, was blamed for believing in the sibylline oracles. He claimed that the Erythraean sibyl had composed this poem in Greek which, translated literally, reads:

> With five loaves and two fishes
> He will feed five thousand people in the wilderness,
> And gathering up the leftovers
> He will fill a dozen baskets.*

The first Christians were also blamed for giving credence to a supposed acrostic by an ancient sibyl, each line of which began with the first letters, in order, of the name 'Jesus Christ'.

But such unscholarly zeal on the part of a few Christians did not stop the church making progress as God intended. At first Christians worshipped in remote dwellings, or in cellars, at night. That's why, according to Minutius Felix, they were characterized as 'lucifugals'. Philo called them Gesseans. Among the Gentiles, during the first four centuries, they were most commonly known as Galileans, or Nazarenes, but eventually the term 'Christians' prevailed over all others.

Neither their hierarchy nor their customs were established straight away; the apostolic age was different from the ones that followed. St Paul tells us in 1 Corinthians that when the brethren, circumcised or not, were gathered together and several prophets wished to speak, only two or three should do so, and if during this time anyone had a revelation, the prophet who was speaking had then to hold his peace.

Some Christian communities which still today hold assemblies without hierarchy take their cue from this practice of the primitive church. It was open to any male worshipper to speak in church; women were not permitted to.

The ceremony that today is high mass—celebrated in the morning—was a service conducted in the evening; practices changed as the church grew stronger. A more extended society required more regulation, and wise pastors bowed to the needs of their own place and time.

St Jerome and Eusebius inform us that as the churches took shape five different orders gradually emerged. The supervisors, *Episcopoi*, early precursors of bishops; the elders of the society; the *Presbyteroi*, the priests, servers or deacons; the *Pistoi*, the believers, the initiates, that is to say the baptized, who took part in the agape feasts; and the catechumens and energumens who were awaiting baptism. None of these five orders dressed any differently from the others, and none was required to embrace celibacy, as we can see from the example of the apostles and of Tertullian, who dedicated a book to his wife. During the first three centuries AD there were no representations in painting or sculpture in their assemblies. The Christians carefully hid their books from the Gentiles and entrusted them solely to the initiated; it wasn't even permissible for the catechumens to recite Sunday prayers.

What made Christians stand out the most was something that has lasted until our own day: the power to drive out demons with the sign of the cross. Origen, in his treatise *Against Celsus*, admits at no. 133 that Antinous, deified by the Emperor Hadrian, produced miracles in Egypt by dint of magic and spells; but he says that to drive out demons from the bodies of the possessed it is enough to pronounce the name of Jesus.

Tertullian goes further and, from the depths of his African retreat, wrote in his *Apologeticus*, chapter. 23, 'If in the presence of a true Christian your gods refuse to admit that they are devils, we're quite happy for you to spill that Christian's blood. Can there be a clearer demonstration?'

Indeed, Christ sent his apostles to drive out demons. In his day Jews too had the power of driving them out; for when Jesus had freed people who were possessed and had sent the devils into the bodies of a herd of pigs, and done similar acts of healing, the Pharisees said, 'He's casting out devils by the power of Beelzebub.' 'If I by Beelzebub cast them out,' replied Jesus, 'by whom do your children cast them out?'* It's incontestable that the Jews boasted of this power; they had exorcists and exorcisms. They invoked the name of the God of Jacob and Abraham. They put consecrated herbs in the nostrils of demoniacs (Josephus records part of these ceremonies). This power over demons, which the Jews have lost, was passed on to the Christians, who also seem to have lost it recently.

Included in the power to cast out demons was that of undermining the workings of magic, because among all the nations of the world magic always enjoyed vigorous health. All the church fathers praise magic. In the *Apology*, Book 3, St Justin admits that the souls of the dead are frequently invoked, and sees in that an argument for the immortality of the soul. In book 7 of *The Divine Institutions* Lactantius writes: 'If you were so bold as to deny that souls continue to exist after death, the magician would soon convince you that they do by making them appear.' Irenaeus, Clement of Alexandria, Tertullian, and Bishop Cyprian all say the same thing. It's true that today everything's changed and that there are no more magicians about than there are demoniacs, but if it please God some will manifest themselves.

When Christian societies became more numerous and several of them rose up against the pagan worship of the Roman Empire, the law came down hard on them and the people, above all, persecuted them. The Jews, who had special privileges and kept themselves to themselves in their synagogues, were not persecuted; they were allowed to practise their religion, as they are in Rome today. All the various forms of worship found within the empire were tolerated even though they were not adopted by the senate.

But the Christians, who made clear their hostility to all these cults, and in particular the official religion, were several times exposed to great hardship.

One of the first and most famous of the martyrs was Ignatius, bishop of Antioch, condemned by the Emperor Trajan himself, who was in Asia Minor at the time, and sent on his orders to Rome to be fed to the lions at a time when other Christians were not being massacred in Rome. We don't know what he was accused of when he appeared before the emperor, a man otherwise well known for his clemency; St Ignatius must have had some pretty violent enemies. However that may be, in the account of his martyrdom it says that they found the name of Jesus Christ engraved on his heart in letters of gold, as a result of which in a few places Christians took the name that Ignatius gave himself: 'theophorics'.

A letter of his has survived in which he asks Christians and the bishops not to oppose his martyrdom, either because the Christians were already powerful enough to get him released, or because some of them had sufficient influence to secure his pardon. What is still pretty remarkable is that the Christians of Rome were allowed to go and welcome him when he was brought to the capital, which obviously proves that it was he himself, and not his sect, that was being punished.

The persecutions did not last long. In book 3 of *Against Celsus* Origen says, 'It is not difficult to count the number of Christians put to death for their religion because there were so few of them, and then only occasionally, with gaps in between.'

God took such good care of his church that in spite of its enemies it held five councils in the first century AD, sixteen in the second, and thirty in the third; that is, assemblies which the authorities tolerated. Sometimes these assemblies were banned when over-cautious magistrates feared they might become stormy. Few reports by the proconsuls or praetors who condemned Christians to death have survived. They would be the only documents that could tell us what they were accused of and how they were punished.

We do have a fragment by Denis of Alexandria in which he quotes an extract from the registry of a proconsul who served in Egypt during the reign of the Emperor Valerian. Here it is:

'When Denis, Faustus, Maximus, Marcellus, and Cheremon had been led into court, the prefect Emilianus said to them: "You'll know from my discussions with you and from the letters I've sent you how much kindness our rulers have shown you; I'm quite happy to say it again: they insist that your preservation and salvation depends on yourselves and that your fate is in your own hands; all they ask of you is something any sensible person would find reasonable, and that is that you worship the empire's guardian deities and that you abandon this other religion, which goes against nature and common sense."

'Denis replied: "Not everyone has the same gods, but people worship those they believe to be truly divine."

'The prefect Emilianus answered: "It's clear you're an ungrateful bunch, abusing our emperors' kindness towards you. Very well: you won't stay a day longer in this town; I'm sending you to Cephro in the heart of Libya. In accordance with the order I've received from our emperors, you're being banished there. What's more, don't even think of holding your meetings there, or of saying your prayers in those places you call cemeteries. That's absolutely forbidden, and I won't allow anyone to do it." '*

This account, which bears all the marks of truth, shows that there was a time when assemblies were banned. In much the same way our Calvinists are forbidden to hold meetings in the Languedoc; we have sometimes even hanged or broken on the wheel the ministers and preachers who held meetings in defiance of the law. In England and Ireland, similarly, Roman Catholic services are forbidden, and there have been occasions where offenders have been put to death.

In spite of the prohibitions enshrined in Roman law God inspired several emperors to show indulgence towards Christians. Even Diocletian, whom people that know nothing about it consider a persecutor, and whose first year on the throne still fell within the martyrdom era, was for over eighteen years an avowed protector of Christianity, so much so that many Christians held leading positions at his court. He even allowed a superb church to be built in the city of his residence, Nicomedia, right opposite his palace, and he married a Christian.

Caesar Galerius, who unfortunately nursed a grudge towards Christians and so was biased against them, persuaded Diocletian to have the cathedral in Nicomedia demolished. Showing more zeal than wisdom, a Christian man tore up the imperial edict, thereby provoking the notorious persecution in which, throughout the length and breadth of the Roman Empire, more than two hundred people were condemned to death, on top of those who were murdered with total disregard for due process by the ever-fanatical and barbarous populace in their fury.

There was at various times such a large number of martyrs that one has to be careful not to undermine, by a dangerous mix of fable and false martyrs, the truth of the stories of those genuinely confessing our holy religion.

The Benedictine Dom Ruinart, for example, an otherwise learned, worthy, and zealous man, ought to have been more discerning in his choice of 'sincere acts'. Even if an exact copy of a manuscript belonging to the Feuillants is found in the abbey at Saint-Benoît-sur-Loire or in a Celestine convent in Paris, that's not enough to make it genuine; such a document must be ancient, written in a contemporary hand, and bear all the marks of truth.

He could have passed up the idea of reporting the adventure of the lad Romanus in AD 303. This young Roman had been pardoned by Diocletian in Antioch. But he says that the judge Asclepiades condemned him to be burned at the stake. Some Jews who were present mocked the young St Romanus and criticized the Christians for the fact that their God let them burn, whereas he had rescued Shadrach, Meshach, and Abednego from the furnace. But out of a clear blue sky a storm arose and put the fire out. The judge then ordered young Romanus' tongue to be cut out. The emperor's top physician, who happened to be there, took on the job of unofficial executioner. He cut the boy's tongue out at the root. The young man, who had been a stammerer before, started speaking at once with great fluency. The emperor was staggered that anyone without a tongue could speak so well. To repeat the experiment the doctor cut out the tongue of a passer-by, who promptly died.

The Benedictine Ruinart lifted this tale from Eusebius, who had sufficient respect for the genuine miracles featured in the Old and the New Testament (on which no one will ever cast doubt) not to let them get mixed up with dubious stories like these, which could give scandal to the feeble-minded.

This last persecution did not extend throughout the empire. There was at the time some Christian belief in England, but it soon faded, resurfacing later under the Saxon kings. Spain and the southern parts of Gaul were filled with Christians. The Caesar Constantius Chlorus afforded them considerable protection in all these provinces. He had a Christian concubine; she was the mother of Emperor Constantine I, and is known to us as St Helena. She and Constantius were never officially married. He even sent her away in AD 292, when he married the daughter of Maximianus Herculius, but she continued to exert a strong influence over him and inspired in him great affection for our holy religion.

Divine Providence prepared the way for the triumph of its church by seemingly human means. Constantius Chlorus died at York, England, in AD 306, at a time when the children a Caesar's daughter had borne him were too young to lay claim to the empire. Constantine had the confidence to get himself elected at York by five or six thousand mainly German, Gaulish, and English soldiers. It seemed unlikely that this election, made without the consent of Rome, the senate, or the armies, would prevail; but God gave him victory over Maxentius who'd been elected in Rome, and eventually freed him from all his colleagues. I can't conceal the fact that he made himself unworthy at first of heaven's favours by having his wife, his son, and all his close relations killed.

What Zosimus says on the subject cannot be doubted. He says that Constantine was so racked with guilt over so many crimes that he asked the high priests of the empire if there was any form of atonement he could make, and they replied that they knew of none. It's certainly true that there weren't any available to Nero either, and that he hadn't had the temerity to join in the sacred mysteries in Greece. Nevertheless, the practice of tauroboly* was widespread, and it's hard to believe that an all-powerful emperor couldn't find a priest willing to conduct the expiatory sacrifices. It's even still more incredible, perhaps, that Constantine, surrounded by sycophants, and focused as he was on war, his ambitions, and his projects, had the time to feel remorse. Zosimus adds that an Egyptian priest who'd arrived from Spain had access to his door and promised him that in the Christian religion he would find atonement for all his crimes. This priest is thought to have been Ozius, bishop of Cordoba.

However that may be, Constantine took communion with the Christians, although he was never more than a catechumen, and reserved his baptism for his deathbed. He had the city of Constantinople built and it became the centre of the empire and of the Christian religion. So the Church took on an august appearance.

It is worthy of note that as early as AD 314, before Constantine took up residence in his new town, those who had persecuted the Christians were punished for their acts of cruelty. The Christians threw Maximian's wife into the Orontes; they slaughtered all her relatives; in Egypt and Palestine they massacred the judges who had been most open about their opposition to Christianity. Diocletian's widow and daughter had taken refuge in Thessalonica, but they were soon recognized and their bodies were thrown into the sea. One would have liked the Christians to have been less receptive to the spirit of revenge, but God, who punishes with even-handed justice, wanted the Christians' hands to be tainted with the blood of their persecutors as soon as they were in a position to act.

Constantine summoned and assembled, in Nicaea opposite Constantinople, the first ecumenical council, with Ozius in the chair. It decided the big question that was exercising the Church, namely the divinity of Jesus. Some espoused the view of Origen who says, in *Against Celsus*, chapter 6, 'We offer our prayers to God through Jesus, who stands in the middle between nature created and uncreated, who brings us the grace of his father and who, in his capacity as our high priest, submits our prayers to almighty God.' They backed up their view, too, by several passages in St Paul, several of which I've already quoted, and above all by these words of Jesus: 'My father is greater than I.' They looked upon Jesus as creation's first born, as the purest emanation of the Supreme Being, but not exactly as God.

Others, who were orthodox, quoted passages more in conformity with the eternal divinity of Jesus, such as this: 'I and my father are one', words which their opponents interpreted as meaning 'My father and I have the same wishes and the same purpose; I have no other desires than those of my father'. The orthodox group was headed by

Alexander, bishop of Alexandria, followed by Athanasius; Eusebius, bishop of Nicomedia, along with seventeen other bishops, the priest Arius, and several others, were in the opposite camp. The quarrel was very bitter at first, because St Alexander called his opponents Antichrists.

Finally, after a great deal of argument in the council, this is how the issue was resolved by the Holy Ghost. Two hundred and ninety-nine bishops voted for the following statement, with eighteen against: 'Jesus is God's only son, born of the father, that is of the substance of the father, God of God, light of light, true God of true God, consubstantial with the father; we believe also in the Holy Ghost, etc.' This was the form of words adopted by the council. This example shows that the ordinary priests were no match for the bishops: according to two Alexandrian patriarchs who wrote a history of Alexandria in Arabic, two thousand second-order people backed Arius' view. Arius was banished by Constantine, and Athanasius likewise soon afterwards, but Arius was recalled to Constantinople. But before Arius could enter the cathedral St Macarius prayed so fervently to God to make him die that God granted the request: the man collapsed on his way to church in AD 330. The Emperor Constantine's life came to an end in 337. He handed his will to an Arian priest and died in the arms of Eusebius, bishop of Nicomedia, the Arians' leader. He got himself baptized only on his deathbed and left the Church triumphant, but divided.

The supporters of Athanasius and those of Eusebius fought each other bitterly: what we call Arianism was for a long time well established throughout the empire.

The philosopher Julian, also known as the Apostate, tried in vain to suppress these divisions.

The second ecumenical council was held in Constantinople in AD 381, where it was explained that the council of Nicaea had not seen fit to pronounce on the Holy Spirit. So to the Nicaean formula these words were added: 'The Holy Spirit is vivifying Lord, who comes from the Father, and he is worshipped and glorified with the Father and the Son.'

It was only around the ninth century that the Latin church came by degrees to establish that the Holy Spirit proceeds from the Father and the Son.

In AD 431 the third ecumenical council held in Ephesus ruled that Mary was truly the mother of God and that Jesus possessed two natures and one person.

Nestorius, the bishop of Constantinople, tried to have the Holy Virgin designated 'the mother of Christ', but the Council called him 'Judas', and the two natures were further confirmed by the council of Chalcedonia.

I'll skip lightly over the next few centuries since they're fairly well known. Sadly all these disputes led to war, and the Church was always forced to take up the cudgels. In the ninth century God sanctioned a definitive split between the Greek and Latin churches to test the patience of the faithful. He also did nothing to prevent the occurrence of twenty-nine bloody schisms over the incumbency of the see of Rome.

While the entire African church and virtually the whole of the Greek church were enslaved, first by the Arabs and then by the Turks, who established the religion of Mahomet on the ruins of Christianity, the Latin church survived, but it was sullied by more than six centuries of bloody disagreements between the western Empire and the priesthood. These squabbles made the Church even more powerful. The bishops and the abbots in Germany all turned themselves into princes, and the popes gradually acquired absolute power over Rome and over three hundred miles of countryside around it. In that way God tested the Church through humiliation, unrest, and splendour.

In the sixteenth century the same Latin church lost Denmark, Sweden, England, Scotland, Ireland, Switzerland, Holland, and half of Germany, but thanks to Spanish conquests it gained more territory in America than it lost in Europe. Despite having more land, however, it ended up with far fewer subjects.

Japan, Siam, India, and China seemed destined by divine Providence to pay obeisance to the Pope to compensate him for the loss of Asia Minor, Syria, Greece, Egypt, Africa, Russia, and the other lost states I've mentioned. The Holy Gospel was taken to the East Indies by St Francis Xavier, and when the Portuguese went to trade in Japan he achieved many miracles there, all attested by the Jesuit Reverend Fathers; some say that he raised nine people from the dead, but in *Flowers of the Saints* the Reverend Father Ribadeneira contents himself with the claim that he raised four, which is still pretty good. In less than a hundred years, by the will of Providence, there were thousands of Roman Catholics in the Japanese islands, but the devil sowed his tares among the good seed. The Christians hatched a plot that led to civil war in which, in 1638, they were all killed. Japan then closed its ports to all foreigners except the Dutch, whom they looked upon as traders and not Christians: they were made to trample on the cross before getting permission to sell their merchandise in the prison into which, on first landing at Nagasaki, they were thrown.

The Roman Catholic Apostolic religion was recently banned in China, albeit in a less cruel manner. The Jesuit Reverend Fathers had, in truth, not raised anyone from the dead at the court in Peking; they confined themselves to being mandarins, teaching astronomy and cannon-foundry. Their unfortunate squabbles with the Dominicans and others so shocked the great Emperor Yongzheng, who was justice and goodness incarnate, that he was blinded into forbidding any further teaching of our religion because our missionaries could not agree with each other. He sent them packing with fatherly kindness, providing them with subsistence and transport to the frontiers of his empire.

The whole of Asia and Africa, half of Europe, all the English and Dutch possessions in America, all the unconquered American tribes, and all the southern regions (a fifth of the globe) remain the prey of the devil, in fulfilment of the words in Holy Scripture, 'many are called but few chosen'. If there are about sixteen hundred million people on earth, as some scholars claim, the universal Holy Roman Catholic Church can lay claim to about sixty million, which makes more than the two hundred and thirtieth part of the population of the known world.

CONVULSIONS

ROUND about 1724 there was dancing at the St Médard cemetery, to the accompaniment of many miracles; here's one, as related in a song by the Duchess of Maine:

> A boot-boy with a goatee
> And lame in his left heel
> By special grace got leave
> To limp on t'other keel.

As we know, the miraculous convulsions continued until they posted a guard outside the cemetery gates.

> By His Majesty's royal command,
> God's forbidden here to hang around.

As we also know, the Jesuits, no longer able to work such miracles after the Company's grace account dipped into the red as a result of St Francis Xavier resurrecting nine dead men, took it into their heads to equal the Jansenists' credit balance by having an engraving made of Christ dressed as a Jesuit. A joker in the Jansenist party, as is also well known, put at the bottom of the engraving:

> Admire the great artifice
> Of these clever monks, Lord,
> Who, afraid people'll love you,
> Have dressed you up so's
> You look just like they do.

The better to prove that Christ could never have donned Jesuit garb, the Jansenists filled Paris with convulsions; a lot of people were drawn to their cloister. Carré de Montgeron, a councillor in the Paris *parlement*, went to the king and presented him with a quarto volume containing an account of all these miracles, attested by a thousand witnesses; he was, as you might expect, sent to a fortress where in an attempt to sort his head out he was put on a diet. People invited home Sister Rose, Sister Visionary, Sister Trothed, Sister Piety; they had themselves flogged but showed no weals the next day; they were beaten with cudgels on their toughened and well-padded stomachs and were none the worse for it; having had their faces smeared with ointment, they were made to lie in front of a hot fire, but they didn't get burned; then—since steady improvement is the rule in all arts—they were finally run through with swords and crucified. Also a famous theologian had the advantage of being nailed to a cross: all this in order to convince people that a certain papal bull was ridiculous, something that could have been proved at less cost. Nevertheless, Jesuits and Jansenists came together to condemn *The Spirit of the Laws*,* and . . . and . . . and . . . and . . . And after that we have the nerve to make fun of the Lapps, the Nenets, and the Negroes!

CRITICISM
(CRITIQUE)

I don't claim to speak here of the criticism of scholiasts, who carry out shaky reconstructions of words in an ancient author that were perfectly well understood before. I don't deal either with the genuine critics who have disentangled whatever can be disentangled in ancient history and philosophy. I have in mind critics who have a taste for satire.

A lover of literature who was reading Tasso with me one day lit upon this stanza:

> The shrill blast of Hell's trumpet bellowing forth
> Summons the denizens of the eternal shades
> The vast and gloomy caverns tremble
> The sombre air shudders with a sound
> Louder by far than any thunderclap
> Raining down from heaven's loftiest peak
> Louder too than the volcano's roar
> When gravid earth spews its lava forth.*

He then read at random several stanzas as powerful and harmonious as this one. 'Ah,' he exclaimed, 'is that what your Boileau calls "flashy"?* Is that how he seeks to belittle a great man who lived a hundred years earlier in order the better to elevate another great man who lived sixteen hundred years before and who would himself have done justice to Tasso?'

'Don't let it get you down,' I said, 'let's take Quinault's operas.' We opened the book and found something to fan our anger about criticism: we were looking at the admirable poem *Armide*, and we hit upon this passage:

> SIDONIE: Hatred is barbarous, awful.
> But on the hearts it conquers
> Love inflicts cruel suffering.
> If in your own hands
> Your fate happens to lie,
> Choose indifference:
> It ensures a better outcome.

ARMIDE: No, no, it's impossible
For me to escape this turmoil
And find a state of calm.
My heart can no longer be still.
Renaud causes me great offence:
He's simply too lovable.
So I'm being forced to choose:
Either to love him, or hate him.*

We read the whole of *Armide*, in which Tasso's genius, thanks to Quinault, acquires even greater charms. 'Well,' I said to my friend, 'this is the same Quinault that Boileau was always trying to do down in everybody's eyes; he even persuaded Louis XIV that this gracious, touching, moving, and elegant writer owed such merits as he possessed to the composer Lully.' 'I can see that pretty clearly,' my friend replied; 'Boileau wasn't jealous of Lully; he *was* jealous of Quinault. What faith can we have in the judgement of a man who, in order to find words that rhymed ending in "-*ault*", denigrated either Boursault, or Hainault, or Quinault, depending on how good his relations were with each of them at the time?'

So as not to allow your ardour against injustice to cool, just put your head out of the window and look at the beautiful façade of the Louvre which has ensured Perrault's immortality. This clever man's brother was a learned academician whom Boileau fell out with, and that was enough to be called an 'ignorant architect'.*

My friend mused a while, then added with a sigh: 'That's human nature, alas. In his memoirs the Duc de Sully finds the Cardinal d'Ossat and secretary Villeroi bad ministers; and Louvois did his utmost not to hold the great Colbert in high esteem.' 'They published nothing against each other during their lifetime,' I replied, 'it's a kind of foolishness that attaches itself only to literature, theology, and quibbling.'

'We did have a man of worth: La Motte. He wrote some beautiful verse:

Oft a young beauty, bent upon
Resisting a charmer's ardour,
Takes up arms against herself and
With a firmness hard to bear

Eschews the shame she loathes.
This extreme duress, alas
Robs her of the vice she loves.
Her cruelty is but for show
So the honour of seeming chaste
Makes her chaste indeed.

In vain does this harsh Stoic
Downcast at so many flaws
Boast of his heroic stance, his
Consuming passion for virtue.
It's not virtue he loves.
His self-intoxicated heart
Aspires the altar to usurp
And with frivolous wisdom
Desires but to adorn the idol
He offers to mortals' worship.

Pharsalus and Arbela fields
Saw two heroes triumph
Worthy models, fit both
To inspire the noblest hearts.
But glory's the fruit of success.
Had the seal of victory not
Consecrated these demigods,
In the eyes of the vulgar
Alexander would be deemed
A reckless fool, and Caesar
A base seditious knave.*

'This author', he said, 'was a wise man who on many an occasion adorned philosophy with the charm of poetry. Had he always written verse of this quality, he would now be considered the greatest of lyric poets. But it was while he was giving the world these fine pieces that one of his contemporaries called him:

A certain gosling, farmyard game . . .

In another place he says of La Motte:

The tedious beauty of his discourse . . .

And in another:

> . . . I see but one defect
> It's that the author should have
> Written them in prose.
> Those odes smack
> Too much of Quinault.*

He harasses him everywhere, reproaching him with dryness and lack of harmony.

'Would you be curious to see the odes which were written a few years later by the same critic who hailed La Motte as a master and disparaged him as an enemy? Just look at this:

> The sovereign influence he wields
> For him is but an illustrious chain
> Binding him to others' wellbeing;
> All the sparkle that embellishes him
> All the talents that ennoble him
> Are in him, but to him do not belong.

> There's nothing that time does not absorb and devour,
>   And the things you don't know
> Are little different from those that never occurred.

> The goodness shining in her
> From her most gentle charms
> Is a reflection of the one
> She sees shining in you.
> And by you alone enriched
> Her courtesy freed
> From every single shadow
> Is the light reflected
> From your sublime brightness.

> They have seen
> The fear of their peoples
> Living in dread
> Happily dissipated
> By your good faith

And banished for ever
The hatred so often
A relic of peace.

Reveal to my eager gaze
Those adopted deities
Synonyms of thought
Symbols of abstraction.

Isn't it fortunate
When two halves bear
The burden of a common load?
When the lesser claims it
And when the body alone
Bears the cost
Of the soul's happiness?*

'It was probably not a good idea', my lover of literature said, 'to offer such loathsome works as models to someone criticized with such bitterness; it would have been better to let his adversary enjoy his merits in peace and hold on to the ones he had; but there you are, the *genus irritabile vatum** is ill with the same bile that plagued it in the past. The public forgive such weaknesses in people of talent because the public think only of their own amusement; in an allegory entitled *Pluto* they see judges condemned to be flayed alive and to sit in hell on a seat covered with their own skin instead of fleurs-de-lys;* the reader isn't bothered whether those judges deserve their fate or not, or whether the complainant who summons them to appear before Pluto is right or wrong. People read poetry for pleasure, and if it gives them pleasure, they ask for nothing more; if they don't like it, they drop the allegory and wouldn't lift a finger to confirm or quash the sentence.

'Racine's inimitable tragedies were all criticized, and very harshly; and it was always rivals who did so. It's true that artists are competent judges of art, but these competent judges are nearly always corrupt.

'An excellent critic would be an artist of great taste and learning, and without prejudice or envy. But such a person would be hard to find.'

FATE
(DESTIN)

OF all the books that have come down to us, Homer's are the most ancient. It's in them we encounter the customs of profane antiquity, as well as coarse heroes, and coarser gods, made in man's image. But it's also in them that we find the seeds of philosophy, and above all the idea of fate as the master of the gods, just as the gods are the masters of the world.

In vain did Jupiter try to save Hector: he consulted the fates; he weighed in the balance the destiny of Hector and Achilles; he found that the Trojan absolutely had to be killed by the Greek; he couldn't prevent it; and from that moment onwards Hector's guardian spirit, Apollo, was forced to abandon him (*Iliad*, Book 22). It's not that Homer, following the privilege of the ancients, isn't frequently guilty of contradicting himself in the poem; but he is the first to put forward the notion of fate, which was very much in vogue at the time.

Among the Jewish common people the Pharisees adopted fate only several centuries later. The Pharisees themselves, as the leading Jewish men of letters, were quite a new phenomenon. In Alexandria they fused ancient Jewish ideas with parts of the Stoics' teachings. St Jerome even claims that their sect barely pre-dates the birth of Christ.*

The philosophers never needed Homer or the Pharisees to convince them that everything happens according to unchanging laws, that everything is preordained, and that everything is a necessary effect.

Either the world subsists by its own nature and by its physical laws, or a Supreme Being shaped it according to his supreme laws; in either case, the laws are immutable and everything is necessary; heavy bodies tend towards the centre of the earth and do not tend to hang in the air. Pineapples can never grow on pear trees. A spaniel cannot have the instincts of an ostrich; everything is ordered, connected, and circumscribed.

A man can have only a certain number of teeth, horses, and ideas; and there comes a time when, of necessity, he loses his teeth, his horses, and his ideas.

It would be contradictory to say that what existed yesterday may never have been, or that what exists today does not, or that what must be may not be.

If you could alter the destiny of a fly, there would be no reason why you couldn't be arbiter of the fate of all the other flies, of all the other animals, of all human beings, and of all nature; you would find yourself in the end more powerful than God.

Stupid people say: 'My doctor cured my aunt of a fatal illness and allowed her to live ten years more than she would otherwise have done'; others, oozing competence, say, 'The prudent make their own fate':

> Nullum numen abest si sit prudentia, sed nos
> Te facimus fortuna Deam coeloque locamus.*

Some people of a subtle political turn of mind argue that if Cromwell, Ludlow, Ireton, and a dozen other parliamentarians had been murdered a week before Charles I's head was cut off, he could have gone on living and died in his bed. They're right; they could add that if the whole of England had been swallowed up by the sea the king would not have perished on a scaffold in Whitehall; matters were so ordained, though, that Charles's head had to be cut off.

Cardinal d'Ossat* was no doubt wiser than a madman in the Petites-Maisons asylum; but isn't it obvious that the wise d'Ossat's organs were differently constructed from those of that birdbrain, in the same way as the organs of a fox differ from those of a crane or a skylark?

Your doctor saved your aunt, but in doing so he wasn't upsetting the order of nature, he was following it. It's obvious that your aunt couldn't help getting born in such-and-such a town, that she couldn't help catching a particular illness at such-and-such a time, that the doctor couldn't be anywhere but in the town he was in, and that your aunt had to call him and he had to prescribe the medicines which cured her.

A farmer believes that the hailstorm has hit his field by chance, but the philosopher knows that there's no such thing as chance and that, given the way the world is constituted, it was impossible for it not to hail at that spot on that particular day.

There are people who, being afraid of this truth, concede half of it (like debtors who offer to pay half the money they owe their creditors and ask for time to pay the rest). There are—they say—some events that are necessary, and others that aren't; it would be nice if one part of the world were preordained and the other part not, and if part of what has to happen does happen, while a part of what happens was not supposed to happen. On closer inspection, the arguments against fate are absurd, but there are many people fated to reason badly, others not to reason at all, and yet others to persecute those who do reason.

You ask me what will become of liberty. I don't understand. I don't know what the liberty you're referring to is; you've been arguing about its nature for so long I'm sure *you* don't know what it is. If you wish—or rather, if you can—reason with me calmly, move to the letter L.*

GOD
(DIEU)

UNDER the Emperor Arcadius, a theologian from Constantinople called Logomachos went to Scythia and stopped at the foot of the Caucasus mountains in the fertile plains of Zephirim, on the border with Colchis. In his spacious lower hall, between his big sheepfold and his vast barn, that worthy old gentleman Dondindac, after a light lunch, was kneeling with his wife, five sons, five daughters, extended family and servants, and they were all singing God's praises. 'What are you doing, you idolater, you?' asked Logomachos. 'I'm no idolater,' said Dondindac. 'You must be,' said Logomachos, 'because you're Scythian and not Greek. Tell me, what you were chanting in your barbarous Scythian tongue?' 'All languages are equal to God's ears,' the Scythian replied; 'we were singing his praises.' 'Well, that's quite extraordinary,' said the theologian; 'a Scythian family praying to God without having been taught by us!' Since the theologian knew a little Scythian and Dondindac a little Greek, he soon started a conversation with the old man. Their dialogue has been found in a manuscript in the Constantinople library.

LOGOMACHOS: Let's see if you know your catechism. Why do you pray to God?

DONDINDAC: Because it's right to worship the Supreme Being to whom we owe everything.

LOGOMACHOS: Not bad for a barbarian! And what do you ask him for?

DONDINDAC: I thank him for the good things I enjoy, and even for the bad things he sends to try me; but I take good care not to ask him for anything; he knows better than we do what we need; anyway, I'd be afraid of asking him for fine weather when my neighbour is praying for rain.

LOGOMACHOS: Ah, I guessed he was going to say something silly. Let's go back a bit. Barbarian, who told you there's a God?

DONDINDAC: The whole of nature.

LOGOMACHOS: That's not good enough. What idea do you have of God?

DONDINDAC: That he's my creator, my master, who'll reward me if I do well, and chastise me if I do ill.

LOGOMACHOS: Rubbish! Tripe! Let's cut to the chase. Is God infinite *secundum quid*, or by essence?*

DONDINDAC: I don't get you.

LOGOMACHOS: Stupid idiot! Is God in a place, or in no place, or in every place?

DONDINDAC: I haven't a clue . . . Whatever you like.

LOGOMACHOS: Ignorant pig! Can he make not be what has been, and a stick not to have two ends? Does he see the future as future or as present? How does he derive being from nothingness, and nullify being?

DONDINDAC: I've never thought about that.

LOGOMACHOS: What an oaf! Oh well, I'll have to adjust, and get down to your level. Tell me, friend, do you believe matter can be eternal?

DONDINDAC: What does it matter to me if it exists from all eternity or not? *I* don't exist from all eternity. God is my master always; he gave me the concept of justice, and I must follow it; I don't want to be a philosopher, I want to be a man.

LOGOMACHOS: People as cussed as this are *such* hard work! Let's take it one step at a time. What is God?

DONDINDAC: My lord, my judge, my father.

LOGOMACHOS: That's not what I'm asking you. What is his nature?

DONDINDAC: To be powerful and good.

LOGOMACHOS: But is he corporeal or spiritual?

DONDINDAC: How am I expected to know?

LOGOMACHOS: What! You don't know what a spirit is?

DONDINDAC: Not a clue. What good would it do me? Would I be a juster person for it? A better husband, a better father, a better master, a better citizen?

LOGOMACHOS: I really must teach you what a spirit is. Listen: it's . . . it's . . . it's . . . I'll tell you some other time.

DONDINDAC: I'm pretty afraid you're going to tell me what it isn't rather than what it is. So let me in my turn ask you a question. I once saw one of your temples. Why do you portray God with a big beard?

LOGOMACHOS: That's very difficult to answer. I'll need notice of the question.

DONDINDAC: While you're thinking about it, I'll tell you what happened to me one day. I'd just built a shed at the bottom of my garden, and heard a mole arguing with a cockchafer. 'What a beautiful piece of work,' said the mole; 'it must have been a very powerful mole who made that.' 'Don't make me laugh,' said the cockchafer; 'a cockchafer of genius designed it.' Ever since then I've resolved never to get into an argument.

EQUALITY
(ÉGALITÉ)

WHAT does a dog owe a dog, or a horse a horse? Nothing, because no animal depends upon its fellow creatures. Human beings have received from the Deity the beam of light called Reason, but what's been the outcome? Slavery, over virtually the whole of planet earth.

If that planet were what it would seem it should be, that is if human beings everywhere enjoyed a convenient and assured level of subsistence and a climate suited to their nature, it's obvious that it would be impossible for one person to enslave another person. If the globe were laden with produce that did us all good, if the air that's needed to sustain life didn't give us sickness and death, and if people required no other lodging and no other bed than that which suffices the roe or the fallow deer, then the Genghis Khans and the Tamburlaines of this world would have no other retainers than their children, who would be decent enough to look after them in their old age.

In that most natural state which all quadrupeds, birds, and reptiles enjoy, human beings would be as contented as they are, and domination would be a chimera, an absurdity, and no one would give it a thought, because what would be the point of looking for servants when you've got no need of service?

If anyone with a strong arm and of a tyrannical cast of mind took it into his head to enslave a neighbour less strong than himself, he'd find it impossible, because the oppressed person would be hundreds of miles away before the oppressor had taken the necessary steps.

If they had no needs, all human beings would necessarily be equal. It is poverty, indissociable from our species, that makes one person subordinate to another; it is not inequality that is the real evil, but dependence. It matters little that this man is called 'His Highness' and that man 'His Holiness'; but it's hard having to serve one or the other.

A large family has cultivated a good piece of land; two small neighbouring families have infertile, difficult fields; the two poor families have to work for their opulent neighbours, or they must kill them, that's not difficult. In order to eat, one of the needy families goes and offers to work for the rich one; the other goes and attacks it and is beaten; the working family is where domestic servants and labourers come from; the beaten family is where slavery originates.

In our unhappy world, it's impossible for people living in society not to be divided into two classes, the oppressors on the one hand and the oppressed on the other; these two are subdivided into a thousand more classes, and those subdivisions present a thousand different variants in their turn.

Not all poor people are absolutely wretched. Most are born into that condition, and having to work all the time stops them noticing how bad their situation is; but when they do realize it, wars break out, as happened between the people's party and the senators' party in Rome, and in peasants' revolts in Germany, England, and France. Sooner or later all these wars end in the enslavement of the common people, because those in power have the money, and money is all-powerful in a state; I say in a state, because the situation is not the same from one country to another. The country that makes the best use of iron will always subjugate the one that has more gold but less guts.

All men are born with a fairly violent penchant for wealth, pleasure, and domination over others, and a great taste for idleness; consequently every man would like to seize the money, wives, and daughters of his fellow men, to lord it over them, to subject them to his every whim, and to have nothing whatever to do, or at least to have only very pleasant things to do. Given such fine tendencies you can see that it's impossible for human beings to be equal, and that it's impossible for two preachers or two theology professors not to be jealous of each other.

The human race, being what it is, cannot survive without an infinite number of people who possess nothing but their skills, because a comfortably-off man will certainly not leave his field to plough yours, and if you need a pair of shoes, you won't get a QC to make them for you. So equality is both the most natural of things and the most chimerical.

Since, whenever they can, human beings go to extremes in everything they do, inequalities have intensified, and in several countries it has been decreed that citizens cannot leave the place where they were born;* obviously what this law means is that 'the place is so badly governed that we forbid any individual to leave it in case everyone follows suit'. It's far better to make your subjects want to stay put and foreigners to enter the country.

In their heart of hearts all human beings have the right to think themselves absolutely equal to everyone else, and although it doesn't follow that a cardinal's cook can order his master to get dinner, the cook can say 'I am a man, like my master; I was born in tears, as he was; when we die we'll suffer the same anguish and be accompanied by the same ceremonies; we share the same animal functions; if the Turks seize Rome and I become a cardinal and my master a cook, I'll be happy to hire him.' That's reasonable and just; but until the Grand Turk conquers Rome, the cook must do his duty, or all human society is subverted.

With respect to a man who is neither a cook nor a cardinal nor the holder of any other office of state; with respect to an individual who has no particular agenda but who's annoyed at encountering everywhere an air of condescension and contempt, who sees clearly that several monsignori have no more wit, learning, or virtue than he has, and who is sometimes forced to kick his heels in their antechamber, what ought he to do? Just go and leave them to it.

HELL
(ENFER)

As soon as human beings began forming social groups, they couldn't help but notice that lots of guilty people managed to evade the long arm of the law. Public offences could be dealt with, but secret crimes had to be curbed too, and only religion could do that. The Persians, Chaldeans, Egyptians, and Greeks came up with the notion of punishments inflicted in the afterlife but, amongst all the ancient peoples we know of, the Jews alone admired penalties imposed in this world. It's ridiculous to believe or pretend to believe, on the basis of a handful of very obscure passages, that the existence of hell was acknowledged by the ancient laws of the Jews, in Leviticus or in the Decalogue, when the author of those laws says nothing that could have the slightest connection with punishments in the life to come. We'd be within our rights to say to the compiler of the Pentateuch: 'You're inconsistent, and you lack integrity and good sense, so you're unworthy of the name of "legislator" which you falsely lay claim to. What? You're familiar with a doctrine as repressive and as indispensable to people as eternal damnation is, and you don't trumpet it from the rooftops? And whereas it's a dogma accepted by every nation around you, you're content to let it be divined by a handful of commentators who'll come along four thousand years after you've gone and twist some of your words to make them say what you haven't said? Either you're an ignoramus who doesn't know that this belief was widespread in Egypt, Chaldea, and Persia, or you're a very stupid person who though conversant with this doctrine fails to make it the basis of his religion.'

The people who wrote the Jewish laws could at best reply: 'We admit that we're very ignorant, that for a long time we couldn't read or write, that we're a savage and barbarous race who for half a century wandered over trackless deserts and who finally seized and plundered a small country in the most appalling manner and with the most loathsome acts of cruelty the world has ever seen. We had no dealings with civilized countries, so how do you expect us (the most earth-bound of peoples) to be able to invent a wholly spiritual system?

'We only use the word which corresponds to "soul" to designate "life"; we only knew our God and his ministers, his angels, as corporeal beings; the distinction between the body and the soul, the idea of an afterlife, can only be the fruit of long meditation and a very subtle system of thought. Ask the Hottentots and the Negroes, who live in a country a hundred times bigger than ours, whether they know anything of the life to come. We thought we'd done enough persuading our people that God punished evildoers unto the fourth generation by visiting upon them either leprosy or sudden death or the destruction of what little they possessed.'

The reply to this apologia might be: 'You've invented a system that is patently absurd, because an evildoer who enjoys good health and whose family prospers is bound to laugh at you.'

The apologist for Judaic law would then reply: 'You're wrong, because for every criminal that could reason correctly, there would be a hundred who couldn't reason at all. Anyone who, having committed a crime, felt that he wasn't going to be punished and that his son wasn't either, would fear for his grandson. Furthermore, were he not to suffer today from a stinking ulcer (something we're very prone to), he would do so in a few years' time: there are always misfortunes in a family, and we would easily get him to believe that these misfortunes were sent by a divine hand avenging hidden crimes.'

It would be easy to counter this and say: 'Your answer is worthless, because every day it happens that very decent people lose their health and worldly goods; and if there's no family that hasn't suffered misfortune, and misfortune is God's punishment, then all your families are scoundrels.'

The Jewish priest could return to the attack: he could say that there are misfortunes attaching to human nature and others that are sent expressly by God. But one could point out to this quibbler how ridiculous it is to believe that fever and hail are sometimes punishments from on high and sometimes natural phenomena.*

Finally, amongst the Jews the Pharisees and Essenians allowed belief in a hell of their own devising: this doctrine had already passed from the Greeks to the Romans, and the Christians then adopted it.

Several of the church fathers did not believe in eternal punishment; it seemed absurd to them that a poor fellow could roast in hell for ever just for stealing a goat. It's no use Virgil saying in the *Aeneid*:

Sedet aeternumque sedebit infelix Theseus.*

In vain does he claim that Theseus is seated for ever on a chair and that this posture is his form of torture. Others believed that Theseus is a hero who isn't sitting in hell, but is residing in the Elysian Fields.

Not long ago a good, decent Huguenot minister preached and wrote that the damned would one day be pardoned, that the penalty had to be proportionate to the sin, and that the lapse of a moment did not deserve eternal punishment. His brother pastors unseated this indulgent judge; one of them said to him, 'My friend, I don't believe in eternal damnation any more than you do, but it's better if your maidservant, your tailor and even your procurator do believe in it.'*

STATES, GOVERNMENTS
(ÉTATS, GOUVERNEMENTS)

Which is the best?

UP till now I've not known anyone who has governed a state. I'm not talking about ministers who, in some cases, hold office for two or three years, in other cases six months, or in other cases six weeks; I'm talking about all the men who at supper or in their study lay out their system of government, reforming the army, the Church, financial services, and the legal profession.

In the name of Cardinal Richelieu the Abbé de Bourzeis* began to rule France around 1645 and made a *Political Testament* in which he sought to conscript the nobility into the cavalry for three years, to make excise payable by the Chambers of Audit and the *parlements*, and to deprive the king of the proceeds of the salt tax. He affirms too that to launch a military campaign with fifty thousand men, economy dictates that a hundred thousand have to be raised, and that 'Provence alone has a lot more fine seaports than Spain and Italy put together'.

The Abbé de Bourzeis had never travelled anywhere. Besides, his testament is riddled with anachronisms and mistakes; it makes Cardinal Richelieu sign in a way he never did and speak in a way he never did. What's more, he devotes a whole chapter to the argument that 'reason must be the rule in a state', and to try and prove this discovery; for a long time this bastard of the Abbé de Bourzeis passed for Cardinal Richelieu's legitimate son, and in his reception address every member of the Académie Française never failed to praise extravagantly this political masterpiece.

On seeing the success of Richelieu's political testament M. Gratien de Courtilz published in The Hague Colbert's testament together with a fine letter from M. Colbert to the king. It's clear that if Colbert had made such a testament, it would have had to be banned; nevertheless the book has been cited by a few authors. Another rascal, whose name is unknown, did not fail to publish Louvois's testament, an even worse document, if that's possible, than Colbert's; and one Abbé de Chèvremont got Charles, Duke of Lorraine to draw up a testament.

M. de Boisguilbert, the author of *Détail de la France* published
in 1695, put forward under the name of Marshal Vauban a wildly
unrealistic proposal for a royal tithe.

An idiot called La Jonchère, who was very hard up, published in
1720 a financial project in four volumes, and a few stupid people
have quoted this work as if it were by the Treasurer-General Gérard-
Michel de La Jonchère, believing that a treasurer cannot write a bad
book about finance.

But it has to be admitted that in France, Spain, and England some
very wise men, worthy perhaps of the highest office, have written
about state administration, and their books have done a lot of good.
But they haven't made the ministers who were in place when those
books appeared alter their ways, because a minister does not, cannot,
alter his ways. Having risen to the top he is unreceptive to lessons or
advice; he hasn't time to listen because he's borne along by the pace
of events; but those fine books do offer instruction to princes and
to young people marked out for office, and so the next generation is
better educated.

In recent times the strengths and weaknesses of all governments
have been closely scrutinized. 'So tell me, you who have travelled
a lot, seen much and read widely, in which state, under what sort
of government would you like to have been born?' I can see that a
member of the landowning aristocracy would not mind being born in
Germany, where he would be a ruler rather than a subject. A French
lord would be very happy to enjoy the privileges of an English peer,
especially that of being able to enact legislation. The lawyer and the
banker would be better off in France than anywhere else.

But what homeland would a wise, free man, of modest means and
without prejudices, choose?

A quite learned member of Pondicherry's governing council was
travelling overland back to Europe in the company of a Brahman
who was better educated than most ordinary Brahmans. 'How do
you rate the government of the Great Mogul?' asked the councillor. 'Abominable,' replied the Brahman; 'how could a state ruled by
Tartars possibly be well governed? Our rajahs, omrahs, and nabobs
are perfectly happy, but the citizenry aren't, and millions of citizens
are quite something.'

The councillor and the Brahman crossed the whole of upper Asia
discussing this. 'I've had a thought,' the Brahman said, 'and it's this:

there's not a republic to be found in the length and breadth of this vast section of the globe.' 'There was Tyre, once,' said the councillor, 'but it didn't last long; there was another, near Arabia Petraea, in a tiny place called Palestine, if you can dignify with the name "republic" a bunch of robbers and loan sharks sometimes ruled by judges, sometimes by sorts of kings, and sometimes by high priests, enslaved seven or eight times, and finally driven out of the land they'd usurped.'

'I can see', the Brahman said, 'that very few republics can be found on this earth. Human beings are rarely worthy of self-government. That happy condition can only appertain to small populations concealed on islands or in deep mountain valleys who, like rabbits hiding from carnivores, are however discovered before long and devoured.'

When the two travellers arrived in Asia Minor the councillor said to the Brahman, 'Would you believe it? That there was once a republic, established in a corner of Italy, which lasted more than five hundred years and owned Asia Minor, where we now are, as well as Asia, Africa, Greece, Gaul, Spain, and the whole of Italy?' 'So it soon turned into a monarchy?' queried the Brahman. 'You've guessed it,' replied the other man, 'but this monarchy collapsed, and every day we're writing yet another impressive analysis of the causes of its decline and fall.' 'You're making very heavy weather of it,' said the Indian gentleman; 'that empire fell simply because it existed. Everything has to fall in the end. I just hope the same will happen to the Great Mogul's empire.'

'By the way,' said the European, 'do you think that there has to be more honour in a despotic state and more virtue in a republic?'* The Indian asked what was meant by 'honour' and, when it had been explained to him, replied that honour was more important in a republic and virtue was more necessary in a monarchy: because, he said, 'a man who aspires to be elected by the people won't be chosen if he's been dishonoured, whereas at court—in accordance with a great prince's maxim that in order to succeed a courtier must have neither honour nor character—a man can easily obtain office. With respect to virtue, he must have prodigious amounts of it if he is ever to summon up the courage to tell the truth at court; in a republic the virtuous man has a much easier time of it, because there's no one he has to flatter.'

'Do you think', the European asked, 'that laws and faiths are designed to suit particular climates in the same way as furs have to be worn in Moscow and gauze in Delhi?' 'Yes, without doubt,' said the Brahman; 'all laws concerning physical matters are calculated for the meridian you inhabit: a German needs only one wife, whereas a Persian has to have three or four.

'It's the same with religious rituals. If I were a Christian, how could I say mass in a country like mine where bread and wine are unknown? Where doctrine is concerned, it's quite different: climate is irrelevant. Didn't your faith originate in Asia, from which it has been banished? And doesn't it exist near the Baltic, where it was once unknown?'

'In what state, under which regime, would you prefer to live?' the councillor asked. 'Anywhere but where I live now,' his companion said, 'and I've found that many Siamese, Tonkinese, Persian, and Turkish people say the same.' 'But, once again,' the European asked, 'what state would you choose?' 'Where the law alone is obeyed,' replied the Brahman. 'That's an old answer,' the councillor said. 'It's none the worse for that,' the Brahman retorted. 'Where is that country?' the councillor asked. The Brahman answered: 'You'll have to look for it.'

ON EZEKIEL
(D'ÉZÉCHIEL)

On some singular passages in this prophet, and on some ancient customs

IT'S generally agreed today that ancient customs must not be judged in the light of present practice. Anyone wishing to reform Alcinous' court on the lines of that of the Sultan or of Louis XIV would get a poor reception from scholars, and anyone finding fault with Virgil for showing King Evander receiving ambassadors dressed in a bearskin and accompanied by two dogs would be considered a bad critic.

The customs of the ancient Jews were even more different from our own than those of King Alcinous or his daughter Nausicaa or that chap Evander. While a slave in Chaldea Ezekiel had a vision near the small river Chebar that flows into the Euphrates.

It's no surprise that he saw animals with four faces, four wings, and calves' feet, and wheels that turned all by themselves and possessed the spirit of life: these symbols are even pleasing to the imagination, but several critics have expressed their disgust at the Lord's command that for three hundred and ninety days he had to eat barley, wheat, and millet bread covered with shit.*

The prophet cried out 'Ugh! Up till now my soul has not been polluted', and the Lord replied, 'All right, I'll give you cow dung rather than human excrement, and you'll knead your bread with that'.

Since it's not customary to eat preserves of that kind on one's bread, most people find these orders unworthy of the Divine Majesty. It has to be admitted, though, that all the Great Mogul's diamonds and a cowpat enjoy exactly the same status in the eyes not only of a divine being but of any true philosopher; and as for God ordering such a lunch for the prophet, it's not for us to reason why.

It's enough for us to demonstrate that these commandments which seem strange to us did not seem so strange to the Jews. It's true that in St Jerome's time the synagogue did allow anyone under thirty to read Ezekiel, but that was because in chapter 18 he says 'the son shall not bear the iniquity of the father', and that it will no longer be said 'the fathers have eaten sour grapes, and the children's teeth are set on edge'.

In saying that he was expressly contradicting Moses who, in Numbers, chapter 28, assures us that 'the iniquity of the fathers shall be visited upon the children unto the third and the fourth generation'.

In chapter 20 Ezekiel attributes to the Lord the statement that he gave the Jews 'statutes that were not good'. That's why the synagogue forbade the young to read something that could make them doubt the irrefragability of the laws of Moses.

The critics of today are even more surprised by Ezekiel chapter 16: this is how the prophet sets about informing people of Jerusalem's misdeeds: he introduces the Lord speaking to a girl and saying, 'as for thy nativity, thy navel was not cut, thou wast not salted at all, nor swaddled at all, I pitied thee; thou hast waxen great, thy breasts are fashioned, and thine hair is grown; now when I passed by thee, and looked upon thee, behold, thy time was the time of love; I covered thy nakedness; I spread my skirt over thee; thou becamest mine; I washed thee, anointed thee, clothed thee and shod thee; I gave thee a cotton scarf, bracelets and a chain on thy neck; I put a jewel on thy nose, earrings in thine ears and a crown upon thine head,' etc.

'But thou didst trust in thy beauty, and pouredst out thy fornications on everyone that passed by . . . thou hast built unto thee a place of ill repute . . . and playedst the harlot in public, and hast opened thy legs to everyone that passed by . . . and thou hast committed fornication with the Egyptians . . . thou hast paid thy lovers and given them gifts that they may lie with thee . . . and in paying rather than being paid thou art contrary from other women . . . the proverb "as is the mother, so is her daughter" is said of thee,' etc.

Chapter 23 has come in for even harsher criticism. A mother had two daughters who lost their virginity early on; the elder was called Aholah and the younger Aholibah: 'Aholah doted on her young lovers, lords, rulers, horsemen . . . and committed her whoredom with Egyptians in the first flush of her youth . . . Aholibah her sister, more corrupt than she, fornicated with captains, rulers, and desirable young horsemen; she revealed her turpitude and multiplied her whoredoms, and doted on the paramours who have members like the members of asses, and who cast their seed like horses . . .'

These descriptions, which so many weak spirits find terrifying, do not only signify the iniquities of Jerusalem and Samaria; the expressions which seem broad to us were not seen to be like that then.

The same ingenuousness is boldly displayed in Scripture: the expression 'opening the vulva' is often used. The terms used to describe the coupling of Boaz and Ruth and of Judah and his daughter-in-law are not unseemly in Hebrew as they would be in our language.*

One does not cover oneself with a veil when one is not ashamed of one's nakedness; how could people in those days have blushed to use the word 'testicles', since it was customary to touch the testicles of those one was making a promise to: it was a mark of respect, a symbol of fidelity, as with us in the past feudal lords placed their hands between those of their suzerain lords.

We have translated the word 'testicle' by 'thigh'. Eliezer put his hand under Abraham's thigh, and Joseph put his hand under Jacob's thigh. It was a very ancient custom in Egypt. The Egyptians were so far from seeing as base the thing we dare neither uncover nor name that they carried in procession a large image of the penis called a 'phallus' to thank the gods for their kindness in making this member serve as the propagator of the human race.

This all proves pretty conclusively that our proprieties are not those of other peoples. In what period did the Romans show more decorum than in the time of the Emperor Augustus? But Horace has no problem saying in a moral piece:

Nec metuo, nedum futuo vir rure recurrat.*

A man using the word that corresponds to *futuo* in our language would be looked upon as a drunken picklock; that word, like several others that Horace and fellow writers use, seems even more indecent than Ezekiel's expressions. Let us shed our prejudices when we read ancient authors or travel in distant lands. Nature is the same the world over, but customs are everywhere different.

FABLES

AREN'T the most ancient fables obviously allegorical? Isn't the first we know about, according to our method of calculating time, the one recorded in Judges, chapter 9? Among the trees a king had to be chosen. The olive tree was unwilling to stop producing oil, the fig tree figs, the vine grapes, and other trees their fruit. So the thistle, which produced nothing useful, was made king, because it had prickles and could do some damage.

Isn't the ancient fable of Venus, as Hesiod retells it,* an allegory of nature as a whole? When genitalia dropped from the sky on to the edge of the sea Venus was born of the precious foam; the first name applied to her was 'sponsor of procreation', and there could be no more fitting image, surely? Because Venus is the goddess of beauty, and without grace beauty is not attractive; beauty gives rise to love; love fires darts that pierce the heart and wears a blindfold that hides a lover's faults.

Wisdom, conceived in the brain of the king of the gods, was given the name Minerva; the human soul was a divine fire revealed by Minerva to Prometheus, who used that fire to breathe life into humankind.

It's impossible not to see in these fables a living picture of nature as a whole. Most of the others are corruptions of old stories, or quirks of the imagination. With ancient fables, it's the same as with our modern narratives: there are some that are charming moral tales, and others that are insipid.

FANATICISM
(FANATISME)

FANATICISM is to superstition what delirium is to running a temperature, or rage is to feeling cross. People who have ecstatic visions, or mistake their dreams for reality and the heated products of their imagination for prophecy, are what we call 'enthusiasts'. Fanatics are people whose madness is fuelled by murder. Jean Diaz, who retired to Nuremberg, firmly persuaded that the Pope was the Antichrist and bore the mark of the beast, was only an enthusiast.* His brother Alfonso, who left Rome to carry out the holy action of murdering Jean, and did indeed kill him for the love of God, was one of the most detestable fanatics that superstition has ever produced.

Corneille's character Polyeucte, who went to the temple on a major feast day to overturn the statues and smash the ornaments,* was a less ghastly enthusiast than Diaz, but just as stupid. Those who assassinated Duc François de Guise, William Prince of Orange, Henri III, Henri IV,* and so many others, were sick people, suffering from the same mad rage as Diaz.

The most loathsome example of fanaticism is that of the burghers of Paris who on the night of St Bartholomew ran hither and thither murdering, defenestrating, and hacking to pieces those among their fellow citizens who did not attend mass.*

Some people are cold-blooded fanatics: they're the judges who condemn to death those whose only offence is to think differently. It seems to me that such magistrates are the more culpable and the more worthy of contempt because, not being stark staring mad like the Cléments, the Châtels, the Ravaillacs, the Gérards, and the Damiens of this world, they ought to be able to listen to the voice of reason.

Once fanaticism has infected the brain, the illness is all but incurable. I've seen Convulsionaries talking about the miracles of St Pâris and getting more and more agitated in spite of themselves; their eyes blazed, their limbs shook, and their faces grew ugly with rage; they would have killed anyone who dared gainsay them.

The only cure for this pandemic malady is the philosophical cast of mind which, as it spreads from one person to another, eventually makes us gentler in our ways and forestalls all attacks of this evil;

because, as soon as the illness starts making progress, we have to flee and wait for the air to clear. Religion and the law are inadequate as a defence against the bubonic plague of the spirit; far from being health-giving nourishment for the soul, in infected brains religion morphs into a poison. Its wretched victims have continually in mind the example of Ehud, King Eglon's assassin, of Judith who slept with Holophernes and cut off his head, and of Samuel who hewed King Agag in pieces; and in justifying their fury by invoking a religion that in fact condemns it, they fail to see that we find such acts revolting, however praiseworthy they may have been in antiquity.

The law is largely impotent against such fits of rage; it's like reading out a court ruling to someone in a frenzy. Such people are convinced that they are filled with the Holy Spirit and so are above the law; indeed, that their enthusiasm is the only law they need obey.

What can you say to a man who tells you that he prefers obeying God rather than men, and that as a result he's certain he'll go to heaven if he cuts your throat?

Normally fanatics are led by scoundrels who supply the weapons and who are like the Old Man of the Mountain who, we're told, made foolish people taste of the joys of paradise and who promised them an eternity of pleasures such as they'd just sampled, on condition that they go and murder anyone he designated. There has been only one faith in the world that has never been sullied by fanaticism, and that's the religion practised by men of letters in China. The philosophers' sects were not only exempt from this plague, they were its remedy.

Philosophy brings peace to the soul; fanaticism and peace are incompatible. If our holy faith has so often been corrupted by this infernal madness, human folly is to blame.

> The plumage he used
> Icarus abused;
> Acquired for his safety
> It served for his injury.*
>
> BERTAUD, Bishop of Sées.

FALSENESS OF HUMAN VIRTUES
(FAUSSETÉ DES VERTUS HUMAINES)

WHEN the Duc de la Rochefoucauld had written down his thoughts on self-love and thereby laid bare what makes human beings tick, a certain Jacques Esprit, a member of the Oratory, wrote a specious book entitled *On the Falseness of Human Virtues*. This Esprit fellow says that there is no such thing as virtue, but by God's grace he ends each chapter by referring to Christian charity. Thus, according to M. Esprit, neither Cato, nor Aristides, nor Marcus Aurelius, nor Epictetus were good people: they were to be found only in the Christian community. Amongst Christians, only the Catholics were virtuous; amongst Catholics the Jesuits, the Oratorians' enemies, had to be excluded; therefore virtue was to be found only amongst those opposed to the Jesuits.

This M. Esprit begins by saying that prudence is not a virtue; that, he argues, is because prudence is often deceived. It's like saying that Caesar was not a great captain because he suffered defeat at Dirrachium.

Had M. Esprit been a philosopher he would have considered prudence not as a virtue, but as a gift, a felicitous, useful quality, because a scoundrel can be very prudent (I've known a few). What madness, to claim that

None shall have virtue but ourselves and our friends!*

What is virtue, my friend? It's doing the right thing. So let's do it, and that'll suffice. The reasons don't matter. What? Is there no difference, according to you, between President Thou and Ravaillac? Between Cicero and Popilius, whose life he'd saved and who was paid to cut his head off? And you'd declare Epictetus and Porphyry rascals for not having espoused our doctrines? Such arrogance is revolting. I'll say no more, because I'm starting to get angry.

END, FINAL CAUSES
(FIN, CAUSES FINALES)

It seems you must be out of your mind to deny that stomachs are made for digestion, eyes for seeing, and ears for hearing.

On the other hand you must have a strange affection for final causes to assert that stone was created to build houses and silkworms were bred in China so that we can wear satin in Europe.

But it's said that if God has done something obviously on purpose, he has done everything on purpose. It's ridiculous to accept Providence in some cases and deny it in others. Everything that is done has been foreseen and prearranged. No arrangement is without object; no effect is without cause: everything is therefore the result, the product, of a final cause, so it's just as true to say that noses were made for wearing glasses* and fingers for wearing diamonds as to say that ears were made to hear sounds and eyes to receive light.

I think it's easy to clear up the difficulty: where the effects are always the same, in every place and at every moment, and where these uniform effects are independent of the beings they belong to, then there is obviously a final cause.

All animals have eyes, and they can see; they all have ears, and they can hear; they all have a mouth to eat with, a stomach (or something like it) to digest food with, an orifice to expel excrement, and an instrument for reproduction: these gifts of nature operate without any skill being required. Here we have clearly established final causes, and denying such a universal truth is a perversion of our thinking faculties.

But stones exist everywhere and at all times and don't just make up buildings; not all noses support glasses; not all fingers wear rings; not all legs are clad in silk stockings. So a silkworm is not made to cover my legs in the same way as your mouth is made for eating and your bottom for going to the toilet. So there are some effects produced by final causes, just as there are many other effects of which that cannot be said.

But they are all part of the plan of general Providence: there can be no doubt that nothing is done in spite of her, or even without her. Everything that pertains to nature is uniform, unchanging, and the direct work of the master: it is he who has created the laws which make the moon responsible for three-quarters of the tidal movements of the oceans and the sun responsible for a quarter of them. It is he who has caused the sun to rotate and to dispatch rays of light to the eyes of human beings, crocodiles, and cats within five and a half minutes.

But if after many centuries we have taken it into our heads to invent shears and spits in order to clip sheep's wool with the former and with the latter to cook and eat mutton, what else can we infer, other than that God made us in such a way that we should one day necessarily become industrious and carnivorous?

No doubt sheep were not created essentially to be cooked and eaten, since several countries shrink with horror from such a practice. Human beings were not expressly created to massacre each other, because the Brahmans and Quakers kill no one; but the dough from which we are kneaded often gives rise to murder as it does to stupidity, calumny, vanity, and persecution. It isn't precisely the way human beings are made that is the final cause of our acts of folly and rage, because a final cause is, everywhere and at all times, universal and invariable: but the horrors and absurdities of humankind are none the less in the eternal order of things. When we thresh our corn the flail is the final cause of the separation of the wheat from the chaff, but if in threshing my corn the same flail crushes a thousand insects it's not because I've decided upon it, but neither does it happen by chance: it's because on that occasion those insects find themselves under my flail and are meant to be there.

It's in the nature of things that a man can be ambitious and sometimes enlist other men to fight alongside him, and he can then either win or lose; but it can never be said that man was created by God to be killed on active service.

The instruments given to us by nature cannot always be final causes progressing towards an ineluctable outcome. The eyes we're given to see with aren't always open; every sense has its moments of repose. There are even senses that never get used. For example, a wretched mad girl shut up at fourteen in a convent closes for ever the door in herself from which a new generation should emerge; but the final cause remains and will function as soon as she is free.

MADNESS
(FOLIE)

THERE'S no question of reviving Erasmus' book,* which people today would find insipid and platitudinous.

What we call madness is an illness of the cerebral organs which necessarily stops a person thinking and acting as others do; if people cannot manage their property, they are divested of it; if they can't entertain ideas acceptable to society, they are excluded; if they're dangerous, they get locked up; and if they're raving, they are put in a straitjacket.

What's important to note is that such people are not deprived of ideas; they have them, as everybody else does, when they're awake, and often when they're asleep. You may well ask; how it is that their spiritual, immortal soul, lodged in their brain, receives through their senses very clear and distinct ideas, but is never capable of formulating a clear judgement about them? Their soul sees objects as the soul of Aristotle, Plato, Locke, and Newton saw them; it hears the same sounds and has the same sense of touch; so how, receiving all the perceptions experienced by the wisest, does it make a crazy assemblage out of them that they can't get rid of? If this simple, eternal substance possesses the same tools for action as the wisest of brains, it ought to reason like them. What possibly can prevent it? I can conceive only too vividly that if mad people see red when wise people see blue; if when a wise person is listening to music the mad person hears an ass braying; if they're sitting in a church and the mad individual thinks it's a playhouse; if they hear 'yes', and the other hears 'no'; then that person must be getting it all wrong. But the mad person has the same perceptions as they have; there's no apparent reason why that individual's soul, having received all its tools through its senses, is incapable of using them. It is pure, people say, and is not by itself subject to any infirmity; it has all necessary assistance at its disposal; something that happens in its body cannot change its essence; but, for all that, it gets carried off to the madhouse in its husk.

This thought might lead one to suspect that the faculty of thought given to humankind by God is, like the other senses, prone to derangement. A mad person is someone whose brain is sick, just as a gout sufferer is someone whose hands and feet are not well; such people were using their brains for thinking, their feet for walking, without knowing anything of their incomprehensible ability to walk or of their no less incomprehensible power of thought. One can get gout on the brain as well as in the feet. In the end, after much argument, it would seem that perhaps only faith can persuade us that a simple and immaterial substance can be ill.

People of science and learning will say to the mad person, 'My friend, although you've lost your marbles, your soul is still as spiritual, immortal, and pure as ours; but ours is well housed and yours is not; the windows of its dwelling are sealed and it is stifled for want of fresh air.' The mad person, in better moments, could reply, 'My friends, you're begging the question as usual. My windows are as wide open as yours, since I see the same objects and hear the same words. So my soul can't be making good use of its senses, or else my soul must itself be tainted and depraved. In a word, either my soul is in itself mad, or I have no soul.'

One of the learned might answer: 'My dear colleague, God has perhaps created mad souls, just as he has wise ones.' The mad person might then reply, 'If I believed what you're telling me I'd be even madder than I am. For pity's sake, you who know so much, tell me why I'm mad?'

If the learned still have a grain of sense, they will answer, 'We don't know'. They won't be able to understand why one brain has incoherent ideas, even less why another has coherent, consistent ones. They will think themselves wise, but they're no saner than the mad person.

FRAUD
(FRAUDE)

Should pious frauds be practised on the common people?

ONE day the fakir Bambabef met a disciple of Kung Futsu (known to us as Confucius). The disciple's name was Wang. Bambabef maintained that the common people needed to be deceived, and Wang claimed that no one should ever be misled. Here's a summary of their debate.

BAMBABEF: We should imitate the Supreme Being. He doesn't show us things as they are: we see the sun as being two to three feet in diameter, whereas it's a million times bigger than earth; we see the moon and stars as if stuck on the same blue background, whereas they are at different distances from us. He wants a square tower to appear round from afar, and fire to seem hot even though it's neither hot nor cold; he surrounds us, in a word, with errors fitted to our nature.

WANG: What you call error isn't that at all. The sun, placed as it is many trillions of feet from our globe, is not what we see. We truly perceive—are able to perceive—only the sun painted on our retina at a particular angle. Our eyes weren't given to us so that we could measure size and distance; we need other means for that.

Bambabef was very surprised at this. Wang, who was very patient, explained the theory of optics to him, and Bambabef, who was quite bright, accepted the demonstration provided by Kung Futsu's disciple, and proceeded to debate with him as follows:

BAMBABEF: If God doesn't, as I believed, deceive us through our senses, you'll at least admit that doctors always mislead children for their own good; they say they're giving them sugar whereas they're really dosing them with rhubarb. So as a fakir I can pull the wool over the eyes of the common people, who are ignorant like children.

WANG: I have two sons; I've never deceived them; when they've been ill I've told them, 'Here's bitter medicine, you must be brave, and take it; if it was sweet it wouldn't do you any good.' I've never allowed their nursemaids or tutors to frighten them with spirits, ghosts, witches, or goblins; that way I've made them into wise and courageous citizens.

BAMBABEF: The common herd weren't born lucky like your children.

WANG: All human beings are alike, born with the same gifts. It's the fakirs who corrupt human nature.

BAMBABEF: We teach people things that aren't correct, I admit, but it's for their own good. We lead them to believe that if they don't buy our consecrated needles, if they don't expiate their sins by giving us money, they will become post-horses, dogs, or lizards in another life. That intimidates them and they become good men and women.

WANG: Don't you see that you're corrupting these poor people? Among them there are far more than you credit who can think, who couldn't care less about your holy needles and your miracles, and who know perfectly well that they won't be changed into lizards or post-horses. So what's the result? They've enough good sense to see that you're teaching them an absurd set of beliefs, but they haven't enough to raise themselves to the level of a pure faith, free of superstition, like ours. Their passions make them think there's no such thing as religion, since the only one taught by you is ridiculous; so you're responsible for all the vices they succumb to.

BAMBABEF: Not at all, because we only teach them sound ethics.

WANG: You'd be stoned by the common people if you taught impure morals, because human beings are so made that they're keen to commit evil but they don't want it preached from the pulpit. All you need do is refrain from mixing sensible morality with absurd fables, because by those quite unnecessary acts of deceit you weaken the morality you have to teach.

BAMBABEF: What? You believe that one can teach people the truth without the help of fables?

WANG: Yes, I really do. Our educated people are made of the same stuff as our tailors, weavers, and peasants. They pray to a God of creation, punishment, and reward. They don't defile their worship with absurd systems or elaborate ceremonies, and there are far fewer crimes committed by the educated than by the common people. So why shouldn't we deign to give our workers an education like that available to the learned?

BAMBABEF: You'd be very foolish if you did so: it would be like teaching them refined manners, or turning them into professors of jurisprudence, which is neither possible nor fitting. There must be white bread for those upstairs and black bread for those downstairs.

WANG: I admit that human beings shouldn't all possess the same knowledge, but there are some things everyone should have. It's necessary for everyone to be just, and the surest way of making them so is to inspire them with a religion free of superstition.

BAMBABEF: That's a noble aspiration, but it's not very feasible. Do you think that it's enough for human beings to believe in a God who dispenses punishments and rewards? You said to me that often it's the cleverest amongst the common people who rebel against my fables; they'll rebel against your truth in the same way, and ask: 'Who'll prove to me that God hands out punishments and rewards? Where's the evidence? What's your authority? What have you done to make me believe you?' They'll laugh at you more than at me.

WANG: That's where you're wrong. You imagine that people will throw aside a straightforward, plausible idea, one that's generally helpful and chimes with their way of thinking, just because they reject disingenuous, absurd, unhelpful, and dangerous notions that go against all common sense?

The common people are highly disposed to trust the powers that be; when they're presented with a reasonable article of belief they embrace it willingly. No one needs miracles to believe in a just God that can see into the hearts of men and women; the idea is too natural to be resisted. It's not necessary to specify precisely how God will punish and reward us: it's enough to believe in his justice. I assure you I've seen whole cities with hardly any other doctrine, and they're the ones where I've encountered the greatest virtue.

BAMBABEF: Beware! You'll find in those towns philosophers who will deny both your punishments and your rewards.

WANG: You'll admit that those philosophers will deny your inventions even more vehemently, so you're no better off. Even if there were any philosophers who didn't agree with my principles, they'd still be good people for all that; they would not cultivate virtue any less, because virtue must be embraced from love, not fear. And, what's more, I submit to you that no philosopher could ever be sure that Providence doesn't punish the wicked and reward the good, because if they were to ask me who said God punishes people, I'd reply, 'Who told you he doesn't?' I submit to you—in a word—that far from contradicting me, the philosophers will bear me out. Would you like to be a philosopher?

BAMBABEF: Very much. But don't tell the other fakirs.

GLORY
(GLOIRE)

BEN-AL-BETIF, the dervishes' august leader, said to them one day: 'Brothers, it's a very good thing that you often use the sacred formula in the Qur'an, "In the name of God, the most merciful", because God does indeed exercise mercy, and you learn to do so as well by repeating frequently these words that commend a virtue without which there would be few people left on earth. But, brothers, beware of imitating those rash individuals who, at the drop of a hat, boast that they're working for the greater glory of God. If a young idiot defends a thesis on categories before a jury presided over by an ignoramus swathed in rabbit's fur, he does not fail to write in big letters at the top of his dissertation, "Ek allhà abron doza: Ad majorem Dei gloriam".* If a good Muslim whitewashes his living room, he carves this piece of silliness over the door; even a *saqqa* carries water for the greater glory of God. That's a devout use of an ungodly practice. What would you say of a little chiaus* who yelled "To the greater glory of our invincible monarch!" as he emptied our Sultan's commode? And the distance between the Sultan and God is certainly greater than that between the Sultan and the little chiaus.

'You wretched worms called human beings, what have you got in common with the glory of the Supreme Being? Can it love glory? Can it receive it from you? Can it taste it? You featherless bipeds, for how much longer will you go on making God in your own image? What? Because you're vain and love glory, you want God to love it too! If there were several gods, each of them would perhaps strive to gain the others' votes. That would be a god's glory. If infinite greatness can be compared to extreme baseness, that god would be like King Alexander or Scander, who wished to compete in the stadium only with kings. But you poor souls, what glory can you give to God? So stop profaning his sacred name. An emperor called Octavius Augustus forbade anyone from praising him in the schools of Rome because he was afraid it would demean his name. But you can't demean the Supreme Being, or honour it. Annihilate yourselves, worship, and hold your tongues.'

Thus spoke Ben-al-Betif, and the dervishes cried out, 'Glory to God! Well said, Ben-al-Betif!'

WAR
(GUERRE)

FAMINE, pestilence, and war are the three most famous components of the world here below. Under the heading 'famine' can be listed the bad foods which in times of dearth we are forced to have recourse to in the hope of sustaining life (even though they tend to shorten it).

'Pestilence' includes all the contagious diseases, of which there are two or three thousand. Famine and pestilence are gifts of Providence; but it is to the imagination of the three or four hundred people spread over the globe known as princes and ministers that we owe war, in which all the presents are combined. It's perhaps for this reason that in many dedicatory prefaces they're called the living images of the Deity.

The most assiduous of flatterers will readily agree that war always drags famine and pestilence in its wake; one has only to see the military hospitals in Germany and travel through a few villages that have been the scene of some grand feat of arms.

Laying waste the countryside, razing homesteads, and killing forty per cent of the population in an average year is no doubt a very accomplished art. At first this novel idea was cultivated by nations gathered in assemblies for their common good: for example, the Greek diet declared to the diet of Phrygia and its neighbouring peoples that it was going to set sail in a thousand fishing boats to wipe them out if it could.

The assembly of the Roman people judged it in their interest to fight the Volcae, or the citizens of Veii, before the harvest. And a few years later all the Romans, incensed at the Carthaginians, fought them on land and sea for a long time. It's not the same today.

A genealogist proves to a prince that he descends in direct line from a count whose forebears made an alliance with a house passed into oblivion long since. This house had distant claims on a province the last ruler of which has died of a stroke. The prince and his council take little persuading that this territory belongs to him by divine right. The province, several hundred miles distant, protests in vain that it doesn't know him and has no wish to be governed by him; that the minimum requirement to be able to rule over a people is their consent; these protests don't even reach the ears of the prince, whose right is incontestable. He soon finds a large number of men with nothing to lose, dresses them in rough blue cloth at fifty pence a yard, trims their caps with coarse white thread, turns them left and right, and marches off to glory.

The other princes get to hear of this venture and join in to the best of their ability, covering a small stretch of land with more homicidal mercenaries than Genghis Khan, Tamburlaine, and Bajazet ever had following them.

People some way off hear that there's going to be a fight and that if they wish to join in there's six or seven pence a day in it for them; they divide themselves at once into two groups like harvesters and set off to sell their services to anyone willing to employ them.

These hordes attack each other furiously, even though they have no interest in the outcome and have no idea what it's all about.

There are five or six belligerents, sometimes three against three, sometimes two against four, and sometimes one against five, all cordially detesting each other, uniting together and attacking each other by turns, all agreed on one thing: to do as much harm as possible.

The most amazing thing about this hellish enterprise is that every assassins' leader gets his flags blessed and solemnly invokes the Deity before setting off to exterminate his neighbour. If he succeeds in killing only two or three thousand men, he doesn't give thanks to God; but when about ten thousand people have been annihilated by fire and sword and when, to crown it all, a town or two has been razed to the ground, then he arranges for the performance of a fairly long hymn in four parts, composed in a language unknown to any of the combatants, and stuffed with barbarisms to boot. As well as for murders, the same music is used for weddings and christenings; that's unpardonable, especially in a country best known for its original compositions.

Everywhere a certain number of haranguers are paid to celebrate these bloody occasions; some are dressed in a long black garment topped with a jacket, and others wear a shirt over a gown; a few have a brightly coloured stole draped over their shirt. They all talk at length and cite, apropos of a battle in the Wetterau, something that happened in Palestine a long time ago.

The rest of the year these people thunder against vice. They demonstrate in three points and by thesis and antithesis that ladies who put a little rouge on their fresh cheeks will be punished by the Almighty for all eternity; that *Polyeucte* and *Athalie** are the work of the devil; that a man on whose table fifty pounds' worth of fish is served on Lenten days is certain of going to heaven; and that a poor fellow who eats two pennyworth of mutton is for ever condemned to hell.

Of the five or six thousand declamations of this kind, there are at most three or four, written by a Frenchman called Massillon,* that a gentleman can read without feeling disgusted; but in all these sermons there's not one where the orator has the courage to protest against this curse, this war crime, that embraces every scourge and act of wickedness. Those wretched haranguers preach ceaselessly against love, which is human beings' sole consolation and means of putting things right; they say not a word about the abominable efforts we make to destroy ourselves.

You've written a very unpleasant sermon on impurity, Bourdaloue,* but none on the many ways of killing people, on plunder, banditry, and the universal madness that's destroying the world. All the vices of every time and place combined will never equal the evils arising from a single military campaign.

Wretched physicians of the soul, you rant for an hour and a quarter about a few pinpricks but say nothing about a sickness that's tearing us apart! Moralizing philosophers, burn all your books! As long as, at a whim, a handful of people can cause the death of thousands of our brothers and sisters, the section of the human race devoted to heroism will remain the most hideous thing in the whole of nature. How can kindness, generosity, modesty, temperance, gentleness, wisdom, and piety possibly matter to me when a half-pound of lead fired at six hundred paces smashes me to pieces and I die at twenty in terrible pain surrounded by five or six thousand dying men, whilst my eyes open one last time to see the town of my birth destroyed by fire and flame, and the last sounds reaching my ears are the cries of women and children expiring under the rubble, and all that to further the so-called interests of a man we don't know?

What's worse is that war is an unavoidable scourge. On looking into it we can see that men have always worshipped Mars, god of war. Among the Jews, Sabaoth means 'Lord of Hosts'. But in Homer Minerva calls Mars a raging, demented, infernal god.

GRACE
(GRÂCE)

You holy papal advisers in post in the Rome of today, you illustrious and infallible theologians, I defer to no one in my respect for your divine decisions; but if the city to whose reputation they once made a not insignificant contribution were to see the return of Paulus Emilius, Scipio, Cato, Cicero, Caesar, Titus, Trajan, and Marcus Aurelius,* you must admit that your decisions about grace would take them somewhat aback. What would they say if they heard of Aquinas's grace of health, Cajetan's medicinal grace, the grace efficacious that is sometimes without effect, the grace sufficient that sometimes does not suffice, and the grace exterior, interior, gratuitous, sanctifying, actual, habitual, cooperant, versatile, congruent? In all honesty, would they understand it any better than you or I?

What need do these poor people have of your sublime teachings? I think I can hear them saying:

'Reverend Fathers, you're frightfully clever: in our foolishness we thought that the Eternal Being never behaves in accordance with particular rules, as lowly humans do, but follows laws that are general and eternal like itself. No one amongst us has ever imagined that God was like a crazy master who gives a peculium to one slave and refuses another food, or who orders someone with no arms to knead dough, a dumb person to read to him, or a legless cripple to be his courier.

'All is grace on God's part: he has had the grace to shape the globe we live on, to feed the animals, and to make the trees grow. But if a wolf finds in its path a lamb for supper, and another is dying of hunger, can it be said that God grants a particular grace to that wolf? Was it by grace prevenient that he undertook to make one oak grow in preference to another that lacked sap? If throughout nature all beings are subject to general laws, how could a single species of animal not be subject to them?

'Why would the absolute master of all things have been more concerned with the governance of one person's inner being than with the conduct of the rest of nature as a whole? By what vagary would he alter something in the heart of a Courlander or a Biscayan while making no changes to the laws he's imposed on the sun and the stars?

'How pathetic it is to suppose that he continually makes, unmakes, and remakes the feelings within us! Even then it's only for those who go to confession that all these changes have been dreamt up. On Monday a Savoyard or a Bergamask will have the grace to have mass said for a shilling; on Tuesday he'll go to the tavern and lack grace; on Wednesday he'll have cooperant grace that will lead him to the confessional, but he won't have the efficacious grace of perfect contrition; on Thursday it will be a sufficient grace that won't suffice him, as has already been said. God will work continually inside the head of the Bergamask, sometimes forcibly, sometimes feebly, and the rest of the earth will be of no concern to him! He won't deign to get involved with the inner being of a person in India or China. If you've a grain of sense left, Reverend Fathers, won't you find this system utterly ridiculous?

'You wretched lot, just look at this oak with its head touching the clouds and this reed clinging to its roots; you don't say that efficacious grace has been given to the oak but denied to the reed. Lift your eyes to heaven and see the eternal Demiurge creating thousands of worlds gravitating around each other in accordance with laws that are general and eternal. See the same light reflected from the sun to Saturn, from Saturn to us; and in this concord of so many stars in rapid movement, in this general obeisance of the whole of nature, dare to believe—if you can—that God bothers to grant versatile grace to Sister Theresa and concomitant grace to Sister Agnes!

'You, atom to whom a silly atom has said that the Eternal has particular laws for a few atoms in your vicinity; that he gives his grace to this one and denies it to that; and that the one who did not have grace yesterday will have it tomorrow: don't repeat such foolishness. God made the universe and isn't going to create new winds to shift a few wisps of straw in a corner of it. The theologians are like Homer's warriors, who believed at one moment that the gods were arming themselves against them and at another coming out in their support. If Homer weren't regarded as a poet he would be seen as a blasphemer.'

It's Marcus Aurelius talking, not me; for God, who inspires you, has given me the grace to believe everything you say, everything you have said, and everything you will say.

HISTORY OF THE JEWISH KINGS AND CHRONICLES

(HISTOIRE DES ROIS JUIFS ET PARALIPOMÈNES)

ALL peoples have written their history as soon as they were able to write. The Jews too have written theirs. Before they had kings they lived under a theocracy: they were considered to be governed by God himself.

When the Jews wanted to have a king like the other neighbouring peoples, the prophet Samuel told them on God's behalf that it was God himself that they were rejecting; thus theocracy ended for the Jews when the monarchy began.

So it can be said without blasphemy that the history of the Jewish kings was written like that of other peoples, and that God did not take the trouble to dictate himself the history of a people he no longer governed.

Such a view is put forward only with the utmost scepticism. What might confirm it is that the Chronicles often contradict the Book of Kings in facts and chronology,* just as our profane historians some-times contradict each other. Furthermore, if God has always written the history of the Jews, it has to be the case that he's still doing so, because the Jews have always been his chosen people. They are due to be converted one day, and it seems that they'll then be just as entitled to view the history of their dispersion as sacred as they are to say that God wrote the history of their kings.

A further reflection can be made: that since God was for a long time the Jews' only ruler and then their historian, we must hold them all in the deepest respect. Any Jewish fripperer stands infinitely higher than Caesar and Alexander. How could anyone not prostrate them-selves before a ragman who proves to you that his history was written by the Deity in person, whereas the Greek and Roman histories have been handed down to us by mere mortals?

If the style of the history of the Kings and the Chronicles is divine, it's nonetheless possible that the actions recorded in these books are not divine. David killed Uriah. Ish-bosheth and Mephibosheth were murdered. Absalom slew Amnon, Joab Absalom, Solomon Adonijah his brother, Baasha Nadab, Zimri Elah, Omri Zimri, Ahab Naboth, Jehu Ahab and Jehoram, and the inhabitants of Jerusalem Amaziah son of Joas. Shallum son of Jabesh killed Zachariah son of Jeroboam. Menahem slew Shallum son of Jabesh. Pekah son of Remaliah killed Pekahiah son of Menahem. Hoshea son of Elah slew Pekah son of Remaliah.* We'll pass over in silence many other trifling assassinations. It has to be admitted that if the Holy Spirit wrote this history, he didn't choose a very edifying subject.

IDOL, IDOLATER, IDOLATRY
(IDOLE, IDOLÂTRE, IDOLÂTRIE)

IDOL comes from the Greek εἶδος (form), εἴδωλον (representation of a form), and λατρεύειν (to serve, revere, adore). The word 'adore' comes from *adorare* in Latin, where it has several different meanings: to lift one's hand to one's mouth as a sign of respect when speaking, to bow, to kneel, to greet, and finally, more commonly, to offer supreme worship.

There's no need to point out here that the article in the Trévoux Dictionary* starts by saying that pagans have always been idolaters and that India is still a nation of idolaters. First of all, before Theodosius the Younger no one was called a pagan; that name was given to *pagorum incolae pagani*, the inhabitants of places in Italy who kept their old religion. Secondly, Hindustan is Muslim, and Muslims are implacable enemies of idolatry. Thirdly, one can't call idolaters many of the peoples in India who adhere to the ancient religion of the Parsees, or certain castes that have no idols.

INQUIRY

Has there ever been an idolatrous government?

It appears that there is no people on earth that has ever adopted the name 'idolater'. The word is an insult, an offensive term, like the word *gavache* that the Spaniards used to give the French, or the term *maranes* which the French gave the Spaniards. If the Roman senate or the Athenian areopagus or the court of the Persian kings had been asked 'Are you idolaters?' they would have hardly understood the question. No one would have answered, 'We worship idols, graven images.' The words 'idolater' and 'idolatry' are not found in Homer, Hesiod, Herodotus, or any other author of the Gentile religion. There has never been any edict or law requiring people to worship idols, wait upon them like gods or look upon them as gods.

When the Roman and Carthaginian captains made a treaty, they called all their gods to witness. 'It's in their presence', they said, 'that we swear peace.' Now, the statues of all those gods, of whom there was a long list, were not in the generals' tent. They considered the gods to be present at the actions of human beings, as witnesses and as judges, but a graven image certainly did not constitute divinity.

How did they look upon the statues in the temples of their false deities? The same way—if I may say so—that we look upon the images of the things we venerate. Their error lay not in worshipping a piece of wood or a lump of marble, but in worshipping a false god represented by the wood or the marble. The difference between them and us is not that they had images and we don't: the difference is that their images pictured the fantastic creatures of a false religion whereas ours stand for real people professing a true faith. The Greeks had the statue of Hercules, and we have St Christopher's; they had Asclepius and his goat and we have St Roch and his dog; they, Jupiter wielding a thunderbolt and we, St Anthony of Padua and St James of Compostela.

When in the introduction to the *Panegyric of Trajan* the consul Pliny prays to 'the immortal gods', it's not images he's addressing: those images were not immortal.

In paganism, both in recent times and in the most remote, not one instance can be adduced that would make it possible to conclude that people worshipped idols. Homer speaks only of the gods dwelling on Mount Olympus. The Palladium, though dropped from heaven, was merely a sacred token of Pallas' protection: it was she who was the object of veneration in the Palladium.

But the Romans and Greeks knelt before their statues, put wreaths on their heads, surrounded them with flowers and incense, and carried them in triumph through the streets. We have sanctified these practices, but we're not idolaters.

Women, in times of drought, and after a period of fasting, were wont to carry the statues of the gods. They walked barefoot and with their hair loose. Straightaway it started to rain pailfuls: in Petronius' words, 'et statim urceatim pluebat'. Have we not consecrated this practice, illegitimate amongst the Gentiles, but legitimate with us? In how many towns do barefoot people not carry the reliquaries of saints in order to obtain through their intercession the blessings of heaven? If a Turk or a Mandarin beheld such ceremonies they might at first, in their ignorance, accuse us of putting our faith in the images borne in this manner in procession, but a word in their ear would suffice to disabuse them.

It's surprising what a prodigious number of diatribes have been uttered throughout the ages against the idolatry of the Greeks and

Romans; it's even more surprising to learn afterwards that they were not idolaters.

Some temples were more privileged than others. The great Diana of Ephesus had greater prestige than a village Diana. More miracles were performed in Asclepius' temple at Epidaurus than in any of his other temples. The statue of Olympian Zeus attracted more offerings than that of Paphlagonian Zeus. But since we must always contrast here the customs of a false religion with those of a true one, have we not, for several centuries, shown greater devotion to some altars than to others? Do we not bring more offerings to Our Lady of Loreto than to Our Lady of the Snows? Should we not accept that someone might use that as a pretext for accusing us of idolatry?

Only one Diana, one Apollo, and one Asclepius were recognized, not as many Dianas, Apollos, and Asclepiuses as there were temples and statues of them. So it's proven—as much as anything in history can be—that the ancients did not believe that a statue was divine or that a statue could be worshipped as an idol; consequently, the ancients were not idolaters.

A coarse, superstitious populace that was incapable of reason, doubt, denial, or belief, that flocked to the temples out of idleness and, because the lowly are equal to the great there, made offerings out of habit and spoke continually of miracles without looking closely into any, and that was hardly on a much higher plane than the sacrificial animals they brought with them: such a populace, I say, could well, at the sight of the great Diana or Jupiter the Thunderer, be struck with religious dread and, without realizing it, worship the statue itself. Sometimes that is what has happened, too, with our coarse peasants in our temples, and then they're told unfailingly that it is from the blessed immortals ascended into heaven that they must seek intercession, not from wooden or stone figures; that, in other words, they must worship God alone.

The Greeks and Romans increased the number of their gods by apotheosis; the Greeks deified conquerors like Bacchus, Hercules, and Perseus, and the Romans built altars to their emperors. Our acts of apotheosis are different: we have saints instead of demigods (their secondary deities), but we pay no regard to rank or military prowess: we've built temples to people who are simply virtuous and who would mostly be unknown on earth if they hadn't gone to heaven. The ancients' apotheoses were done out of flattery, ours out of respect for virtue, but their apotheoses are yet further telling evidence that the

Greeks and Romans were not really idolaters: it's quite clear that they no more recognized divine qualities in the statues of Augustus and Claudius than they did in the medals struck in their honour.

In his philosophical works Cicero makes it clear that there are no grounds for misunderstanding the role of statues or for confusing them with the gods themselves. His dialogists thunder against established religion, but none imagines that the Romans can be accused of mistaking marble and bronze for deities. Lucretius—he who reproaches the superstitious with everything—does not upbraid anyone for such foolishness. So, once again, no one held that opinion; the notion did not exist: there were no idolaters.

Horace puts these words into the mouth of a statue of Priapus: 'I was once the trunk of a fig tree; a carpenter, not knowing whether to make me into a god or a bench, finally decided to make me a god,'* etc. What conclusions should be drawn from this quip? Priapus was one of those lesser, subaltern deities, the butt of many a joke; and this one is the strongest proof that the figure of Priapus—which was used as a scarecrow in vegetable gardens—was not anything greatly revered.

In a spirit of commentary Dacier has not failed to observe that Baruch predicted this outcome, saying 'They will only be what the craftsmen want them to be;* but he could also have noted that the same can be said of all statues.

From a block of marble one can just as well make a basin as a figure of Alexander or Jupiter, or anything else more respectable. The substance from which the cherubim of the Holy of Holies were fashioned could just as well have been used for the lowliest of purposes. Is a throne or altar less revered because the craftsman could have made a kitchen table out of it?

So instead of concluding that the Romans worshipped the statue of Priapus and that Baruch had predicted it, Dacier should have concluded that the Romans didn't care a hoot. Consult all the authors who talk about statues of their gods and you won't find a single one that mentions idolatry: they say the exact opposite. You see in Martial:

> Qui finxit sacros auro vel marmore vultus,
> Non facit ille deos.*

In Ovid:

> Colitur pro Jove forma Jovis.*

In Statius:

> Nulla autem effigies, nulla commissa metallo.
> Forma Dei mentes habitare ac numina gaudet.*

In Lucan:

> Estne Dei sedes, nisi terra et pontus et aer?*

A whole volume could be compiled of passages which testify that images were only images.

It's only in cases where statues pronounced oracles that people may have been led to believe the statues had in themselves something divine. But certainly the prevailing view was that the gods had chosen certain altars and certain images to sometimes take up residence, grant audiences to human beings, and answer their questions. All one sees in Homer and in the choruses of Greek tragedies are prayers to Apollo, who utters his oracles on mountains, or in this temple or that city; nowhere in the whole of antiquity is there the least trace of a prayer addressed to a statue.

Those who practised magic, and thought it a science (or pretended to), claimed to know how to make gods enter statues—not the great gods, but the secondary ones, the genii. That's what Hermes Trismegistus called 'god-making' and what St Augustine refutes in *The City of God*. But what that obviously shows is that the images had nothing divine about them, since a magician was needed to animate them; and it seems to me that it was pretty rare for a magician to be skilful enough to give a statue a soul so that it could speak.

In a word, the images of the gods were not gods; Jupiter, not his statue, hurled thunderbolts; it wasn't the statue of Neptune that lashed the sea to fury any more than it was Apollo's that offered the gift of light. The Greeks and Romans were Gentiles and polytheists; they were not idolaters.

Were the Persians, Sabines, Egyptians, Tartars, and Turks idolaters?
What is the ancient origin of images called idols?
The history of their cult.

It's a great error to call peoples who worship the sun and the stars idolaters. For a long time these nations possessed neither images nor temples. If they were mistaken, it was in rendering to stars what they should have rendered to their creator; even so, the doctrine of

Zoroaster or Zerdust, collected in the *Sadder*, includes belief in an avenging, rewarding Supreme Being, a long way off idolatry. The Chinese never had idols; they have always kept to the simple worship of the master of heaven, King-tien. The Tartar Genghis Khan wasn't an idolater and possessed no images. The Muslims who swept across Greece, Asia Minor, Syria, Persia, India, and Africa called the Christians idolaters, *giaours*, because they believed that Christians worshipped images. They smashed several statues they found in the Hagia Sophia in Constantinople, in the church of the Holy Apostles, and in other places that they converted into mosques. As human beings always are, they were deceived by appearances, which led them to believe that temples dedicated to saints who had once been ordinary people, images of such saints being venerated on bended knee, and miracles being performed in those buildings, were proof positive of the most flagrant idolatry. But nothing could be further from the truth. In fact, Christians worship only the one God, and in the blest they revere solely the virtue of God himself active in his saints. The iconoclasts and Protestants have made the same accusation of idolatry against the Roman Catholic Church and met with the same response.

Because human beings have rarely had clear ideas, and even less expressed those ideas in precise and unequivocal language, they call the Gentiles, and above all the polytheists, 'idolaters'. Huge tomes have been written, various opinions have been offered about the origins of the worship of God, or of several gods in the form of images; all that this plethora of books and opinions proves is people's ignorance.

We don't know who invented shoes and socks, so how can we know who invented idols? Of what significance is a passage in Sanchoniatho, who lived before the Trojan war broke out? What does he tell us really when he says that chaos, the spirit (that is breath), enamoured of its principles, derived the primal clay from it, made the air luminous, that the wind Colp and his wife Bau begat Eon, and Eon begat Genos? That Chronos, their descendant, had two eyes in the back of his head and two in front, that he became a god and gave Egypt to his son Taut? And that's one of the most respected monuments in antiquity.

Orpheus precedes Sanchoniatho, but we will not learn anything more from his *Theogony* than Damascius has passed on to us. In it he represents the principle of the world as a dragon with gilded wings on his shoulders and with two heads, one a bull's and the other a lion's, with a face in the middle which he calls 'god-face'.

But from these bizarre ideas two great truths derive: one, that visible images and hieroglyphs are of the utmost antiquity; two, that all ancient philosophers have recognized a first principle.

As for polytheism, common sense tells you that as soon as there were human beings, that is feeble creatures, capable of both reason and folly, subject to every mishap and to disease and death, they realized their weakness and dependency, and had no difficulty acknowledging that there was something more potent than themselves. They felt a power in the earth that supplied their food, another in the air that often destroyed them, a third in the fire that consumed them, and a fourth in the water that drowned them. What could be more natural for ignorant humans than to imagine beings who presided over these elements? What could be more natural than to revere the invisible power that made the sun and stars to shine? And as soon as people tried to form an idea of these forces that were superior to humankind, what was more natural than to give them a visible shape? How else could they have set about it? The Jewish religion which preceded our own, and was handed down by God himself, is replete with images of him. He deigned to speak from a bush in human language; he appeared on a mountain. The celestial creatures sent by him all come in human form; the temple is filled with cherubim who have wings and animal heads but otherwise inhabit human bodies; that's what gave rise to the mistake made by Plutarch, Tacitus, Appian, and so many others when they accused the Jews of worshipping an ass's head. So, despite his prohibition of graven images, God deigned to bow to the human weakness for things that can be seen and touched.

In Isaiah (ch. 6) the prophet sees 'the Lord sitting upon a throne: his train filled the temple'. In Jeremiah (ch. 1) 'the Lord puts forth his hand and touches my mouth'. Ezekiel speaks of 'the likeness of a throne, as the appearance of a sapphire stone', and God as 'the appearance of a man upon it' (ch. 1). The purity of the Jewish religion is in no way compromised by these images, because the Jews have never used paintings, statues, or idols to represent God to the people.

The Chinese mandarins, the Parsees and the ancient Egyptians never had any idols; but soon images were made of Isis and Osiris, and before long there was a huge colossus of Bel in Babylon. Brahma was a bizarre monster in the Indian peninsula. The Greeks above all multiplied statues, temples, and gods' names, but always attributed supreme authority to their Zeus (the Roman Jupiter), the master of the gods and of humankind. The Romans copied the Greeks. Both peoples always placed their gods in heaven, without knowing what they meant by heaven or by Olympus; it's hardly likely that these superior beings lived in the clouds, which are nothing but water vapour. At first seven of them were placed in the seven planets, including the sun; but later on the home of the gods was extended to the whole of heaven.

The Romans had twelve major deities, called *dii majorum gentium*, six male and six female: Jupiter, Neptune, Apollo, Vulcan, Mars, and Mercury; Juno, Vesta, Minerva, Ceres, Venus, and Diana. Pluto was overlooked: Vesta took his place.

Next came the *minorum gentium* gods, the indigete gods (heroes, that is), like Bacchus, Hercules, and Aesculapius; the infernal gods, Pluto and Proserpine; the gods of the sea like Thetis, Amphitrite, and the Nereids, and the gods of shepherds and gardens; there was one for every profession and stage in life, for children, maidens, matrons, and women brought to bed; there was even a god of flatulence. Lastly, the emperors were deified. Neither these emperors, nor the god Fart, nor the goddess Pertunda, nor Priapus, nor Rumilia the goddess of milkful breasts, nor Stercutius the god of the privy, were in truth regarded as the masters of heaven and earth. The emperors sometimes had temples and the little household gods had none, but they all had a statue or idol representing them.

These were small figurines kept in people's cabinets as an amusement for old women and children; they were not meant for public worship. Individuals were free to practise any superstition they liked. Such tiny idols are still to be found in the ruins of ancient cities.

If no one can be sure when human beings started making idols, we do know that they are very ancient. Abraham's father Terah made them at Ur in Chaldea. Rachel stole and carried off the idols of her father-in-law Laban. You can't go back much further than that.

But what notion precisely did ancient peoples have of all these images? What virtue, what power did they attribute to them? Did they believe that the gods descended from heaven to hide in those statues? Or that they communicated a little of divine spirit to them? Or communicated nothing at all? Much useless rubbish has been written on the subject; it's clear that every opinion was based on that person's degree of rationality, credulity, or fanaticism, and that in order to maximize offerings priests attached as much divinity as they could to their statues. We know that philosophers condemned such superstitions, that warriors derided them, that judges tolerated them, and that the ever-foolish populace had no idea what they were doing. That, in a nutshell, is the history of all the nations to which God has not revealed himself.

We can get much the same idea from Egypt, where ox-worship was widespread, and from the many towns where a dog, a monkey, or onions were venerated. It's highly likely that these were emblems at first. Then, while continuing to eat onions and beef, people began worshipping a certain bull named Apis and a certain dog called Anubis; but it's hard to know what the old women of Egypt thought of bulls and sacred onions.

Idols would often speak. In Rome, on Cybele's feast day, people commemorated the beautiful words the statue had uttered when it was transferred from the palace of King Attalus.

> Ipsa pati volui, ne sit mora, mitte volentem,
> Dignus Roma locus, quo deus omnis eat.

That is to say, 'I wanted to be moved, take me quickly: Rome is a worthy home for any god.'*

The statue of Fortune had spoken; it's true that the likes of Scipio, Cicero, and Caesar didn't believe a word, but the old woman given a crown by Encolpius to buy geese and gods probably did.

Idols also gave out oracles, and the priests hidden inside the statues spoke on the deity's behalf.

How was it that, in the midst of so many gods and so many different theogonies and special cults, there was never a war of religion between peoples described as idolaters? That state of peace was something good that came of evil and from error itself: since every nation recognized several inferior gods they had no problem with their neighbours having theirs. If you except Cambyses who was blamed for the death of the bull Apis, there's no instance in human history of a conqueror mistreating the gods of a defeated people. The Gentiles weren't exclusive in religion, and all the priests cared about was how to maximize offerings and sacrifices.

The first offerings consisted of fruit. Soon afterwards the priests wanted for their table animals which they slaughtered themselves;

then they introduced the loathsome practice of human sacrifice, especially of children and young girls. The Chinese and the Parsees were never guilty of such an abomination. But according to Porphyry men were immolated at Hieropolis in Egypt.

In Tauris foreigners were sacrificed. Fortunately the priests there couldn't have had many takers. The early Greeks, the Cypriots, the Phoenicians, the Tyrians, and the Carthaginians all practised this loathsome superstition. The Romans too committed this religious crime: Plutarch records that they sacrificed two Greeks and two Gauls to expiate the amorous frolics of three vestal virgins. Procopius, a contemporary of the Frankish King Theodobert, says that on crossing into Italy under his command the Franks conducted human sacrifices. The Gauls and Germans commonly did the same. It's hard to read about things like that without feeling horror for the human race.

It's true that among the Jews Jephthah sacrificed his daughter and Saul was ready to do the same with his son, and that those pledged to the Lord by anathema could not be redeemed, as animals could, but had to die. King Agag, a prisoner of war whom Saul had spared, was hacked to death with a holy cleaver by the Jewish priest Samuel, and Saul was reproved for having observed international law where this monarch was concerned; but God, ruler of all humankind, can take people's lives when he likes, how he likes, and with the help of whom he likes, and it's not for human beings to take the place of the master of life and death and usurp the prerogatives of the Supreme Being.

As some consolation to the human race for this terrible state of affairs and these pious acts of sacrilege, it's important to realize that amongst nearly all nations considered idolatrous there was a sacred theology and popular error, a secret cult and public ceremonies, the religion of the wise and the faith of the common herd. Only one God was taught to the initiates in the mysteries: you have only to look at the hymn attributed to the ancient Orpheus that was sung in the mysteries of Ceres Eleusinus, famed throughout Europe and Asia: 'Contemplate divine nature, illuminate your spirit, rule over your heart and walk in the path of justice; may the God of heaven and earth be forever present before you; he is unique, he lives by and through himself alone; all creatures owe their existence to him and he sustains them all; he has never been seen by mortal eyes but all things are visible to him.'*

Read again this passage in the letter addressed to St Augustine by the philosopher Maxime de Madaure: 'What man is so coarse and stupid as to doubt the existence of a supreme, eternal, infinite God who has engendered nothing resembling himself and who is the common father of all things?'

There are a thousand testimonies that the wise abhorred not only idolatry but polytheism too.

Epictetus, a model of resignation and patience, a man so great in a condition so lowly, never talks but of one God. Here's one of his maxims: 'God created me, God is above me, I carry him everywhere within me. How could I sully him with obscene thoughts, unjust actions, and shameful desires? It's my duty to thank God for everything, to praise him for everything, and to cease blessing him only when I myself cease to live.'* All Epictetus' ideas revolve around that principle.

Marcus Aurelius, as great perhaps on the Roman imperial throne as was Epictetus in the condition of slavery, often talks, it's true, about gods, either in conformance with everyday language or to describe creatures halfway between humans and the Supreme Being; but in how many places does he not show that he recognizes only an eternal, infinite God? 'The soul', he says, 'is an emanation of the divine. My children, my body, and my wits come from God.'*

The Stoics and the Platonists believed in a divine, universal nature; the Epicureans denied it. The high priests talked only of one God in their mysteries. So where were the idolaters?

Moreover one of the big mistakes in Moreri's dictionary* is where it's stated that in the time of Theodosius the Younger there were no longer any idolaters except in the remote parts of Asia and Europe. Even in the seventh century there were still many Gentile peoples in Italy. Northern Germany beyond the Weser wasn't Christianized in Charlemagne's time, and Poland and the whole of the north remained in what's called idolatry for a long while afterwards. Half of Africa, all the kingdoms beyond the Ganges, Japan, the population of China, and many Tartar hordes have preserved their ancient forms of worship. In Europe only a few Lapps, Samoyeds, and Tartars have persevered in the faith of their ancestors.

Let me end by noting that in the period known as the Middle Ages we called the Islamic lands 'Pagania'. We treated as idolaters and worshippers of graven images people who hold such things in horror.

Let's admit, once and for all, that the Turks can readily be forgiven for thinking us idolaters when they see our altars laden with paintings and statues.

JEPHTHAH, OR ON HUMAN SACRIFICES
(JEPHTÉ, OU DES SACRIFICES DE SANG HUMAIN)

FROM the text of the Book of Judges (ch. 11), it's clear that Jephthah promised to sacrifice the first person to emerge from his house to congratulate him on his victory over the children of Ammon. His only daughter came out to meet him; he rent his clothes and sacrificed her after allowing her to bewail upon the mountains the misfortune of dying a virgin. For a long while, during four days in every year, Jewish girls marked the event in public lamentation over the fate of Jephthah's daughter.

This story was eventually written down. Whether it served as a model for the Greek story of Agamemnon and Idomeneus or was based upon it, and whether it pre-dated or came after similar Assyrian tales, is not my concern here. I'm sticking to the text in Judges: Jephthah swore to sacrifice his daughter, and he carried out his promise.

It was expressly ordained in Jewish law that people vowed to the Lord were to be sacrificed: 'None devoted, which shall be devoted of men, shall be redeemed, but shall surely be put to death' or, in the Latin of the Vulgate, 'non redimetur, sed morte morietur' (Leviticus 27: 29).

It was by virtue of this law that Samuel cut King Agag into pieces, even though Saul had granted the man a pardon; and it was for sparing Agag that Saul was reproved by the Lord and made to forfeit his kingdom.

So we see here, clearly established, the reality of human blood sacrifice; no other historical fact is better authenticated; it's only on the basis of the archival record and by what it itself reports that a nation should be judged.

FLOOD
(INONDATION)

COULD there ever have been a time when the entire planet was under water? It's a physical impossibility. It may have been the case that every plot of land was covered, in turn, one after the other, by the sea, but it can only have been by a gradual process that took place over very many centuries. Over a period of some five hundred years the sea has withdrawn from Aigues-Mortes, Fréjus, and Ravenna, places which were once great ports, and left a few square miles of land high and dry. At that rate of progress it's obvious that it would take two million two hundred and fifty thousand years to get round the whole world. What's remarkable about this—something we've suspected for half a century—is that the earth's axis takes much the same length of time to right itself and coincide with the equator; this can only happen in the space of more than two million three hundred thousand years.

The fossil-shell beds discovered in many places a hundred and thirty, a hundred and eighty, and even two hundred and thirty miles from the sea are proof positive that these marine products were deposited on land once under water. But the idea that the whole earth was covered in this way is a physical impossibility, defying the laws of gravitation and fluid mechanics, and betraying ignorance of the fact that there wouldn't be enough water to do it. None of this casts doubt on the veracity of the account of the universal flood given in the Pentateuch: quite the reverse. That was a miracle, so must be believed; and, being a miracle, it's not subject to the laws of physics.

Indeed, everything about the history of the Flood is miraculous. It was a miracle that forty days of rain led to the four quarters of the globe being flooded and that the water rose to a height of fifteen cubits above the tallest mountain-tops. It was a miracle, too, that there were fountains, doors, and windows in heaven, that every animal from all parts of the earth went into the ark, that Noah was able to feed them for ten months, that they all managed to fit into the ark with their provisions, that most of them survived, and that they found enough to eat when they left the ark. It was a miracle, finally, though of a rather different kind, that a certain Jean Le Pelletier thought he could explain how all the animals were able to fit into the ark and to feed naturally there.

But, since the deluge is the most miraculous story ever told, it would be mad to explain it; such mysteries are articles of faith; faith consists in believing what reason does not believe: that, too, is a miracle.

So the history of the worldwide flood is like that of the tower of Babel, Balaam's she-ass, the sound of trumpets bringing down the walls of Jericho, rivers turning to blood, the crossing of the Red Sea, and all the other prodigies the Lord deigned to perform on behalf of the elect among his people. These are depths which the human spirit cannot hope to plumb.

JOSEPH

EVEN when viewed merely as literature or as an object of curiosity, the story of Joseph is one of the most precious monuments of antiquity to have come down to us.* It seems to be the model for all Eastern writers; it's more moving than Homer's *Odyssey*, because a hero who offers forgiveness is more touching than one who seeks vengeance.

We consider the Arabs to be the earliest writers of ingenious fictions to have passed into every language, but I see none by them which is comparable to the adventures of Joseph. Everything in them is marvellous, and the end can make you cry. Joseph is a youth of sixteen whose brothers are jealous of him; they sell him to a caravan of Midianites; he's taken to Egypt and bought by one of the king's eunuchs. This eunuch was married, which is not at all surprising; the Kislar-aga, a complete eunuch with everything removed, has a harem in Constantinople today: they've left him with his eyes and hands, and Nature has lost none of her rights over his heart. The other eunuchs, who've only had the two pendants of the organ of reproduction cut off, often make use of the latter; and Potiphar, who'd bought Joseph, could very well have been a eunuch like that.

Potiphar's wife fell in love with Joseph who, through fidelity to his master and benefactor, rejected her advances. She got angry and accused him of trying to rape her. It's the story of Hippolytus and Phaedra, Bellerophon and Stheneboea, Hebrus and Damasippa, Tanis and Peribea, Myrtilus and Hippodamia, Peleus and Astydamia.

Out of all these tales it's difficult to know which is the original version, but among the ancient Arab authors there is a very ingenious twist to the story of Joseph and Potiphar's wife. The writer supposes that Potiphar, uncertain as to whom to believe—his wife or Joseph—did not consider Joseph's tunic, which she had ripped apart, to be proof of the young man's assault on her. There was an infant in a cradle in the bedroom of the woman. According to Joseph, the woman had torn his tunic off in front of the child, who was very advanced for his age; and he said to Potiphar, 'See if the tunic is torn at the front or the back; if it's torn at the front, that proves Joseph was trying to rape your wife and she was defending herself; if at the back, that shows your wife was running after him.' Thanks to the genius of this child, Potiphar accepted that Joseph was innocent. That's how, following the ancient Arab author, the story is related in the Qur'an.* He doesn't bother telling us to whom the child belonged that showed such penetrating judgement. If he was the son of Potiphar's wife, Joseph wasn't the first man she'd had it in for.

Whatever the truth about that, according to Genesis Joseph was sent to prison and found himself in the company of the king of Egypt's bread-waiter and his cupbearer. That night both these royal prisoners had a dream. Joseph interpreted their dreams, predicting that in three days the cupbearer would be pardoned and the bread-waiter hanged. And that's indeed what happened.

Two years later the king of Egypt had a dream too. His cupbearer told him that there was a young Jew in prison who was the best in the world when it came to interpreting dreams; the king summoned the young man, who predicted seven years of plenty and seven years of famine.

Let's pause for a moment in this story to see how prodigiously ancient the interpretation of dreams* is. Jacob had seen in a dream the mysterious ladder at the top of which was God in person; he learned in a dream a method of getting sheep to multiply that never worked for anyone else but him; Joseph himself learned via a dream that he would one day have dominion over his brothers. And a long time before that Abimelech had been warned in a dream that Sarah was Abraham's wife (see the entry 'Dreams' (*Songes*)).

To get back to Joseph: as soon as he'd explained Pharaoh's dream he was made first minister. It's doubtful if you could find a king today, even in Asia, who'd give a post like that to someone just for interpreting a dream. Pharaoh had Joseph marry a daughter of Potiphar's. It's said that this Potiphar was the high priest in Heliopolis, so he was not the same person as the eunuch, Joseph's first master; or if he was, he must have had another title than that of high priest, and his wife must have had more than one child.

However, as had been predicted, the famine arrived, and to earn the king's good graces Joseph made everyone sell their land to Pharaoh, and the entire populace became slaves in order to get corn. That, apparently, is how despotism originated. It must be admitted that no king ever struck a better bargain, but at the same time the people probably had scant reason to bless the first minister.

In the end Joseph's father and brothers needed corn, for 'in all the land the famine was very sore'. There's no need for me to retell here the manner in which Joseph received his brothers, and how he pardoned and enriched them. One finds in this story everything that makes an epic poem interesting: exposition, crux, recognition, peripeteia, and the supernatural. Nothing bears the stamp of oriental genius more.

The reply given by Joseph's father Jacob to a question from the Pharaoh can't fail to strike the reader. 'How old are you?' the king asked. 'I'm a hundred and thirty,' the old man said, 'and I haven't enjoyed a single day's happiness during this brief pilgrimage.'

ON FREE WILL
(DE LA LIBERTÉ)

A. There's a gun battery firing at our ears; are you at liberty to hear it or not to hear it?

B. Of course I can't help hearing it.

A. Do you want that gun to blow your head off, together with that of your future wife and daughter walking beside you?

B. What are you suggesting? So long as I'm of sound mind I couldn't wish for such a thing—it's impossible.

A. Good. You necessarily hear that gun firing and you necessarily wish you and your family not to die from a cannon-shot while out walking, and you have neither the ability not to hear it nor the ability to wish to stay here.

B. That's obvious.

A. As a result, you've moved some thirty yards to get out of the line of fire, and you've been able to walk these few paces with me?

B. That's pretty obvious too.

A. And if you'd been paralysed you couldn't have avoided being exposed to the battery, and you'd necessarily have heard and received a cannon-shot, and you'd necessarily be dead.

B. True enough.

A. So what does your liberty amount to, if it isn't the power you've exercised as an individual to do what your will demanded as an absolute necessity?

B. You're confusing me. So liberty is nothing but the ability to do what I want?*

A. Think about it, and see if liberty can be understood any other way.

B. In that case my gun dog is as free as I am; on seeing a hare it necessarily has the will to run forward and, unless it's lame, the ability to do so. Therefore I'm no better than my dog: you reduce me to the level of dumb animals.

A. Those are the poor sophisms of the poor sophists who taught you. You're peeved at being as free as your dog. But don't you resemble your dog in so many ways? Don't you share with it hunger, thirst, wakefulness, sleep, and the five senses? Do you wish to be able to smell things otherwise than through your nose? Why do you want to be free in a different way from your dog?

B. But I have a soul that reasons a lot, and my dog hardly thinks at all. It only has simple notions, whereas I have innumerable metaphysical ideas.

A. Well, you're a great deal freer than it is, that's to say you have a great deal more brainpower than it has, but you're not free in a different way.

B. What? I'm not free to wish as I like?

A. What do you mean?

B. I mean what everyone else means. Doesn't the proverb say 'wishes are free'?

A. A proverb isn't a reason. Explain yourself more clearly.

B. I mean that I'm free to wish as I please.

A. With all due respect, that makes no sense. Don't you see it's silly to say, 'I want to will'? Your will is necessarily a consequence of the ideas presented to you. You want to get married, don't you? Yes or no?

B. What if I told you that I don't care either way?

A. That would be like saying, 'Some believe that Cardinal Mazarin is dead, and others think he's alive, but I don't share either opinion.'

B. All right, I want to get married.

A. Ah, a straight answer at last. Why do you want to get married?

B. Because I'm in love with a young lady who's pretty, kind, well brought up and fairly wealthy, who sings beautifully and whose parents are very nice people, and because I flatter myself that she loves me and that her family likes me a lot.

A. Those are good reasons for getting married. You see that you can't wish for something without having a reason. I declare that you're free to marry, that is, you have the power to sign the contract.

B. What? I can't wish without reason? So what is the point of that other proverb, *sit pro ratione voluntas*, 'my will is my reason, I wish because I wish'?*

A. My dear friend, that's absurd. That would mean there is in you an effect with no cause.

B. What? If I bet odds or evens, I've a reason to choose evens rather than odds?

A. Undoubtedly.

B. So what's the reason, then?

A. It's that the idea of odds has presented itself to your mind rather than the opposite one. It would be funny if there were cases where you willed because there was good cause, and others where you willed without good cause. When you wish to get married you obviously feel the dominant reason for it; you don't feel it when you bet odds and evens, but there has to be a reason.

B. But, once more, I'm not free, then?

A. Your will isn't free, but your actions are; you're free to act when you have the power to do so.

B. But all the books I've read about the freedom of indifference . . .

A. Nonsense, all of them. There's no such thing. It's a word devoid of sense, invented by people who themselves had hardly any.

ON LAWS
(LOIS, DES)

In the days of Vespasian and Titus when the Romans were eviscerating the Jews, a very rich Israelite, who didn't want to be cut open, fled with all the money he'd made as a usurer and went to the port of Ezion-geber with his whole family, made up of his elderly wife, a son, and a daughter; his suite consisted of two eunuchs, one who worked as cook and the other as ploughman and wine-grower. A good Essene who knew the Pentateuch by heart served as his chaplain. They all embarked at Ezion-geber, crossed the so-called Red Sea (it isn't red), and entered the Persian Gulf in search of the land of Ophir, without knowing where it was. You can imagine that a terrible storm blew up and drove the family towards the Indian coast. They were shipwrecked on one of the islands in the Maldives, now called Padrabranca, which was then uninhabited.

Old moneybags and his elderly wife died; the son and daughter, the two eunuchs, and the priest survived; they pulled, as best they could, a few provisions from the vessel, built small huts on the island, and lived fairly comfortably. You know that the island of Padrabranca is five degrees above the equator and grows the best coconuts and pineapples in the world; it was very pleasant living there while the rest of the chosen people were being murdered; but the Essene wept at the thought that they would perhaps be the only Jews left on earth and that the seed of Abraham would die out.

'It's up to you to revive it,' said the young Jew. 'Marry my sister.'
'I'd love to,' said the Essene, but it's against the law. As an Essene, I've made a vow never to get married, and the law says that a vow must be respected. The Jewish race will die out if it wants to, but I certainly won't marry your sister, pretty though she is.'

'My two eunuchs can't father children,' said the Jew; 'I'll oblige, if you like, and you'll bless the marriage.'

'I'd rather die a hundred times at the hands of Roman soldiers', said the Essene, 'than help you commit incest; if she were the daughter of your father, fair enough, that's allowed under the law; but she's the daughter of your mother, and that's taboo.'

'I can see that it would be a crime in Jerusalem, where I'd find other girls,' replied the young man, 'but here in Padrabranca, where only coconuts, pineapples, and oysters are to be seen, I think it's perfectly all right.' So he married his sister despite the Essene's objections; they had a daughter, the only child born of a union which the one thought legitimate and the other an abomination.

Fourteen years later the sister died; the brother said to the Essene, 'Have you shaken off your ancient prejudices at last? Do you want to marry my daughter?' 'God forbid,' said the Essene. 'Oh, all right then, I'll marry her myself,' the father said, 'because I don't want the seed of Abraham to be reduced to nothing.' The Essene, horrified at this, ran off. In vain did the bridegroom call after him 'Stay, dear fellow, I'm only obeying natural law and serving my country; don't abandon your friends!' The Essene, still obsessed with the law, took no notice, and swam off to a neighbouring island.

It was the large island of Attole, densely populated and highly civilized. As soon as he landed he was sold into slavery. He learned the rudiments of the Attolean language and complained bitterly about the very inhospitable manner in which he'd been received. He was told 'that's the law', because ever since the island had been on the verge of succumbing to a surprise attack from the inhabitants of the island of Ada, it had been wisely decreed that all foreigners who landed in Attole would be sold into slavery. 'That can't be a proper law,' said the Essene: 'it's not in the Pentateuch.' He was told that it was enshrined in the country's statutes, and he remained a slave. Fortunately he had a kind and very wealthy master who treated him well and to whom he became much attached.

One day some people came to kill the master and steal his riches; they asked the slaves if he was at home and if he had a lot of money. 'We swear to you', said the slaves, 'that he's not at home and has no money.' But the Essene said, 'Lying is forbidden under the law; I swear to you that he is at home and has a lot of money.' So the master was robbed and murdered; the slaves accused the Essene in court of having betrayed him; the Essene said he couldn't tell lies, and wouldn't do so for the world, and he was hanged.

I was told this story, and many others like it, during the last trip I made from India to France.* On arrival I went to Versailles on business and saw a beautiful woman pass by, followed by several other beautiful women. 'Who is that beautiful woman?' I asked my lawyer; he'd come with me because I was involved in a lawsuit in Paris about the clothes I'd had made in India, and I wanted him by my side at all times. 'She's the king's daughter,' he replied; 'she's charming and kind; it's a great pity she can never be queen of France.' 'What,' I said, 'if the country had the misfortune—God forbid—to lose the princes of the blood and all their relatives, could she not inherit her father's kingdom?' 'No,' the lawyer replied, 'Salic law expressly forbids it.' 'And who made this law?' I asked him. 'I've no idea, but it's claimed that among an ancient people known as the Salians, who could neither read not write, there was a written law which said that in Salian lands a girl could not inherit an allod, and this law was adopted in non-Salic lands.' 'Well, I'm repealing it,' I said; 'you've assured me that this princess is charming and kind, so she would have an incontestable right to the throne if she had the misfortune to be the only one left alive of royal blood; my mother was my father's heir, and I want this princess to be her father's too.'

The next day my case came up in court and I lost everything by one vote. My lawyer told me that in another court I would have won everything by one vote. 'That's quite comic,' I said; 'so there's a court for every law.' 'Yes,' he said, 'there are twenty-five commentaries on the common law of the Paris judicature; that's to say, it's been proved twenty-five times that Paris common law is questionable; and if there were twenty-five courts there would be twenty-five different jurisdictions. 'There is'—he went on—'some fifty miles from Paris a province called Normandy, where your case would have been decided very differently from the way it was here.' That made me want to visit Normandy. I went with one of my brothers; we met in the first inn we came to a young man in despair. I asked him what misfortune had befallen him. He replied that it was having an elder brother. 'What's so terribly unfortunate about having a brother?' I asked; 'My brother is older than me and we get along fine.' 'Alas, sir,' he said, 'the law here gives everything to the elder son and leaves nothing for the younger ones.' 'You're right to be angry,' I said; 'where we come from we share things equally, and sometimes brothers don't like each other any better for it.'

These little adventures led me to think deeply about laws; I realized that they're just like clothes: I had to wear a dolman in Constantinople, but a doublet in Paris.

'If all laws are a matter of convention,' I said, 'all you need do is shop around. The burghers of Delhi and Agra say they got a very bad deal from Tamburlaine; the citizens of London are delighted to have done well out of William of Orange. A Londoner said to me one day: "It's necessity that makes laws, and it's force which sees they're obeyed." I asked him if force did not sometimes make laws, and if William the Conqueror hadn't given them orders without doing a deal with them. "Yes," he said, "we were oxen then, and William put a yoke on us and prodded us along with goads; since then we've turned into men, but we've kept our horns and use them to gore anyone who tries to make us plough for him and not for ourselves." '

Full of all these thoughts I was delighted to see that there is a natural law independent of all human conventions: the fruits of my labour have to be mine; I must honour my father and mother; I've no rights over my neighbour's life, nor he over mine; and so on. But I got very depressed when I reflected that from the time of King Chedorlaomer to that of Mentzel,* colonel of hussars, everyone has murdered and robbed his neighbour, with a licence to do so in his pocket.

I was told there is a code of honour among thieves, and that there are laws governing the conduct of war. I asked what these laws were. I was informed that they laid down that a brave officer must be hanged for holding out in a position with no artillery against a royal army;* that a prisoner should be hanged for every one of yours hanged by the enemy; that villagers who hadn't brought you their entire means of subsistence on the appointed day as ordered by the local gracious sovereign should be put to the sword and their homes razed to the ground. 'Good,' I said, 'that's Montesquieu's *Spirit of the Laws.*'

After receiving thorough instruction in the matter, I found that there were wise laws which lay down that a shepherd can be sent to the galleys for nine years for having given a little foreign salt to his sheep. My neighbour was ruined by a lawsuit over two oak trees belonging to him that he'd felled in his wood because he'd failed to observe a formality he couldn't have known about; his wife died in poverty and his son leads a wretched life. I admit that these laws are just, even if they're applied rather harshly; but I'm not a bit grateful for laws that allow a hundred thousand men to go and cheerfully murder a hundred thousand of their neighbours. It's always seemed to me that nature has granted most people enough common sense to make laws; but not everyone has enough wisdom to make good laws.

Bring together, from the four corners of the earth, a group of simple, peaceful farmers; they will all readily agree that people should be allowed to sell their surplus corn to their neighbours, and that the law forbidding it is absurd and inhumane; that the coinage used in such transactions may no more be tampered with than should the fruits of the earth be; that heads of household should exercise authority in their own home; that religion should bring human beings together in order to unite them, not to turn them into persecuting fanatics; that those who work hard should not be deprived of the fruits of their labour to subsidize idleness and superstition in others; in an hour those farmers will pass thirty laws like that, all of them useful to the human race.

But if Tamburlaine comes and conquers India, all you'll see are arbitrary laws. One will bleed a province white in order to enrich one of his lieutenants; another will make it a crime of *lèse-majesté* to speak ill of the mistress of a rajah's first valet; a third will rob farmers of half their crop and dispute their right to the rest; finally, there will be laws allowing a Tartar subordinate to seize your children in the cradle and turn those that are better built into soldiers and the weaker ones into eunuchs, leaving father and mother helpless and inconsolable.

Now, which is it better to be, Tamburlaine's dog, or one of his subjects? It's obvious that the dog's situation is far preferable.

CIVIL AND ECCLESIASTICAL LAWS
(LOIS CIVILES ET ECCLÉSIASTIQUES)

IT's worth taking a look at these notes, found amongst the papers of a jurist.

'That no ecclesiastical law shall be enforceable unless and until it has the government's express approval. Because they adhered to that principle Athens and Rome never got embroiled in religious argument.

'Such squabbles are the lot of barbarous nations, or nations that have fallen into barbarism.

'That only a magistrate may allow or forbid people to work on feast days, because it's not the job of priests to stop people cultivating their fields.

'That everything to do with marriage should be the sole preserve of a magistrate; priests should stick to the noble function of blessing newly-weds.

'That lending with interest should be subject to the civil law, because it alone presides over commercial activity.

'That ecclesiastics should without exception submit to the secular authority, because they are subjects of the state.

'That the practice of handing over to a foreign pontiff the first year's revenue from a property given to a local priest by his fellow citizens, is shameful and ridiculous, and should never be allowed.

'That no priest shall ever take away any prerogative from citizens on the grounds that they are sinners, because the sinning priest must pray for sinners and not sit in judgement over them.

'That magistrates, ploughmen, and priests should all pay tax to the state on an equal basis, because they all belong to the state.

'That there should only be one standard of weights and measures, and one common law.

'That a useful purpose is served in subjecting criminals to physical punishment. A hanged man is no use at all, but a prisoner ordered to do work in the community is still able to serve the country, and serves as a living lesson to others.

'That every law should be clear, uniform, and precise. To interpret it is always to corrupt it.

'That nothing should be despicable but vice.

'That taxes should only ever be proportionate.

'That law should never conflict with custom, because if custom is sound, law is unnecessary.'

LUXURY

(LUXE)

FOR two thousand years censorious people have railed at luxury, in verse and in prose, but it's always been very popular.

What has not been said of the first Romans, who ravaged and pillaged their neighbours' crops and who, in order to develop their own poor village, destroyed the poor villages of the Volsci and the Samnites? They were disinterested, virtuous people; they were not yet able to steal gold, silver, and precious stones because there were none in the townships they sacked. Their woods and marshes produced neither partridge nor pheasant, and they're much praised for their frugality.

When step by step they had looted everything and robbed everyone from the Adriatic to the Euphrates, and when they'd had enough wit to enjoy the fruits of their rapine for seven or eight hundred years; when they had cultivated all the arts, tasted of all the pleasures and even helped the vanquished to taste them too, they then—it's said—stopped being good, wise people.

All that such censorious clamour amounts to is the assertion that a robber must never eat the dinner he's stolen, wear the coat he's taken, or slip on the ring he's filched. In order to live an honest life he ought, it's said, to throw all that in the river, whereas he should be told not to steal. By all means condemn brigands when they rob people, but don't treat them as mad when they enjoy in good faith what they've stolen. When a large number of English seamen were made rich by the seizure of Pondicherry and Havana, were they wrong to have had a good time in London afterwards as a reward for the pain they'd suffered in the wilds of Asia and America?

Do the ranters wish to see buried deep the wealth amassed by feats of arms, agriculture, trade, and industry? They cite Sparta; why don't they also point to the republic of San Marino? What good did Sparta do for Greece? Did it ever produce a Demosthenes, Sophocles, Apelles, or Phidias? The luxury of Athens produced great men of every kind; Sparta had a few captains, but even so fewer of them than the other cities. But it's fine that such a small republic as Sparta was able to hang on to its poverty-stricken status: in the end, you get to die lacking everything just as easily as you do enjoying what makes life pleasant. A Canadian savage living at a subsistence level can attain old age just as easily as an English citizen can on an income of fifty thousand guineas a year. But who would ever compare the land of the Iroquois to England?

If the republic of Ragusa and the canton of Zug pass laws against conspicuous consumption, they're right to do so, because poor people mustn't be allowed to spend money they don't have; but I read somewhere:

> Know this: a large state's enriched
> By luxury, but a small one's destroyed.*

If by luxury you mean excess, it's well known that excess of any kind is pernicious, be it exaggerated abstinence or gluttony, thrift or liberality. I don't know how it comes about, but in my villages where the soils are poor, the taxes heavy, and the prohibition on exporting the corn that one's sown intolerable, nearly every inhabitant is well dressed, well shod, and well fed. If such a person goes out to plough in a fine suit, white linen, and a curly powdered wig, that would certainly be the height of luxury and the acme of cheek, but if a Parisian or Londoner went to the theatre dressed like a peasant, that would be stinginess of the grossest and silliest kind.

> Est modus in rebus, sunt certi denique fines,
> Quos ultra citraque nequit cosistere rectum.*

When scissors were invented—and they're certainly not at all ancient—what diatribes weren't hurled against the first people to use them to trim their nails or to cut the hair falling over their eyes? They were no doubt called spendthrift dandies who paid far too much for an instrument of vanity which ruined the Creator's handiwork. What a terrible sin, shortening the horn designed by God to grow at the end of our fingers! It was an outrage against the Deity. It was even worse when shirts and slippers were invented. It's well known with what fury old councillors who'd never worn them railed against young magistrates who went in for this pernicious luxury.

MATTER
(MATIÈRE)

WHEN wise people are asked what the soul is, their answer is that they have no idea. If they're asked what matter is, they say the same. It's true that teachers, and above all pupils, know all that perfectly well; and when they've repeated that matter is extended and divisible, they think they've said all there is to say; but when asked what extension is, they are at a bit of a loss. 'It's composed of parts,' they mumble. 'And those parts, what are they made up of? Are the elements of those parts divisible?' Then they fall silent, or they talk a lot, which is just as suspect. 'Is this almost unknown being, called matter, eternal?' 'The entire ancient world believed so.' 'Does it of itself have active force?' 'Several philosophers have thought so.' 'Those who deny it, have they the right to? You don't conceive that matter can of itself have anything. But how can you be sure that it has not, of itself, the properties necessary to it? You do not know what its nature is, and yet you refuse modes that are in its nature; for after all, as soon as it exists, it has to exist in a certain way, it has to be configured; and as soon as it's necessarily configured, is it impossible that there aren't modes attached to its configuration? Matter exists; you know it only through sensation. Alas, what use are all these mental subtleties, ever since people were able to reason? Geometry has taught us many truths, metaphysics very few. We weigh matter, measure it, and decompose it, and if we wish to go beyond these crude operations we find ourselves face to face with our impotence, gazing into the abyss.

'Please forgive the whole universe for getting it wrong in believing matter to exist of itself. Could it have been otherwise? How could it have imagined that what is without succession may not always have existed? If it wasn't necessary for matter to exist, why does it exist? And if it was necessary, why hasn't it always existed? There is no axiom more widely held than this: "Nothing comes from nothing." Indeed, the opposite is incomprehensible. Amongst all peoples chaos has preceded the arranging by a divine hand of the entire world. The eternity of matter has never anywhere done any harm to the worship of the Deity. Religion has never shied away from the idea of an eternal God being recognized as the lord of a matter that is eternal.

Today we are fortunate enough to know through faith that God created matter from nothingness, but no nation was ever taught the doctrine, and even the Jews weren't aware of it. The first verse in Genesis states that the gods Elohim, and not Eloï, created the heaven and the earth; it doesn't say that the heaven and the earth were created from nothing.'

Philo, who arrived during the only period when the Jews had a smattering of erudition, says in his chapter on creation, 'God, being by nature good, has never envied substance, matter, which of itself possessed nothing good, and by its nature was merely inertia, confusion, and disorder. He deigned to make it good rather than bad as it was before.'

The idea of chaos unravelled by a God is found in all ancient theogonies. Hesiod endorsed oriental thinking when he said in his *Theogony* 'chaos was what existed at first'.* Ovid conveyed the views of the entire Roman empire when he wrote:

> Sic ubi dispositam quisquis fuit ille deorum
> Congeriem secuit.*

So matter was regarded as being moulded by God's hands in the same way as clay is turned on the potter's wheel (if it's permissible to use these feeble metaphors to express the divine power).*

Matter, being eternal, had to have eternal properties, such as configuration, inertia, movement, and divisibility. But divisibility is only the consequence of movement; for without movement nothing can be divided, separated, or arranged. So movement was seen as being indispensable to matter. Chaos had been uncoordinated movement, and the arranging of the universe a regularity of movement being stamped on all bodies by the master of the world. But how could matter have movement of itself, as—according to all the ancients—it had extension and impenetrability?

But can't it be conceived without extension, and can it be conceived without movement? The reply to this was that it was impossible for matter not to be permeable; so, being permeable, something had to be passing continually through its pores; for what use are channels if nothing is channelled through them?

Of replying to replies, there is no end; like all systems, the system of eternal matter presents very considerable difficulties. That of matter formed from nothing is no less incomprehensible. It has to be accepted—we shouldn't flatter ourselves that it can be explained: philosophy doesn't elucidate everything. How many incomprehensible things are we not obliged to admit, even in geometry? Can we conceive of two lines getting ever closer together and never meeting?

In truth the geometers will tell you that the properties of asymptotes are proven, and you can't not believe them; but the Creation is not proven, so why do you believe it? What's your problem in accepting, as everyone did in antiquity, that matter is eternal? From the other corner the theologian will put pressure on you and say 'If you believe matter to be eternal, you're thereby recognizing two principles, God and matter, and you're falling into the error of Zoroaster and Manes.'*

We won't say anything to the geometers, because those people know only their lines, surfaces, and solids; but we can ask a theologian, 'In what way am I a Manichaean? Those stones over there—no architect made them, but he used them to build a huge edifice; I don't acknowledge two architects; the rough stones have bowed to the power of genius.'

Fortunately whatever system you adopt, none offends morality, for what concern is it whether matter is made or simply arranged? God is always our absolute master. We must be equally virtuous in a ravelled chaos as in a chaos created from nothing, since none of these metaphysical questions affects the conduct of life; these disputes are like empty chatter round a dinner table: after the meal people always forget what they've said, and follow wherever their interest and their taste lead.

WICKED
(MÉCHANT)

WE'RE continually being told that human nature is essentially perverse, that human beings are the children of the devil and that they're wicked. Nothing is sillier. Because, my friend, when you preach at me that everyone is born perverse, you're warning me that you were born like that and I must be as wary of you as I would be of a fox or a crocodile. Not at all, you reply, I'm born again, I'm neither a heretic nor an unbeliever, you can have faith in me. But the rest of the human race who are either heretics or what you call unbelievers will be but a bunch of monsters, and every time you talk to a Lutheran, or a Turk, you can be sure that they'll rob you and kill you, because they are the children of the devil, and born wicked; the Lutheran isn't born again, and the Turk is degenerate. It would be much nicer and much more reasonable to say to people, 'You're all born good, see how horrid it would be to corrupt the purity of your being.' The human race should be treated as one would treat everyone individually. Does a canon lead a scandalous life? He's told, 'How can you dishonour the dignity of a canon?' A man of the law is reminded that he has the honour to be a king's councillor and should set a good example. To encourage a soldier, he's told: 'Remember you're in the Champagne regiment.' Every individual should be encouraged to bear in mind his dignity as a man or her dignity as a woman.

And indeed, however you look at it, everything comes back to that, because what is the meaning of the expression, heard so often, 'retreat into yourself'? If you were born the child of the devil, if your origins were criminal, if hell's liquor ran in your veins, this phrase, 'retreat into yourself' would mean 'follow and be guided by your diabolical nature, be an imposter, thief and murderer, because that's the law of your fathers'.

Human beings are not born wicked, they become so, just as one becomes ill. Doctors appear and say, 'You're born sick.' It's a racing certainty that whatever such doctors say or do, they won't cure people if their illness is inherent in their nature; these reasoners are very sick themselves.

Bring together all the children in the universe: all you'll see in them is innocence, gentleness, and respect; if they'd been born wicked, malevolent, and cruel, they'd show signs of it, as do little snakes to bite and baby tigers to claw. But since Nature has not given to human beings any more offensive weapons than it has to pigeons and rabbits, it can't have invested them with a killer instinct either.

So human beings are not born evil; how is it, then, that several are infected with the disease of wickedness? It's because those that rule over us are sick and pass the illness to the rest of humanity, like the carrier who spread from one end of Europe to the other the malady brought back from America by Columbus. The earth was similarly corrupted by the first person with an ambitious streak.

You're going to tell me that the first monster deployed the germ of pride, rapine, fraud, and cruelty that is in all of us. I admit that in general most of our brothers and sisters can acquire these defects; but has everyone got typhus, calculus, and gravel just because everyone is exposed to them?

There are whole nations that are not wicked: the Philadelphians and the Banians* have never killed anyone. The Chinese and the people of Tonkin, Laos, Siam, and even Japan have not known war for over a hundred years. The cities of Rome, Venice, Paris, London, and Amsterdam, where cupidity, mother of all crime, is extreme, have for all that in ten years hardly seen one of those spectacular offences that people find so staggering.

If human beings were essentially wicked, if they were all born in thrall to a being as malevolent as it was miserable who, in order to seek revenge for its suffering, instilled in them all its fury, we'd be seeing every day husbands murdered by their wives, and fathers by their children, just as we see at dawn chickens killed by a stone marten who's sucked their blood.

If there are a billion people in the world, that's a lot; that makes about five hundred million women who sew, spin, feed their little ones, keep their house or hut clean, and gossip a little about their neighbours: I don't see what great wickedness these poor innocents commit on earth. Out of the total world population there are at least two hundred million children, and they certainly don't pillage or kill, and about the same number of elderly and sick people, and they haven't the ability to do so. That leaves at most a hundred million young men who are robust and capable of crime. Of this number there are ninety million continually occupied in making the earth by their prodigious efforts furnish them with food and clothing, and they certainly don't have the time for wrongdoing.

The remaining ten million include people of leisure and good company who wish just to enjoy a quiet existence, men of talent busy in their profession, and magistrates and priests visibly interested in leading—at least in appearance—a pure and unblemished life. So the only really wicked people left are a few politicians, religious and lay, who are always out to make a nuisance of themselves, and a few thousand adventurers in the pay of those politicians. Now, there are never at any one time a million such wild beasts in employment; in this number I include highwaymen. So, during the most troubled times on earth, you have, at the outside, one person in a thousand who can be called wicked, and even then, not always.

So there's a great deal less wickedness on earth than is both said and widely believed. That's still too much, probably; we see great misfortune and horrible crimes; but the desire to moan and exaggerate is so great that at the slightest scratch you howl that the earth is running with blood. Have you been misled? We're all forsworn. A depressive who has suffered an injustice sees a world overrun by the damned, just as a young libertine supping after the opera with his lady-friend cannot conceive that there is such a thing as unhappiness.

MESSIAH

(MESSIE)

IN Hebrew, 'messiah' or 'meshiah'; in Greek, 'christos' or 'eleimen-nos'; 'unctus' ('anointed') in Latin.

In the Old Testament we see that the name 'messiah' was often given to princes who were idolaters or unbelievers. It's written in 1 Kings 19: 15-16 that God sent a prophet to anoint Jehu king of Israel and that he announced the sacred anointing to Hazael, King of Damascus and Syria (these two rulers being 'messiahs' of the Most High), in order to punish the house of Ahab.

In Isaiah 45: 1 the name 'messiah' is expressly given to Cyrus: 'Thus saith the Lord to his anointed, to Cyrus, whose right hand I have holden, to subdue nations before him', etc.

In the revelations of Ezekiel (ch. 28) the name 'messiah' is given to the king of Tyre (also called 'cherub'). 'Son of man,' the prophet is told, 'say unto the prince of Tyrus, Thus saith the Lord God, Thou sealest up the sum, full of wisdom, and perfect in beauty; thou hast been in Eden the garden of God' (or in other versions 'Thou wert the Lord's whole delights'). 'Every precious stone was thy covering, the sardius, the topaz, the jasper, the chrysolite, the onyx, the beryl, the sapphire, the carbuncle, the emerald, and gold; the workmanship of thy tabrets and of thy pipes was prepared in thee in the day that thou wast created; thou art the anointed cherub, a messiah.'

This name—'messiah', 'christ'—was given to the kings, prophets, and high priests of the Hebrews. We read in 1 Samuel 12: 5 that 'the Lord is witness and his anointed is witness', that is the Lord and the king set up by him. And elsewhere: 'Touch not mine anointed, and do my prophets no harm.' In more than one passage David, filled with God's spirit, gives his father-in-law Saul, the reprobate who persecuted him, the name and quality of 'messiah', the Lord's anointed: 'The Lord forbid', he often says, 'that I should stretch forth mine hand against him, seeing he is the anointed of the Lord, the "messiah" of God!'

If the name 'messiah', anointed of the Lord, was given to idolaters and reprobates, it's been very often used in our ancient oracles to designate the Lord's true anointed, the 'messiah' par excellence, the Christ, son of God and himself God.

If one brings together the various oracles applied ordinarily to 'messiah', certain seeming difficulties can arise which the Jews have cited in justification, if that's possible, of their obstinacy. Many leading theologians are ready to grant the Jewish people that given the state of oppression under which they laboured, after all the promises the Lord had so often made them, it was understandable that they longed for the coming of a conquering, liberating 'messiah', and therefore that it was in a way excusable that they failed to recognize, in the person of Jesus, their liberator.

It was in God's plan that the blind multitude had no knowledge of the true Messiah's spiritual ideas, so much so that the Jewish men of learning hit on the notion of denying that the passages which we cite should be understood as referring to a 'messiah'. Several claim that the Messiah has already come in the person of Hezekiah; that was the famous Hillel's opinion. Others, in great number, assert that the belief in the coming of a 'messiah' is not a fundamental article of faith, since it's neither in the Ten Commandments nor in Leviticus, but is only a comforting aspiration.

Several rabbis will tell you that they have no doubt that, in accordance with the ancient oracles, the 'Messiah' did come at the appointed time, but that he remains hidden on this earth and does not age; he is waiting until Israel celebrates the Sabbath correctly to manifest himself.

The famous rabbi Shlomo Yitzhaki, or Rashi, who lived at the start of the twelfth century, writes in his commentary on the Talmud that the ancient Hebrews believed that the Messiah was born on the day of Jerusalem's final destruction at the hands of the Roman armies; it was, to coin a phrase, like shutting the stable door after the horse had bolted.

Rabbi Kimchi, who also lived in the twelfth century, announced that the 'Messiah', whose coming he believed imminent, would drive out of Judaea the Christians who were occupying it at the time; it's true that they lost the Holy Land, but it was Saladin who defeated them: if only he had protected the Jews and taken their side, it's likely that in their enthusiasm they would have made him their messiah.

The sacred writers, and our Lord Jesus himself, often compare the Messiah's reign and eternal bliss to wedding and feast days; but the Talmudists have strangely overdone these parables: according to them the Messiah will give his people assembled in the land of Canaan a

meal served with a wine made by Adam himself in the earthly paradise and stored in vast cellars hollowed out of the earth's core by the
angels.

As entrée will be served the celebrated fish called the great
Leviathan which carries all the seas on its back and swallows in one
go a fish smaller than itself but still nine hundred miles long. In the
beginning God created two Leviathans, one male and one female, but
fearing that they would knock the earth over and fill the universe with
their progeny, God killed the female and salted it for the Messiah's
banquet.

The rabbis add that for this meal the bull Behemoth will be slaughtered; it is so huge that it eats a thousand mountains of hay every day;
the female of this bull was killed when the world began so that such an
enormous species could not multiply and harm other creatures; but
they assure us that the Lord did not salt it, because salt beef is not as
good as salt Leviathan. The Jews still give such credence to all these
rabbinical fantasies that they often swear oaths on their share of the
bull Behemoth.

After such crude ideas about the coming of the Messiah and about
his reign it's hardly surprising that the Jews, both ancient and modern,
and even several early Christians unfortunately imbued with the same
fantasies, have not been able to embrace the idea of the godly nature of
the Lord's anointed and have shown themselves incapable of attribut-
ing divine qualities to the Messiah. See how the Jews talk about this in
the work entitled *Judaei Lusitani quaestiones ad Christianos* (*Quaest.* 1.
2. 4, pp. 1, 3): 'To acknowledge a God-made-flesh is to deceive oneself,
to create a monster, a centaur, the bizarre combination of two natures
never intended to be joined together.' They add that the prophets do
not teach that the Messiah is God made flesh: they make a clear distinction between God and David, declaring God to be the master and
David his servant; and so on.

It's well known that the Jews adhere slavishly to a literal interpretation of Scripture and so, unlike us, have never penetrated the true
meaning of Holy Writ.

When the Saviour appeared the Jews were prejudiced against him.
In order not to offend their susceptibilities Jesus himself seems to
have kept very quiet about his divinity; according to St Chrysostom,
he wanted 'gradually to get his hearers to believe in a mystery so far
above the limits of human reason'. When he took it upon himself to

exercise God's authority for the forgiveness of sins he aroused the resentment of those who'd witnessed it; even people who'd benefited most from his very obvious miracles failed to be convinced of his divinity. When he appeared before the Sanhedrin and with self-deprecating evasion let it be understood that he was the son of God, the high priest tore his clothes and cried 'blasphemy!' Before the arrival of the Holy Spirit even the apostles did not suspect that their master was divine; he asked them what the people thought of him, and they replied that some took him for Elijah and others for Jeremiah or some other prophet. St Peter needed a special revelation before he was able to acknowledge that Jesus was the Christ, son of the living God.

Jews hostile to the notion that Jesus was divine have had recourse to all sorts of subterfuges to demolish this great mystery; they twist the meaning of their own oracles, or refuse to apply them to the Messiah; they claim that the name of God, Elohi, was not specific to the deity but was even given to judges, magistrates, and generally to all those in authority; to back up this observation they cite a very large number of passages in Holy Scripture that do not however undermine in any way the clear and explicit terms in which the ancient oracles speak of the Messiah.

Finally, they claim that if the Saviour, as well as the evangelists, apostles, and first Christians, called Jesus 'the son of God', this august term meant no more in Gospel times than the opposite of the children of Belial, that is a good man, a servant of God, in contrast to a wicked man who fears not the Lord.

In denying Jesus the status of Messiah and God the Jews have left no stone unturned in their efforts to make him appear despicable and to cast aspersions on his birth, life, and death, with all the slanderous mockery their dogged wickedness has been able to dream up.

Of all the works spawned by the blindness of Jewry there is none more loathsome or outrageous than an ancient tome entitled *Sepher Toldos Jeshut*, which was rescued from obscurity by Herr Wagenseil in the second volume of his *Tela Ignea Satanae*.

It's there you'll read a horrendous biography of Our Lord compiled with all the spite and bad faith possible: thus the author has dared to write, for example, that someone living in Bethlehem called Panthera or Pandera fell in love with a young woman married to Jochanan. From these impure shenanigans a son was born, called Jesua or Jesu. The father of this child was forced to flee, and retired to Babylon.

As for the young Jesu, he was sent to school but (the author adds) was insolent, looking up and taking off his headgear in front of the officiating priests rather than keeping his eyes lowered in their presence and covering himself, as custom demanded. He was soundly rebuked for his impudence; the circumstances of his birth were then looked into and found not to be whiter than white, so he was promptly disgraced.

The detestable book *Sepher Toldos Jeshut* was known as early as the second century; Celsus quotes it with confidence and Origen refutes it in *Contra Celsum*, chapter 9.

There's another book, called *Toledos Jesu*, published in 1705 by M. Ulrich, which follows the Gospel story more closely, but commits anachronisms and makes some gross errors: Christ was born and died, it says, during the reign of Herod the Great to whom, it argues, were addressed complaints about the adultery of Pandera and Mary the mother of Jesus.

This book—written by someone called Jonathan who claims to be an inhabitant of Jerusalem and a contemporary of Jesus—asserts that Herod consulted the senators of a town in the land of Caesarea about Christ; but we won't pursue an author as absurd in his contradictions as this one.

Nevertheless, it's thanks to all these calumnies that the Jews are able to persist in their implacable hatred of Christians and of the Gospel; and they've never missed a trick when it comes to altering the chronology of the Old Testament and sowing doubt and raising quibbles about the date of the coming of our Saviour.

Ahmed-ben-Cassum-al-Andacusi, a Moor from Granada who lived towards the end of the sixteenth century, quotes an ancient Arab manuscript found with sixteen strips of lead engraved with Arabic characters in a cave near the city. The archbishop of Granada, Don Pedro y Quinones, himself paid tribute to it. The lead objects, known as the Granada *plomos*, were later taken to Rome and after several years' examination, were eventually condemned as apocryphal under the pontificate of Alexander VII; all they contain are fairy tales about Mary and her son.

The name 'messiah' followed by the adjective 'false' is still given to the imposters who have from time to time sought to deceive the Jewish people. There were 'false messiahs' even before the coming of the true Son of God. In Acts (5: 34–6) the sage Gamaliel refers to a certain Theudas whose story is told in Josephus' *Jewish Antiquities* (book 20, ch. 2). He boasted of walking dry-foot across the Jordan and had many followers; but the Romans came upon his little group and scattered it; then they decapitated its unfortunate leader and put his head on display in Jerusalem.

Gamaliel also speaks of Judas the Galilean, no doubt the same person mentioned by Josephus in *The Jewish War* (book 2, ch. 12), where it's said that this false prophet had gathered about thirty thousand men around him; but Josephus is rather given to exaggeration.

In apostolic times there was Simon, known as 'The Sorcerer', who'd so comprehensively taken in the inhabitants of Samaria that they considered him 'the great power of God' (Acts 8: 10).

During the next century, in AD 178 and 179, under the Emperor Hadrian, a false messiah appeared, named Bar Kochba, at the head of an army. Hadrian sent Julius Severus to confront him. After several skirmishes Severus confined the rebels within the town of Bethar. Following a stubborn siege the town was stormed and the Jews were defeated; Bar Kochba was taken prisoner and executed. Hadrian believed that the only way of preventing repeated uprisings by the Jewish people was to issue an edict barring them from Jerusalem, so he set up guard-posts at the gates to stop the survivors of the rebellion from entering the city.

In book 2, chapter 38 of the *Historia Ecclesiastica* by Socrates Scholasticus we read that in AD 434 a false messiah called Moses turned up in Crete; he claimed to be the ancient liberator of the Hebrews returned from the dead to deliver them a second time.

A century later, in AD 530, there arose in Palestine a false messiah called Julian; he declared that he was a great warrior who would lead his nation into battle and wipe out everyone in Christendom by force of arms; the Jews, taken in by these promises, seized their weapons and massacred several Christians. The Emperor Justinian sent troops to confront him; they attacked the false Christ, who was taken prisoner and tortured to death.

At the start of the eighth century the Spanish Jew Serenus made himself out to be the Messiah, preached to his disciples, and died like them in poverty.

Several false messiahs arose in the twelfth century. One appeared in France under Louis VII. He was hanged together with his followers; there is no record of his name, or theirs.

The thirteenth century saw many false messiahs: there were seven or eight who appeared in Arabia, Persia, Spain, and Moravia. One of them was called David el-David and was taken for a very great magician. He beguiled the Jews and found himself at the head of a considerable movement. He too was assassinated.

Jacques Ziegler of Moravia, who lived in the middle of the sixteenth century, announced the imminent return of the Messiah, who was born—so he claimed—fourteen years earlier and whom he'd seen in Strasbourg. He was carefully looking after a sword and sceptre for him and would hand them over to him as soon as the lad was old enough to begin teaching.

In 1624 another Ziegler confirmed the prophecy of the first one.

In 1666 Sabbatai Zevi, born in Aleppo, declared that he was the messiah whom the Zieglers had predicted. He began by preaching in open country and on the high road; the Turks laughed at him while his disciples admired him. It seems that at first he did not get most of the Jews on side, since the leaders of the Smyrna synagogue passed a death sentence on him; but he got away with banishment and with being scared out of his wits.

He contracted three marriages which it's claimed he never consummated, saying that such a thing was beneath him. He took up with a certain Nathan Levi and got him to play the role of the prophet Elijah, the Messiah's trail-blazer. They travelled to Jerusalem and Nathan announced that Sabbatai Zevi was the liberator of the nations. The Jewish rabble came out in his support, but he was anathematized by those who had something to lose.

To flee the storm Zevi retired to Constantinople, and from there went to Smyrna; Nathan Levi sent four ambassadors to him who acknowledged him publicly and saluted him as the Messiah; the envoys impressed the people, and even a few learned men who declared Sabbatai Zevi Messiah and king of the Jews. But the Smyrna synagogue condemned its king to death by impalement.

Sabbatai sought the protection of the cadi of Smyrna and soon had the whole of the Jewish population rooting for him. He had two thrones erected, one for himself and one for his favourite wife; he took the title of king of kings and gave his brother Joseph Zevi the title of king of Judah. He assured the Jews that the conquest of the Ottoman empire was virtually a fait accompli. He even had the impudence to take the name of the emperor out of the Jewish liturgy and put his own in its place.

He was imprisoned in the Dardanelles; the Jews let it be known that his life was being spared because the Turks were convinced that he was immortal. The governor of the Dardanelles grew rich from the gifts heaped on him by Jews whom he allowed to visit their king, their imprisoned Messiah, who in his chains kept his dignity intact and got people to kiss his feet.

However, the Sultan, holding court at Adrianople, wanted to put an end to this farce. He summoned Zevi and told him that if he was the Messiah he must be invulnerable. Zevi agreed. His Sublime Highness arranged for him to serve as target practice for his archers; the 'Messiah' confessed that he wasn't invulnerable at all and protested that God had sent him merely to bear witness to the holy faith of the prophet Mohammed. After a flogging administered by the officers of the law, he became a Muslim. He lived and he died despised in equal measure by Jews and by Muslims, which has had the effect of greatly discrediting the métier of false messiah. So he's the last we're likely to see.

METAMORPHOSIS, METEMPSYCHOSIS
(MÉTAMORPHOSE, MÉTEMPSYCOSE)

Isn't it quite natural that all the metamorphoses by which the world is overwhelmed made the Orient, where everything is imagined, imagine that our souls pass from one body to another? An almost imperceptible dot becomes a worm, that worm becomes a butterfly; an acorn is transformed into an oak, an egg into a bird; water becomes cloud and thunder; wood is changed into fire and ash; everything in nature seems to be metamorphosed in the end. People soon attributed to souls, viewed as rather slight things, what they saw with their senses in grosser bodies. The concept of metempsychosis is perhaps the most ancient doctrine in the known world, and it still holds sway in large parts of India and China.

It's also quite natural that all the metamorphoses we've observed have given rise to the ancient fables which Ovid has collected in his admirable work.* The Jews too have had their metamorphoses.* If Niobe was turned into marble, Lot's wife Edith became a pillar of salt. If Eurydice remained in Hades because she'd looked behind her, it's the same indiscretion that deprived Lot's wife of human form. The town where Baucis and Philemon lived in Phrygia was changed into a lake; the same thing happened in Sodom. Anius' daughters changed water into oil, and in the Scriptures we have a rather similar, if altogether truer and more sacred, metamorphosis. Cadmus was changed into a snake; Aaron's rod became a snake too.

The gods very often changed themselves into men; the Jews have only ever seen angels as having human form; the angels broke bread with Abraham. In his epistle to the Corinthians Paul says that the angel of Satan slapped him: 'Angelos Sathana me colaphiset.'*

MIRACLES

In the literal meaning of the term a miracle is a wonderful thing. So everything is a miracle. The staggering order of nature, the rotation of a hundred million globes around a million suns, the functioning of light, the life of animals: all these are perpetual miracles.

But according to received wisdom miracles involve breaking these eternal, divine laws. If there is a solar eclipse during the full moon, if a dead man walks five miles carrying his head in his arms, that's called a miracle.

Several physicists maintain that in that sense there is no such thing as a miracle. Here are their arguments.

A miracle is the setting aside of mathematical, unchanging, divine, eternal laws. Put that way, a miracle is a contradiction in terms. A law cannot at one and the same time be respected and set aside; 'but', they're asked, 'cannot a law, established by God himself, be suspended by its author?' The physicists have the temerity to say no, it's impossible that the infinitely wise Being would make laws in order to break them. He couldn't—they say—disrupt his machine to make it work better, and it's clear that, being God, he built this huge mechanism to the very best of his ability; if he'd seen that some imperfection might arise from the nature of matter, he would have allowed for this at the outset; so he'll never change anything.

Moreover God can never do anything without a reason, so what possible reason could he have for occasionally distorting the way his own handiwork functions?

'It's for the benefit of human beings,' they're told. 'So it's at least for the benefit of all human beings,' they reply, 'since it's inconceivable that the Deity works for some people in particular rather than for all humanity; and even then, the human race is of no great significance, indeed it's a lot less than a tiny anthill in comparison with all the creatures that fill the vastness of space.' So isn't it the height of folly to imagine that the infinite Being would overturn, in favour of three or four hundred ants on this little dung heap, the everlasting interplay of the immense springs that move the entire universe?

But even supposing God wished to mark out a small number of human beings for special treatment, would he have to alter what he'd set up everywhere for all time? He certainly doesn't need modifications or inconstancy of this kind to offer his creatures favours that are enshrined in his very laws. In them he has arranged and anticipated everything; they all obey unalterably the force he's imprinted in nature for ever.

Why would God go in for miracles? To pull off a certain feat involving a handful of living beings! Would he say: 'In constructing the universe and through my divine decrees and eternal laws, I haven't managed to carry out a certain plan: so I'm going to alter my eternal ideas, my unchanging laws, to try and pull off what I couldn't achieve through them'? That would be an admission of weakness, not of strength. In him it would seem to constitute a quite inconceivable contradiction. Thus, daring to suppose miracles where God is concerned would be a real insult (if it's possible for human beings to insult God). It would be like saying to him: 'You're a weak, inconsistent being.' So it's absurd to believe in miracles: it's dishonouring the Deity, in a way.

These philosophers are pressed further: they're told, 'It's all very well your exalting the immutability of the Supreme Being, the perenniality of his laws and the regularity of his infinite worlds: our tiny mud pile has been swamped by miracles; history is as replete with prodigious occurrences as it is with natural events. The daughters of the high priest Anius changed whatever they felt like into corn, oil or wine; Athalida, Mercury's daughter, rose several times from the dead; Aesculapius revived Hippolytus; Hercules snatched Alcestis from the jaws of death; Heres came back to earth after spending a fortnight in hell; Romulus and Remus were born of a god and a vestal; the Palladium fell from heaven to earth in the city of Troy; the hair of Berenice became a mass of stars; the hut of Baucis and Philemon was changed into a superb temple; the head of Orpheus delivered oracles after his death; to the sound of the flute, in the presence of the Greeks, the walls of Thebes built themselves; the cures effected in the temple of Aesculapius were without number; and there still exist monuments with walls bearing the names of eyewitnesses to Aesculapius' miracles.

'Name us a people in whose country there have never been any incredible prodigies, especially in an era when they could read and write.'

In reply to this the philosophers merely laugh and shrug their shoulders, but the Christian thinkers say: 'We believe in the miracles performed in our holy religion; we believe in them through faith, and not through our reason; we take good care not to pay any heed to that, because when faith speaks it's agreed that reason must be silent; we have total, rock-solid faith in the miracles of Jesus Christ, but allow us to have a few doubts about several others; let us, please, suspend judgement on what a simple man honoured with the title "Great" says. He assures us that a little monk had got so used to doing miracles that the prior eventually told him to stop exercising his talent. The monk obeyed; but on seeing a poor tiler falling off a roof he was torn between holy obedience and his desire to save the man's life. So he simply told the workman to stay hanging in mid-air until further notice and hurried off to tell his prior how matters stood. The prior absolved him from the sin of starting a miracle without permission, but told him to leave it at that and not do it again. We agree with the philosophers that this story should be taken with a pinch of salt.'

'But how dare you deny', the philosophers are asked, 'that St Gervasius and St Protasius appeared in a dream to St Ambrose and told him where their relics were located? That St Ambrose dug them up and they cured a blind man? St Augustine was in Milan at the time; it's he who reports this miracle—"immenso populo teste", he says—in book 2 of *The City of God*. It's one of the best attested miracles.' The philosophers say that they don't believe a word of it; that Gervasius and Protasius never appeared to anyone; that human beings couldn't care less about knowing where the remains of their carcasses are buried; that no more credence should be given to the cure of this blind man than to the story of Vespasian doing the same; that it was a useless miracle, and God never does anything useless; and that they're sticking firmly to their principles. My respect for St Gervasius and St Protasius stops me agreeing with these philosophers; I merely report their disbelief. They set great store by a passage in Lucian that can be found in *The Death of Peregrinus*: 'When a skilled juggler becomes a Christian he's bound to make a fortune.' But Lucian is a profane author, so he lacks all authority in our eyes.

These philosophers can't bring themselves to believe in the miracles carried out in the second century; in vain have eyewitnesses recorded that when the bishop of Smyrna, St Polycarp, was condemned to be cast into the flames and burned to death, they heard a voice crying out, 'Courage, Polycarp, be strong, show yourself a man!'; that the

flames of the pyre then separated from his body and formed a tent of
fire above his head, and a dove flew up from the middle of the pyre;
and that in the end they had to cut Polycarp's head off. 'What was the
point of this miracle?' ask the incredulous; 'Why did the flames lose
their potency whereas the executioner's axe did not? How come that
so many martyrs have emerged unscathed from a tub of boiling oil
but could not resist the edge of a sword?' The answer they're given is:
'It's God's will.' But the philosophers would like to have seen all that
with their own eyes before believing it.

Those who back up their reasoning with science will tell you that
the church fathers themselves often admitted that in their time no one
did miracles any more. St Chrysostom expressly says: 'The extraordinary gifts of the spirit were granted even to the unworthy, because
the Church needed miracles then; but now they're not even given to
the worthy, since the Church does not need them any more.' Then he
admits that no one is resurrecting the dead or even curing the sick.

St Augustine himself, despite the miracle of Gervasius and
Protasius, asks in *The City of God*: 'Why are the miracles done in the
past not seen any longer?' And he gives the same reason. 'Cur, inqui-
unt, nunc illa miracula quae praedicatis facta esse, non fiunt? Possem
quidem dicere, necessaria prius fuisse, quam crederet mundus, ad
hoc ut crederet mundus.'*

It's objected to the philosophers that despite this admission
St Augustine speaks of an old cobbler of Hippo who, having lost all
his clothes, went to pray in the chapel of the Twenty Martyrs, and on
his return found a fish containing a gold ring. The cook who prepared
the fish told the cobbler, 'That's a gift from the twenty martyrs!'

To which the philosophers reply that there's nothing in this story
that contradicts the laws of nature, that physics is not involved if a
fish swallows a gold ring, and that it's not a miracle if a cook gives the
ring to a cobbler.

If the philosophers are reminded that, in the account given by
St Jerome in his *Life of the Hermit Paul*, the hermit had several conversations with satyrs and fauns, and that a raven brought him a half-
loaf every day for his dinner and a whole loaf the day St Anthony
came visiting, they could still reply that all that has nothing to do with
physics; that satyrs and fauns may well have existed, and that in any
case if this story is puerile it's got nothing in common with the true
miracles of the Saviour and his apostles. Many good Christians have

attacked the story of St Simeon Stylites as recorded by Theodoret; many miracles that pass for authentic in the Greek church have been called into question by several members of the Latin church, just as some Latin miracles have been held suspect in the Greek church; the Protestants, who came later, have had little time for the miracles of either church.

A learned Jesuit who has preached for many years in the Indies complains that neither he nor his fellow priests have ever gone in for miracles (Ospiniam, p. 230*). Xavier laments in several of his letters that he has no gift for languages, saying that in Japan he's nothing but a mute statue; yet the Jesuits have written that he had raised nine people from the dead, which is a lot; but it has also to be borne in mind that he resurrected eight people fifteen thousand miles from here. Since then some people have claimed that the abolition of the Jesuits in France was a far greater miracle that those of Xavier or Ignatius.

However that may be, all Christians are agreed that the miracles of Jesus Christ and his apostles are incontestably true, but that some miracles of questionable authenticity in recent times must seriously be open to doubt.

It's dearly to be wished, for example, that for a miracle to be properly certified, it should be done in the presence of the Academy of Sciences in Paris, or the Royal Society in London, or the Faculty of Medicine, assisted by a Guards detachment to keep in order the crowds who might, by their unseemly behaviour, prevent the miracle taking place.

A philosopher was asked one day what he'd do if he saw the sun standing still, that is, if the earth stopped moving round the sun, and if the dead rose as one from the grave, and if every mountain threw itself along with its fellows into the sea, the whole to prove some important truth such as, for example, that of the grace versatile.* 'What I'd do?' asked the philosopher. 'I'd become a Manichaean, and say: what one principle has done, another has undone.'

MOSES
(MOÏSE)

SEVERAL scholars have held that the Pentateuch cannot have been written by Moses. They say that Scripture itself indicates that the earliest known copy was found in the reign of King Josiah and that this document was brought to the king by his secretary Shaphan. Now, between Moses and secretary Shaphan's exploit, there were, according to the Hebrew calendar, eight hundred and sixty-seven years. For God appeared to Moses in the burning bush in the year of creation 2213 and secretary Shaphan published the book of the law in the year 3380. This book, found in the reign of Josiah, was unknown until the return from the Babylonian captivity, and it's said that it was Ezra, inspired by God, who brought the whole of Holy Scripture to light.

But whether it was Ezra or someone else who drafted the text is a matter of absolutely no importance so long as the book is inspired. It's not said in the Pentateuch that Moses is the author, so it's legitimate to attribute it to another person to whom the Divine Spirit will have dictated it.

Some quibblers add that no prophet quotes the books of the Pentateuch, that they're not mentioned in the Psalms, nor in the books attributed to Solomon, nor in Jeremiah, nor in Isaiah, nor indeed in any canonical book. The words corresponding to Genesis, Exodus, Numbers, Leviticus, and Deuteronomy are found in no other texts in the Old or New Testament.

Bolder people have raised the following questions:

1. In an arid desert, which language would Moses have written in? It could only have been Egyptian, because we learn from the book itself that Moses and his entire people were born in Egypt. The Egyptians were not using papyrus yet; they carved hieroglyphs on marble and wood. It's even stated that the Ten Commandments were carved in stone. So five volumes would have to have been engraved on polished stones, which would have required much effort and a lot of time.

2. Is it plausible that in a desert where the Jewish people had neither tailors nor shoemakers, and where the Lord of the Universe was obliged to undertake a continual miracle to preserve the Jews' old

clothes and shoes, sufficient skilled people could have been found to carve the five books of the Pentateuch on marble or wood? It's true that workmen were found to make a golden calf in one night and then grind it to powder, to build the tabernacle, to adorn it with thirty-four bronze columns surmounted by silver capitals, to weave and embroider veils of linen, hyacinth, scarlet, and purple. That only reinforces the quibblers in their opinion; they respond by saying that in a desert where everything is lacking it's not possible to make such rarefied items; that making shoes and tunics ought to have been a top priority; that those who don't have the basics don't go in for luxuries; and that it's a flagrant contradiction to say that there were founders, engravers, sculptors, dyers, embroiderers, but no one to make clothes or bake bread.

3. If Moses had written the first chapter of Genesis, would all young people be forbidden to read it? Would the lawgiver have been shown such disrespect? And if Moses had said that God punishes the iniquity of the fathers 'unto the fourth generation', would Ezekiel have dared contradict him?

4. If Moses had written Leviticus, how could he have contradicted himself in Deuteronomy? Leviticus forbids a man to marry his sister-in-law; Deuteronomy commands it.

5. Would Moses have spoken about cities that didn't exist at the time he was writing his book? Would he have said that towns which, for him, were to the east of the Jordan, were to the west of the river?

6. Would he have assigned forty-eight towns to the Levites in a country which never had even ten cities and in a desert where he had always wandered around without a roof over his head?

7. Would he have prescribed rules for the Jewish kings when not only were there no such kings, but people couldn't bear to think of them and were unlikely ever to change their opinion? What? Would Moses have laid down precepts for the conduct of kings who only appeared about eight hundred years later, and said nothing to guide the judges and high priests who succeeded him? Does not this lead one to think that the Pentateuch was written in the time of the kings, and that the ceremonies instituted by Moses had merely been a tradition?

8. Could Moses really have said to the Jews, 'Under the protection of your God I led you, an army of six hundred thousand combatants, away from the land of Egypt'? Wouldn't this have been the Jews'

answer? 'You must have been very timid not to have led us against the Pharaoh: he couldn't raise a force of two hundred thousand to oppose us. Egypt never had such a large standing army; we would have beaten them easily and would now be masters of the country. What? God, your interlocutor, killed all the firstborn of Egypt just to please us, and if there were three hundred thousand families in that land, that makes three hundred thousand men slaughtered in a single night to avenge us. Why didn't you follow up your God's excellent work? Why didn't you give us that fertile country after it was left defenceless? Why did you make us leave Egypt as robbers and cowards and wander to our deaths, caught in deserts between precipices and mountains? You could at least have led us straight to this land of Canaan which we have no right to but which you promised us and which we still haven't been able to enter?

'It would have made sense for us to walk from the land of Goshen along the Mediterranean towards Tyre and Sidon, but you made us cross almost the whole of the isthmus of Suez, re-enter Egypt and proceed beyond Memphis, only to find ourselves, after walking two hundred and fifty miles in this Egypt we wanted to avoid, at Baal-Zephon, on the shores of the Red Sea, with our backs turned to the land of Canaan and our people close to death between Pharaoh's army and the sea!

'Had you wanted to deliver us into the hands of our enemies you couldn't have set about it better. God saved us by a miracle, you say; the waters parted to let us through; but after such a favour was it necessary to make us die of hunger and exhaustion in the horrible deserts of Etam, Kadesh-Barnea, Marah, Elim, Horeb, and Sinai? Our fathers all died in those desolate wastes, and you come and tell us that God had a particular concern for them!'

That's what these grumbling Israelites, these unfair descendants of the wandering Jews who'd died in the deserts, could have said to Moses if he'd read Genesis and Exodus to them. And what couldn't they have said (and done) when he got on to the business of the golden calf? 'What! You've got the nerve to tell us that your brother made a golden calf for our fathers when you were with God on the mountain; you who say at one moment that you spoke to God face to face and at another that you could only see him from behind! Anyway, you were with this God, and in a single day your brother casts a golden calf for us to worship, and instead of punishing your unworthy brother you make him our high priest and order your Levites to kill twenty thousand of your people; would our fathers have put up with that? Would they have let themselves be battered to death like sacrificial victims by bloodthirsty priests? You tell us that, not content with this orgy of bloodletting, you had another twenty-four thousand of your poor followers murdered because one of them slept with a Midianite even though you'd married one! And you add that you're the gentlest of men. A few more acts of gentleness like that and there'll be no one left alive.

'No, if you were capable of such cruelty and managed to exercise it, you would be the most barbarous of men, and no punishment would suffice to expiate such a strange crime.'

Those, more or less, are the objections that scholars make to those who think that Moses is the author of the Pentateuch. But they're told that the ways of God are not those of human beings; that God tested, led, and abandoned his people through an act of wisdom which is beyond our ken; that for more than two thousand years the Jews themselves have believed that those books were written by Moses; that the Church, successor to the Synagogue and equally infallible, has decided the issue once and for all; and that when the Church has spoken, scholars must for ever after hold their peace.

ONE'S COUNTRY
(PATRIE)

ONE'S country is made up of several families; and just as one supports one's family out of pride where no conflicting interest is involved, one similarly supports out of pride one's town or village, and calls it one's country.

The bigger this country becomes, the less one loves it, because shared love gets steadily weaker. It's impossible to love tenderly a large family one hardly knows.

Those who are dying to be an aedile, tribune, praetor, consul, or dictator, and who shout from the rooftops that they love their country, only love themselves. People want to be sure of sleeping in their own beds without others taking it upon themselves to make them sleep somewhere else. They want the certainty of knowing that their home is their castle. Since everyone feels the same, personal interests become the general interest. When one's formulating wishes only for oneself one is formulating them for the community too.

On this earth it's impossible for a country to be governed in the first instance other than as a republic, a commonwealth: it's the natural order of things. A few families get together to fend off bears and wolves; one that has corn gives some to another and receives wood in exchange.

When we discovered America, we found all the tribes organized into republics; there were only two monarchies in that part of the world: out of the many nations we found only two that had rulers.

It was the same in the ancient world: everywhere in Europe was a republic before the rise of the kinglets of Eritrea and Rome. Republics are still to be found in Africa: Tripoli, Tunis, and Algiers, in the north, are brigand republics; the Hottentots, in the south, still live as we were said to have lived when the world was young: free, equal, without masters, subjects, money, indeed virtually without needs. The meat from their sheep feeds them and the skins clothe them; huts of wood and mud are their shelter; they stink far more than anyone else, but they can't smell it; and they live and die in a more gentle fashion than we do.

In Europe today there are eight republics without monarchs:

Venice, Holland, Switzerland, Genoa, Lucca, Ragusa, Geneva, and San Marino. Poland, Sweden, and England can be seen as monarchical republics, but only Poland is called that.

Now, a monarchy or a republic: which is it better for your country to be? People have been debating that for four thousand years. Ask the rich, and they all prefer aristocratic government; ask the people, and they want democracy; only kings opt for monarchy. So how is it that most of the earth is ruled by kings? Ask the rats who wanted to hang a bell around the cat's neck.* But, in truth, the real reason, as has been said, is that human beings are very rarely capable of self-government.

It's sad that being a good patriot often means that one is the enemy of all other human beings. In the senate that good citizen Cato the Elder always kept saying, 'This is my opinion: Carthage must be destroyed.' Being a good patriot is to want your city to get rich through trade and powerful through arms. It's obvious that a country cannot gain without another losing, and cannot win without making others wretched.

So that's the human condition: wanting greatness for your country means wishing nothing but ill for its neighbours. People who'd like their country to be neither much greater nor much smaller, neither a lot richer nor a lot poorer, would be the true citizens of the universe.

PETER
(PIERRE)

In Italian Piero, *or* Pietro; *in Spanish* Pedro; *in Latin* Petrus;
in Greek Petros; *in Hebrew* Cepha

WHY did Peter's successors have such power in the West and none in the East? It's like asking why the bishops of Wurzburg and Salzburg could take royal powers to themselves during periods of anarchy whereas the status of Greek bishops was always a subordinate one. The time, the occasion, the ambitions of one group and the weakness of another have always been and will always be what counts in this world.

To this confused state of affairs is added public opinion, which reigns supreme among human beings; it's not that they really do have a settled view: words are a sufficient substitute.

In Matthew Jesus tells Peter, 'I will give unto thee the keys of the kingdom of heaven.'* Around the eleventh century the bishop of Rome's supporters maintained that he who gives the greater gives the lesser; that the heavens encircle the earth; and that since Peter held the keys to the container, he also held the keys to its contents. If by 'the heavens' all the stars and all the planets are understood, it's evident, according to Thomasius, that the keys given to Simon Bar-Yonah, known as Peter, were a passe-partout set. If by 'the heavens' are understood the clouds, the atmosphere, the ether, and the space in which the stars revolve, then—according to Meursius—no locksmith could ever make a key to fit those doors.

In Palestine the 'keys' were wooden pegs tied with a strap; Jesus said to Bar-Yonah, 'Whatsoever thou shalt bind on earth shall be bound in heaven.'* From this the Pope's theologians concluded that the popes had been given the right to dispose of kingdoms as they saw fit and to bind and unbind people from the oath of fidelity made to their kings. Very clever! At the Estates-General of France in 1302 the commons said in their petition to the king: 'Boniface VIII is a b—— who believes that God binds and imprisons people in heaven and that he, Boniface, binds people on earth.' In Germany a famous Lutheran—Melanchthon, I think—found it very hard to accept that Jesus said to Simon

Bar-Yonah, Cepha, or Cephas, 'Thou art Peter, and upon this rock (*petros*) I will build my church.' He couldn't conceive that God would make a pun like that, or go in for such a peculiar witticism: he couldn't believe that the Pope's authority was based on a joke.

Peter was supposed to have been bishop of Rome, but it's well enough known that at the time and for a long while afterwards there were no individual bishoprics. Christian society only began to take shape around the end of the second century.

It's possible Peter travelled to Rome; it's even possible that he was crucified head downwards, though that wasn't the practice at the time: we just don't have any proof of all this. We have a letter in his name in which he says he's in Babylon; some astute canon lawyers have claimed that by 'Babylon' Rome is meant. So on the supposition that the letter was dated from Rome, people could conclude that it was written in Babylon. That was the way of the world.

There was a holy man who was made to pay a very high price for a benefice in Rome; it's called Simony. He was asked if he believed Simon Peter had ever been to Rome. He replied: 'I don't know about Peter, but I'm sure Simon has.'

As for Peter himself, it must be admitted that Paul wasn't the only one to have been scandalized by his conduct. He—and his successors—have often been met with resistance. Paul bitterly reproached him with eating forbidden meat, that is pork, black pudding, hare, eels, ixion, and griffin. Peter defended himself by saying that he had seen the skies open around the sixth hour and a great tablecloth come down from the four quarters of heaven filled with eels, quadrupeds, and birds; the voice of an angel had told him, 'Kill and eat'.* It's apparently the very same voice, Wollaston says, that has told so many pontiffs, 'Kill everything, and eat the substance of the people.'*

Casaubon couldn't approve of the way Peter treated Ananias and his wife Sapphira. 'With what right', Casaubon asked, 'did a Jewish slave of the Romans order or permit all those who believed in Jesus to sell their inheritance and lay the proceeds at his feet? If an Anabaptist in London had all his brothers' money brought and put at his feet, wouldn't he be arrested as a crafty seducer and thief and sent to Tyburn? Wasn't it horrible to have Ananias killed just because, after selling his property and giving the money to Peter, he'd kept for himself and his wife a few coins to pay for their basic necessities without telling anyone? Hardly was Ananias's body cold when his wife arrived.

Instead of having the kindness to inform her that he'd just made her husband die of a stroke for hanging on to a few coppers, and to warn her to watch out for herself, he let her fall into a trap: he asked her if Ananias had given all his money to the saints. The good lady said yes, and promptly dropped dead. That's harsh.

Conringius* wonders why Peter, who killed in this way people who'd given him alms, didn't instead murder all the doctors who'd caused Jesus to be put to death and who on more than one occasion had had Peter himself flogged: 'Oh Peter! You make two Christians die who'd given you alms, and you allow those who crucified your God to go on living!'

Seemingly when Conringius asked these rash questions he wasn't in a country where the Inquisition held sway. On the subject of Peter Erasmus drew attention to an extraordinary fact: that the head of the Christian religion began his apostolate by denying Christ, and that the first priest of the Jews had begun his ministry by making and worshipping a golden calf.

However that may be, Peter is portrayed as a poor man who catechized the poor. In that he resembles the founders of religious orders, who lived in poverty, but whose successors have become great lords.

Peter's successors, the popes, have sometimes won and sometimes lost, but apart from their immediate vassals they still have around fifty million people in the world who are in several respects subject to their laws.

Giving oneself a master a thousand miles or so from where one lives; waiting to think until this man has seemed to think; not daring to give a final verdict in a suit between some of one's fellow citizens and leaving it to commissioners appointed by a foreigner to decide; not daring to take possession of fields and vineyards obtained from one's king without paying a considerable amount of money to the same foreign master; violating the laws of one's country that forbid one to marry one's niece and then marrying her legally by paying an even greater sum to this foreign master; not daring to plough one's field on a day when that foreigner wants one to celebrate the memory of an unknown person that he's sent to heaven on his personal authority; that's all part of what is involved in acknowledging a pope; those are the freedoms of the Gallican church.

There are a few other nations that carry their submission even further. We've recently seen a monarch ask the Pope for permission to arraign before his royal courts some monks accused of parricide;* it was refused, so he didn't dare try them!

It's fairly well known that in the past the rights of popes were even more extensive; they were much greater than the gods of antiquity, because those gods were merely said to dispose of empires whereas the popes disposed of them in reality.

Sturbinus* says that, on due consideration, we can pardon people for doubting the divinity and infallibility of the pope; that forty schisms have profaned the chair of St Peter and twenty-seven have drenched it in blood; that Stephen VII, son of a priest, dug up the body of his predecessor Formosus and cut off his head; that to Sergius III, who was convicted of murder, Marozia bore a son, who inherited the papacy; that John X, Theodora's lover, was strangled in his bed; that John XI, son of Sergius III, was notorious for his drunkenness and debauchery; that John XII was assassinated in his mistress's house; that Benedict IX bought the papacy and then sold it on; that Gregory VII provoked five hundred years of civil wars which were continued by his successors; that, finally, among so many ambitious, bloody, and debauched popes there was one Alexander VI, whose name is pronounced with the same horror as those of Nero and Caligula.

It's proof—it's said—of the divinity of the popes that it survived so many crimes; but if the caliphs' behaviour had been even worse, that would have made them even more divine. So runs Dermius' argument; but it's been refuted by the Jesuits.

PREJUDICES
(PRÉJUGÉS)

PREJUDICE is an opinion that's not based on judgement. So through-out the world children are spoon-fed all the opinions under the sun before they are able to acquire the capacity to make judgements.

There are some prejudices that are necessary, universal, and the very essence of virtue. In every country children are taught to acknowledge a God who punishes and hands out rewards in equal measure; to offer love and respect to their mother and father; to look upon theft as a crime and self-seeking deception as a vice; and all this even before they have a clue as to what vice and virtue really are.

So there are some very good prejudices: they're the ones that are sanctioned by reason and judgement.

Sentiment is not simply prejudice: it's something much stronger. A mother doesn't love her son because she's been told she has to: for-tunately she cherishes him in spite of herself. It's not prejudice that impels you to run to the help of a child you don't know who's about to be attacked by a wild animal or fall over a cliff.

But it would be prejudice that inclines you to respect a man just because he wears certain clothes and walks and talks with studied grav-ity. Your parents have told you that you should show deference to such a person, so you respect him before knowing whether he deserves it: you grow in years and wisdom; you realize that the man is a vain, devi-ous and self-interested charlatan; you despise what you once revered, and prejudice gives way to judgement. Prejudice made you believe the fables of your childhood; you were told that the Titans waged war on the gods and that Venus loved Adonis; at twelve you accept these fables as true, at twenty you regard them as clever allegories.

To sort matters out, let's look briefly at the different kinds of preju-dice. We'll then perhaps be like the people who realized after the col-lapse of John Law's bank* that the assets they'd been holding were purely imaginary.

PREJUDICES OF THE SENSES

Isn't it funny that even if we can see perfectly well, our eyes are always deceiving us, whereas our ears never do? If, Madam, your well-formed ear hears 'You're beautiful, I love you', it's certain you haven't been told 'You're ugly, I hate you'; but if you see a smooth mirror, it's been shown that you're mistaken, because it has a very uneven surface. The sun looks to you as if it's about two feet in diameter, whereas it's been proved that it's a million times bigger than the earth.

It seems that God put truth into our ears and error into our eyes; but study optics and you'll see that God hasn't deceived you and that it's impossible in the present state of things for objects to look other than as you see them.

PHYSICAL PREJUDICES

Most stories are believed without close examination, and that belief is a prejudice. Fabius Pictor tells us that several centuries before his time a vestal in the town of Alba went to fill her pitcher with water, was raped, and gave birth to Romulus and Remus who were suckled by a she-wolf, and so on. The Roman people believed the fable and didn't look into the question whether there were any vestals in Latium at the time, whether it was plausible for the daughter of a king to leave her convent with a pitcher, or whether it was likely that a she-wolf would give suck to two infants rather than eat them. The prejudice took hold.

A monk writes that when Clovis was in great danger at the battle of Tolbiac he vowed to become a Christian if he managed to get away; but was it natural in such circumstances to address a foreign god? Isn't the religion one's born into more potent? In a battle against the Turks what Christian would pray to Mohammed rather than to the Holy Virgin? It's also said that a pigeon brought the sacred phial to Clovis in its beak and an angel carried the oriflamme to guide him: prejudice led people to believe every anecdote of this kind. Those who understand human nature are well aware that the usurper Clovis and the usurper Rollon converted to Christianity the better to govern Christians, in the same way as the conquering Turks embraced Islam the better to rule over Muslims.

RELIGIOUS PREJUDICES

If your nurse told you that Ceres presides over the cornfields, or that Vishnu and Xaca were reincarnated several times, or that Sammonocodom came to cut down a whole forest, or that Odin awaits you in a hall in Jutland, or that Mohammed or anyone else was able to fly through the air, and if your tutor then hammered into your brain what your nurse had imprinted on it, you're stuck with it for life. If your judgement tries to rebel against these prejudices your neighbours—especially your female neighbours—will shriek 'Ungodly wretch!' at you and frighten you; your dervish, fearful of seeing his income decline, will denounce you to the cadi, and the cadi will if he can see you impaled, because he wants to command fools and thinks fools are more obedient than other people; and this will go on until your neighbours and the dervish and the cadi begin to understand that folly is no good to anyone and that persecution is awful.

RELIGION

THE bishop of Worcester, Warburton, author of one of the most scholarly works ever compiled, writes as follows on page 8, volume i: 'Whatsoever religion and society have no future state for their support, must be supported by an extraordinary Providence: the Jewish religion and society had no future state for their support. Therefore, the Jewish religion and society were supported by an extraordinary Providence.'*

Many theologians attacked him, and since all arguments can be refuted, his was too; this is how people put it:

'Any religion that is not rooted in the doctrine of the immortality of the soul and in eternal reward and punishment, is necessarily false: Judaism did not know these doctrines, so Judaism, far from being supported by Providence, was by your criteria a false and barbarous religion that attacked Providence.'

Bishop Warburton had a few other adversaries who put it to him that the immortality of the soul was known amongst the Jews even in Moses' time, but he showed them clearly that neither the Ten Commandments, nor Leviticus, nor Deuteronomy say a word about this belief, and that it's ridiculous trying to twist and corrupt a few passages in other books to extract a truth that is not announced in the book of the law.

My lord bishop, having compiled four volumes to prove that Judaic law offered neither punishment nor reward after death, was never able to answer his adversaries very satisfactorily. They told him: 'Either Moses knew this doctrine and deceived the Jews by not revealing it, or he didn't know it, in which case he was too ignorant to found a good religion. If the religion had been good, why was it abolished? A true religion must be so for all times and all places; it must be like the light of the sun, giving light to all peoples and all generations.'

This prelate, enlightened man though he was, had a lot of trouble extricating himself from all these difficulties; but what system doesn't?

SECOND QUESTION

Another scholar, who is more of a philosopher and one of the most profound metaphysicians of the age, puts forward strong arguments

in support of the thesis that polytheism was human beings' first religion, and that people began by believing in several gods before reason
enlightened them sufficiently to enable them to acknowledge only one
Supreme Being.*

I venture to think that, on the contrary, people began by acknowledging one God and that afterwards human weakness led to the adop-
tion of several gods. Here's how I see it:

There can be no doubt that there were hamlets before the great
cities were built, and that all human beings were divided into tiny
republics before they were assembled into great empires. It's natural
that a village terrified of thunder, afflicted by the loss of its crops, ill-
treated by the neighbouring village, conscious every day of its weakness and sensing everywhere an invisible power, soon began to say,
'There is a being above us who does us good and ill.'

It seems impossible to me that it said, 'There are two powers',
for why several? Everything starts with the single, then comes the
multiple, and greater illumination soon brings us back to the single.
That's the way the human spirit works.

What being was the first to be invoked? Was it the sun? The moon?
I don't think so. Let's look at what happens with children. They're
very similar to ignorant adults: they're struck neither by the beauty
nor by the utility of the sun that animates nature, nor by the help
the moon gives us, nor by the regular variations in its course; they
don't think about it; they're too used to it. Only what is feared is
invoked and worshipped; children all see the sky with indifference;
but when the thunder rolls they tremble, run away, and hide. The
earliest human beings no doubt did the same. It can only be philosopher types who noticed the course of the stars and got them admired
and worshipped; but simple farmers, lacking enlightenment, were too
ignorant to embrace such a noble error.

So a village will have been content to say, 'There's a power that
thunders and hails, that makes our children die, let's appease it; but
how? We've seen that with small gifts we've been able to soothe the
anger of irritable people, so let's give small presents to this power.'
It also has to be given a name. The first that offers itself is 'chief',
'master', 'lord'; so this power is called Lord. That's probably the
reason why the earliest Egyptians called their god Knef, the Syrians
Adonai, the neighbouring peoples Baal or Bel or Melch or Moloch,
and the Scythians Papee: all words meaning 'lord', 'master'.

That's why almost the whole of America was found to be divided between a multitude of small tribes, all of whom had their protector god. Even the Mexicans and the Peruvians, who were large nations, had only one god. The one worshipped Manko Kapak, the other the god of war. Just as the Hebrews had called their lord Sabaoth, the Mexicans gave their warrior god the name Vitziliputzli.

It's not thanks to superior reason and culture that all peoples began in this way to acknowledge a single divinity; had they been philosophers they would have worshipped the god of all nature rather than the village deity; they would have examined that which proves the existence of a creative, conserving Being: the infinite relationships between all things; but they examined nothing, they merely felt something. Such is the progress of our feeble understanding: every hamlet felt its weakness and the need it had for a strong protector. It imagined that this terrifying, tutelary being lived in the neighbouring forest, or on a mountain, or in a cloud. It only imagined one, because the hamlet had only one warrior chief. It represented him as corporeal because it was impossible for them to see him in any other way. It couldn't believe that the neighbouring hamlet didn't have its own god too. That's why Jephthah says to the Moabites: 'Will not you possess that which Chemosh your god gives you to possess? So whomsoever the Lord our God shall drive out from before us, them will we possess.'*

This speech addressed by a foreigner to other foreigners is quite remarkable. The indigenous people of the country had been dispossessed by the Jews and the Moabites, neither of whom had any right to the land other than that justified by brute force, and the one said to the other, 'Your god gave you cover in your act of usurpation, suffer our god to do the same.'

Jeremiah and Amos both ask by what right the god Melchom seized the land of Gad. From these passages it seems clear that in antiquity each country was assigned a protector-god. The traces of such a theology can still be found in Homer.

It's quite natural that when human beings' imagination got heated and their minds acquired knowledge of a muddled kind they quickly multiplied their gods and assigned protectors to the elements, the seas, the forests, the springs, and the fields. The more they examined the stars, the more they were struck with admiration: how could people not worship the sun if they worshipped a river god?

Once the first step had been taken, the earth was soon covered in gods, and in the end people progressed downwards from stars to cats and onions.

However, reason was necessarily perfected over time, and eventually philosophers were produced who saw that neither onions, nor cats, not even the stars, had arranged the natural order. All these philosophers—Babylonian, Persian, Egyptian, Scythian, Greek, and Roman—acknowledged a rewarding and avenging supreme deity.

They didn't tell people at first, because anyone rash enough to speak ill of onions and cats would have been stoned to death. Anyone who upbraided certain Egyptians for eating their gods would have been eaten too; indeed, Juvenal tells of an Egyptian who was killed and eaten during a heated argument.

So what did they do? Orpheus and others established mysteries which, uttering fearsome oaths, the initiates swore never to reveal, and the chief of these mysteries was the worship of one god. This great truth spread over half the globe; the number of initiates increased enormously; it's true that the ancient religion survives to this day, but since it doesn't contradict the doctrine of the unity of God, it's left in peace. Indeed, why would anyone abolish it? The Romans acknowledged the *Deus optimus maximus*; the Greeks had their supreme god, Zeus. All the other deities were mere intermediate beings; heroes and gods were promoted to the rank of gods, that is of the blessed; but it's certain that Claudius, Augustus, Tiberius, and Caligula were not regarded as creators of the heavens and the earth.

In a word, it seems proven that in Augustus' time everyone who was religious acknowledged a superior, eternal god and several orders of secondary gods, the worship of whom has since been called 'idolatry'.

The Jews were never idolaters, for though they acknowledged *malakhim*—angels, celestial beings of a lower order—it was not prescribed under their law that these deities should be worshipped. They did worship angels, it's true: whenever they saw any, they bowed before them; but since it didn't happen very often there was no ceremonial or legal service laid down for them. The cherubim of the ark never received homage. It's certain that the Jews openly worshipped one god, just as the numberless crowd of initiates worshipped him in their mysteries.

THIRD QUESTION

It was during this time, when the cult of a supreme God was established among all wise people in Asia, Europe, and Africa, that the Christian religion was born.

Platonism was of considerable assistance in the understanding of these doctrines. The *logos* that in Plato meant wisdom, the intelligence of the Supreme Being, became with us the Word and a second person of God. A profound metaphysic beyond human understanding was an inaccessible sanctuary in which religion was concealed.

I won't repeat what I said above about the way Mary was later declared to be the mother of God, or about the way theologians established the consubstantiality of the Father and the Word, the procession of the *pneuma*, divine organ of the divine *logos*, two natures and two wills resulting from hypostasis, and finally the superior manducation, the soul as well as the body nourished by the limbs and the blood of the man-god worshipped and eaten in the form of bread, present to the eyes, tasteable in the mouth, and nevertheless annihilated. All these mysteries are quite sublime.

As early as the second century people began driving out demons in the name of Jesus; before that they were driven out in the name of Jehovah, or Iahoh, because St Matthew tells us that when Jesus' enemies said he'd driven out demons in the name of the prince of demons, he replied, 'If I by Beelzebub cast out devils, by whom do your children cast them out?'

We don't know when the Jews acknowledged that the prince of demons was Beelzebub, who was a foreign god, but we do know from Josephus that there were in Jerusalem exorcists appointed to drive devils from the bodies of the possessed, that is from people afflicted with strange illnesses, which over large parts of the globe were attributed at the time to malevolent spirits.

So these demons were cast out with the true pronunciation of Jehovah that's now lost and with other ceremonies forgotten today.

This exorcism by Jehovah and by the other names of God was still practised by the Church during the early centuries of its existence. In his book against Celsus Origen says* (para. 262): 'If in invoking God or swearing by him he is named as the God of Abraham, Isaac, and Jacob, certain things can be done by these names; their nature and their strength are such that the demons submit to anyone who

pronounces them; but if another name is used, like god of the noisy
sea or supplanter, it will have no effect. The name Israel translated
into Greek will produce no result, but say it in Hebrew with the other
words required, and the spell will work.'

The same Origen says these remarkable things (para. 19): 'There are
names which possess virtue by their very nature, such as those used by
the Egyptian and Persian sages and by the Brahmans in India. What's
called magic is not a vain and fanciful art as the Stoics and Epicureans
claim: neither the name Sabaoth, nor that of Adonai, has been made
for created beings; but they form part of a mysterious theology connected to the Creator; whence the effectiveness of those names when
they are arranged and pronounced according to the rules,' etc.

In saying this Origen is not giving us his personal opinion; he is
merely conveying the universally held view. All regions known at the
time believed in a sort of magic; a distinction was made between heavenly magic and infernal magic, necromancy and theurgy; everything
was prodigy, divination, and oracle. The Persians did not deny the
miracles of the Egyptians, nor the Egyptians those of the Persians.
God allowed the first Christians to believe in the oracles attributed to
the sibyls and left them with a few other unimportant errors that did
not adversely affect anything fundamental in their religion.

Something even more remarkable is that the Christians of the first
two centuries felt nothing but horror for temples, oracles, and statues, as Origen admits on para. 347.* Everything changed afterwards
when, with tighter discipline, the Church achieved stability.

FOURTH QUESTION

Once a religion is legally established in a state the courts are kept busy
preventing any renewal of most of the things done in that religion
before it became publicly accepted. Its founding members met in
secret despite the judges; now only public gatherings held where the
law can exercise oversight are allowed, and all associations that elude
legal scrutiny are banned. The ancient maxim was that it is better
to obey God than mortal creatures; now the opposite is stated, that
respecting the laws of the state is the sole way of showing obedience
to God. In the past all the talk was of obsession and possession; now
the devil stays at home; prodigies and predictions were needed then;
now they're no longer acceptable. Anyone foretelling calamities on

city squares would be sent to an asylum. The church founders were given money in secret by the faithful; anyone receiving cash in order to use it without legal authorization would be arrested. Thus none of the scaffolding used in building the edifice has any further purpose.

FIFTH QUESTION

After our holy religion, which beyond doubt is the only good one, what would be the least bad?

Would it not be the simplest? Would it not be one that lays great stress on ethics and very little on dogma? One that aims to make people just without making them absurd? One that would not tell them to believe things that are impossible, contradictory, and insulting to the Deity and harmful to humankind, and would not presume to threaten with eternal punishment anyone with a grain of common sense? Would it not be one that did not rely on torturers to enforce belief in its doctrines and would not drench the earth with blood to advance unintelligible sophisms? One in which an ambiguous formula, a pun, and two or three forged charters could not make a priest who is a poisoner, murderer, and sometimes incestuous into a sovereign and a god? One which would not subordinate kings to such a priest? One which would advocate only the worship of a just, tolerant, and humane God?

SIXTH QUESTION

It's said that the religion of the Gentiles was absurd in several respects, self-contradictory and pernicious, but hasn't more wickedness been laid at its door than it was truly responsible for, and more foolish doctrines than it actually preached?

> For, to see Jupiter as a bull,
> Snake, swan or whatever,
> Attractive it certainly isn't:
> Small wonder it provokes comment!
>
> Molière, *Prologue to Amphitryon**

That's rather cheeky no doubt, but can anyone show me a temple in all antiquity dedicated to Leda making love to a bull or a swan? Was a sermon ever preached in Athens or Rome to encourage girls to have babies with the swans in their farmyard? Are the fables collected and ornamented by Ovid religious texts? Are they at all like our *Légende dorée* or our *Fleur des saints*? If a Brahman or dervish objected to the story of St Mary of Egypt who, not having the money to pay her fare to the sailors who took her to Egypt, gave each one in lieu what are called 'her favours', we'd say to the Brahman, 'Reverend Father, you're mistaken, our religion is not the *Légende dorée*.'

We reproach the ancients with their oracles and marvels; if they came back to earth and we could count up the miracles of Our Lady of Loreto and those of Our Lady of Ephesus, which goddess would notch up the highest score?

Human sacrifice has been known in nearly all societies, but very rarely practised. Among the Jews we have only the immolation of Jephthah's daughter and of King Agag, because Isaac and Jonathan were spared. The story of Iphigenia is not well attested among the Greeks. Human sacrifices were very rare among the Romans. In a nutshell, pagan religion spilt very little blood, whereas ours has drenched the earth with it. Ours is without doubt the only good, the only true faith; but we've done so much evil through it that when we speak about other religions, it behoves us to be modest.

SEVENTH QUESTION

If people want to convert foreigners, or their compatriots, to their religion, shouldn't they set about it with the most ingratiating gentleness, the most winning moderation? If they start by saying that what they're announcing is proven beyond doubt, they will be met with utter disbelief; should they have the temerity to tell others that if they reject their doctrine it's only because it condemns their passions, because their hearts have corrupted their minds, and because their reasoning is arrogant and false—should they go about it that way, they'll provoke outrage and meet vigorous opposition, thereby scuppering the whole enterprise.

If the religion they preach is true, will insolence and rage make it even truer? Do you get angry when you say that people must be kind, patient, generous, just, and fulfil all society's duties? No, because everyone shares your views; so why do you hurl insults at your brother when you teach him a metaphysical mystery? It's because his calm good sense ruffles your self-esteem. You have the arrogance to insist that your brother subordinates his intelligence to yours: humiliated arrogance produces anger; nothing else does. A man sustaining twenty gunshot wounds in a battle does not get angry; but a scholar cut to the quick by someone's refusal to agree with him flies into a rage and becomes quite implacable.

RESURRECTION
(RÉSURRECTION)

IT'S said that the Egyptians only built their pyramids to make them into tombs, and that their bodies, embalmed within and without, were waiting for their souls to come and reanimate them after a thousand years. But if their bodies were going to be resurrected, why was the perfumers' first job to pierce their skulls with a hook and draw the brain out? The idea of being resurrected without a brain leads me to suspect (excuse the term) that the Egyptians didn't have much of a one while they were alive; but it must be borne in mind that most of the ancients thought that the soul was in the chest. And why there and not somewhere else? It's because whenever we feel anything strongly we experience a dilatation or a tightening in the cardiac region that makes us think that it's the seat of the soul. This soul had something airy about it; it was a weightless thing that floated about freely until it found its body again.

The belief in the resurrection greatly pre-dates the historical era. Athalida Mercury's daughter could die and rise again at will; Aesculapius brought Hippolytus back to life, as did Hercules Alcestis. Pelops was hacked to pieces by his father and resurrected by the gods. Plato tells us that Heres was resurrected for a fortnight only.

Among the Jews the Pharisees adopted the doctrine of the resurrection only a very long while after Plato.

There is a rather strange fact—one well worth our attention—in the Acts of the Apostles. St James and several of his companions advised St Paul to go into the temple in Jerusalem and, good Christian though he was, to observe all the ceremonies of the old law, so that—they said—'all may know that those things, whereof they were informed concerning thee, are nothing; but that thou thyself also walkest orderly, and keepest the law of Moses' (Acts 21: 24).

So St Paul spent seven days in the temple, but on the last day he was recognized. He was accused of having brought Greeks in with him and to have polluted the holy place. This is how he got out of that tight spot:

'But when Paul perceived that the one part were Sadducees, and the other Pharisees, he cried out in the council, "Men and brethren,

I am a Pharisee, the son of a Pharisee: of the hope and resurrection of the dead I am called in question" (Acts 23: 6). Now, in the entire affair there had never been any question of the resurrection of the dead: Paul only said so in order to set the Pharisees and the Sadducees by the ears.

Acts 23: 7: 'And when Paul had so said, there arose a dissension between the Pharisees and the Sadducees: and the multitude was divided.'

Acts 23: 8: 'For the Sadducees say that there is no resurrection, neither angel, nor spirit: but the Pharisees confess both'; and so on.

It's been claimed that Job, who was very ancient, was familiar with the doctrine of the resurrection. People quote these words: 'I know that my redeemer liveth, and that he shall stand at the latter day upon the earth; and though after my skin worms destroy this body, yet in my flesh shall I see God.'

But several commentators understand by these words that Job hopes that he will soon recover from his illness and will not remain for ever lying on the ground. What follows is proof enough that this is the correct explanation, because the next moment he cries out to his false, hard friends: 'But ye should say, Why persecute we him?' or else, 'For ye will say, Why persecute we him?' Doesn't that obviously mean, 'You'll repent for having insulted me when you see me restored to my earlier state of health and wealth'? A sick person who says, 'I'll get up', doesn't say 'I'll resurrect'. Giving false meanings to passages that are perfectly clear is the surest way of never understanding one another.

St Jerome situates the birth of the sect of the Pharisees only a very short time before the advent of Christ. The rabbi Hillel is considered their founder, and he was a contemporary of Gamaliel, St Paul's teacher.

Many of those Pharisees believed that these Jews alone would resurrect: it wasn't worth raising the rest of humanity from the dead. Others maintained that only in Palestine would people resurrect, and that the bodies of those buried elsewhere would be secretly conveyed to Jerusalem to link up with their souls. But in chapter 4 of the first epistle to the Thessalonians St Paul says that the second coming of Jesus Christ is for them and for him, and that they will witness it:

Verse 16: 'For the Lord himself shall descend from heaven with a shout, with the voice of the archangel, and with the trump of God: and the dead in Christ shall rise first.'

Verse 17: 'Then we which are alive and remain shall be caught up together with them in the clouds, to meet the Lord in the air: and so shall we ever be with the Lord.'

Doesn't this important passage clearly prove that the first Christians expected to see the end of the world? The same is predicted in fact in St Luke, for the very time when Luke was alive.

St Augustine believes that children, even stillborn babies, will rise again as mature adults. The Origens, Jeromes, Athanasiuses, and Basils did not believe that women would resurrect with female genital organs.

Well, there have always been arguments about what we have been, what we are, and what we shall be.

SOLOMON
(SALOMON)

COULD Solomon have been as wealthy as is claimed?

The Chronicles assure us that at a conservative estimate his father King David left him about twenty billion in our money at today's exchange rate. There's not that much cash in the whole world, so it's quite difficult to believe that David could have amassed this sum in the tiny land of Palestine.

According to the third book of the Kings* Solomon had forty thousand stables for his chariots' horses. If each stable had held only ten horses that would have amounted to a mere four hundred thousand which, together with his twelve thousand saddle horses, would have made four hundred and twelve thousand cavalry horses. That's a lot for a Jewish leader who never went to war. Such magnificence is without parallel in a country which can only feed donkeys and which today has no other mounts. But seemingly times have changed; it's true that such a wise prince who had a thousand wives could well have had four hundred and twelve thousand horses too, if only to go riding with his ladies along the Sea of Galilee, or around Lake Sodom, or towards the Kidron stream, which is one of the most delightful places on earth, although truth to tell it's dry for nine months in the year and the ground is rather stony.

But did the wise Solomon do all the things attributed to him? Is it plausible, for example, that he is the author of the Hebrew poem known as the Song of Songs?

It's possible that a monarch who had a thousand wives said to one of them, 'let her kiss me with the kisses of her mouth, for thy breasts are better than wine.'* When it's a matter of a kiss on the mouth, a king or a shepherd are likely to express themselves in much the same terms. It's true that it's rather strange that people claim that it was the girl speaking here, praising the breasts of her lover.

I won't deny either that an amorous king could put these words into his mistress's mouth: 'A bundle of myrrh is my well-beloved unto me; he shall lie all night betwixt my breasts.'* I'm not too sure what a bundle of myrrh is; but when the well-beloved suggests that her well-beloved pass his left hand under her head and embrace her with his right hand, I've no difficulty understanding that.

The author of the Song of Songs could be asked for some clarification when he says, 'Thy navel is like a round goblet, which wanteth not liquor; thy belly is like a heap of wheat, thy breasts are like two young roes, and thy nose is as the tower of Lebanon.'*

I must confess that Virgil's *Eclogues* are written in rather a different register; but each to their own, and a Jew is not obliged to write like Virgil.

It's apparently a fine turn of oriental eloquence to say, 'We have a little sister, and she hath no breasts: what shall we do for our sister? If she be a wall, we will build upon her; if she be a door, we will inclose her.'*

It's fine if Solomon the wisest of men spoke like that in his cups; the Song of Songs was, it's said, his epithalamium for his marriage to the Pharaoh's daughter; but was it natural for the Pharaoh's son-in-law to leave his well-beloved during the night and walk in his walnut-tree garden, for the queen to run barefoot and unchaperoned after him, for her to be beaten by the town guards who took her robe?

Could a king's daughter have said, 'I am black, but comely, as the curtains of Solomon'?* One might overlook such an expression coming from a shepherd, although after all there's not much relation between a girl's beauty and curtains. But the curtains of Solomon could well have been admired in their time; and a Jew from the dregs of society composing verses for his mistress could very well have said in his Jewish language that no Jewish king ever had curtains as beautiful as she; but King Solomon would have had to have been really keen on his curtains to compare them to his mistress; a king who nowadays composed a fine epithalamium on the occasion of his marriage to the daughter of a neighbouring king would certainly not be taken for the best poet in the kingdom.

Several rabbis have maintained not only that this short, voluptuous eclogue is not by King Solomon, but that it's not even authentic. Theodore of Mopsuestia was of this view, and the famous Grotius called the Song of Songs 'a libertine work, *flagitiosus*';* nevertheless, it is hallowed and seen as a perpetual allegory of the marriage between Christ and his church. It has to be admitted that the allegory is a bit risqué, and that it's hard to see what the Church could understand by the phrase that the little sister has no breasts, and that if she's a wall, she must be built upon.

The Book of Wisdom is more serious in flavour, but it's no more by Solomon than the Song of Songs. It's commonly attributed to Jesus son of Sirach, or by others to Philo of Byblos; but whoever the author was, it seems that when he was writing the Pentateuch did not yet exist, because he says in chapter 10 that Abraham wanted to sacrifice Isaac at the time of the deluge; and in another place he speaks of the patriarch Joseph as a king of Egypt.

The Proverbs have been attributed to Isaiah, to Elzia, to Shebna, to Eliakim, to Joah, and to several others. But whoever it was who composed these oriental maxims, it's unlikely that a king took the trouble to do so. Would he have said, 'The fear of a king is as the roaring of a lion'? A subject or a slave who's afraid of his master's wrath speaks like that. Would Solomon have kept saying, 'A whore is a deep ditch'? Would he have said, 'Look not thou upon the wine when it is red, when it giveth his colour to the glass'?*

I doubt very much whether wine glasses existed in Solomon's time; they're a quite recent invention; throughout antiquity people drank from wooden or metal cups; so this passage alone indicates that the Song of Songs was written by a Jew from Alexandria long after Alexander's time.

Then there's Ecclesiastes, which Grotius claims was written under Zerubbabel. We know how freely the author of Ecclesiastes expresses himself; we know he says that human beings are no better off than beasts; that it's better not to have been born than to live; that there is no other life; and that there's nothing so good as enjoying the fruits of one's labours with the woman one loves.

It could be that Solomon did say things like that to some of his wives; it's claimed that these were rhetorical objections he addressed to himself; but these maxims have a rather licentious tone which doesn't exactly square with serious debate; and it's brazen impertinence to read into an author the opposite of what he says.

Besides, several Fathers have claimed that Solomon repented, so he can be forgiven.

But does it matter to us whether these books were written by a Jew? Our Christian faith is based on the Jewish, but not on all the books the Jews have written. Why should the Song of Songs be more sacred than the fables of the Talmud? It's because we've included it in the Hebrew canon. And what is this canon? It's a collection of authentic works. So if a work is authentic, it's divine? Is a story about the kings of Judah and Shechem, for example, anything other than a story? What a strange prejudice! We have a horror of the Jews and yet we want everything written by them and collected by us to bear the stamp of the Deity. There's never been an inconsistency as blatant as this.

SENSATION

IT's said that oysters have two senses, moles four, and other animals, like human beings, six. Some people say there is a sixth, but it's clear that the sensation of pleasure that they're talking about is part of the sense of touch, so five are all we've got. It's impossible to imagine any beyond five, or even to want them.

It's possible that on other worlds there are senses we can have no notion of, that their number increases from globe to globe, and that the being that has innumerable and perfect senses is the *nec plus ultra* of all creatures.

But what is it within our power to do with our five senses? It's always in spite of ourselves that we have sensation and not because we desire to; once we come across an object it's impossible for us not to experience the sensation our nature destines us to receive. Feeling is within us, but it cannot depend on us. We receive it: but how? It's well known that there is no connection between the vibrations in the air made by the words sung to me and the impression made in my brain by those words.

We're amazed at thought, but sensation is just as magical. A divine power is just as manifest in the sensation of the lowest form of insect as it is in the brain of Isaac Newton. But if you see a thousand animals die you're not the least bothered about what will become of their ability to feel, even though that ability is the work of the Supreme Being; you look upon them as nature's machines, born to die and to make room for others.

Why and how could their sensation survive them? What need would the author of all things have to preserve the properties of subjects that have been destroyed? One might as well say that the ability of the so-called sensitive plant to pull its leaves back when they're touched survives the plant's demise. You're no doubt going to ask, 'How can the thought of a human being not perish if the sensation of animals dies with them?' I can't answer that question, I don't know enough about it.* The eternal author of sensation and thought knows how he gives the latter and how he preserves it.

All antiquity has maintained that there's nothing in our minds that did not already exist in our senses. In his fictions Descartes claims that we have metaphysical ideas even before we are put out to nurse. A faculty of theology proscribed this doctrine, not because it was mistaken, but because it was a novelty; later on it embraced the error because the English philosopher Locke had demolished it, and an Englishman obviously had to be wrong. Finally, having changed its mind so often, it reverted to the proscription of the ancient truth that the senses are the doors of the understanding; it behaved like heavily indebted governments that print banknotes at one moment and withdraw them the next; but for a long time now no one has any confidence in the currency issued by that faculty.

All the universities in the world won't stop philosophers seeing that we begin by feeling and that our memory is nothing but continued sensation.* Even if they survived into adulthood, people born without the five senses would never have any ideas. Metaphysical notions only come through the senses. How can you measure a circle or a triangle if you've never seen or touched a circle and a triangle? How can you form an imperfect idea of the infinite without pushing boundaries? And how can you expand limits without seeing or feeling them?

Sensation envelops all our faculties, says the great philosopher Condillac* (*Traité des sensations*, ii. 128).

What can we conclude from all that? You who can read and think, you conclude.

DREAMS
(SONGES)

Somnia quae ludunt animos volitantibis umbris,
Non delubra deum nec ab aethere numina mittunt,
Sed sua quisque facit.*

BUT how is it that when all the senses are dead during sleep, there is an internal sense that is alive? How is it that although your eyes see nothing and your ears hear nothing, you can see and hear things in your dreams? In its dreams the hound is with the hunt, it barks, follows its prey, and is in at the kill. The poet writes verse when asleep, the mathematician sees figures, and the metaphysician reasons well or badly. There are striking examples of this.

Is it solely the organs of the machine that are active? Is this the pure soul, untrammelled by the control of the senses, freely exercising its rights here?

If the organs alone produce the night's dreams, why can they not alone produce the ideas of the daytime? If the pure soul, at peace during the senses' repose, acting on its own, is the sole cause and the unique subject of all the ideas you have when asleep, why are they all nearly always irregular, unreasonable, and incoherent? What? It's at a time like this, when the soul is the least troubled, that there's the most trouble in all its imaginings? It is free, and it is mad? If it was born with metaphysical ideas, as so many writers dreaming with their eyes wide open have said, its pure and luminous ideas of being, of infinity, and of all the first principles ought to awake in it fired with the greatest energy when its body is asleep: only when dreaming would one ever be a good philosopher.

Whatever system you embrace, whatever vain efforts you make to prove to yourself that your brain is set in motion by your memory and that your soul is set in motion by your brain, you must agree that all your ideas come to you in your sleep despite and without you: your will has nothing to do with it. So it's certain that you can think for seven or eight hours at a stretch without the least desire to think and without even being sure that you are thinking. Ponder that, and try to work out how the animal is put together.

Dreams have always—naturally enough—been very much the subject of superstition. A man deeply worried about his mistress's illness dreams that he sees her in her death-throes; if she dies the next day, it's because the gods have predicted her death.

An army general dreams that he is winning a battle, and when he does, it's because the gods have told him that he will.

People only take notice of dreams that turn out to be true and forget the rest. Dreams feature a lot in ancient history, as do oracles.

In Leviticus the end of chapter 19, verse 26 is translated 'ye shall not observe dreams'. But the word 'dream' is not in the Hebrew, and indeed it would be odd if the observation of dreams were reproved in the same book that relates how Joseph became the benefactor of Egypt and of his family for having interpreted three dreams.

The interpretation of dreams was so commonplace that people did not limit themselves to that skill: they also sometimes had to guess what another person had dreamt. Having forgotten a dream he'd had, Nebuchadnezzar ordered his magi to guess it, and threatened them with death if they didn't manage; but the Jew Daniel, a member of the college of magi, saved their lives by guessing what the king's dream had been and interpreting it.* This story and many others serve to show that the Jews did not prohibit oneiromancy, the science of dreams.

SUPERSTITION

Chapter taken from Cicero, Seneca, and Plutarch

ALMOST everything that goes beyond worship of the Supreme Being and the heart's submission to its eternal order is superstition. It's a particularly dangerous one that associates forgiveness of crimes with certain ceremonies.

> Et nigras mactant pecudes, et manibus divis,
> Inferias mittunt.*

> O faciles nimium qui tristia crimina caedis,
> Fluminea tolli posse putatis aqua!*

You think God will forgive you the murder you've committed if you bathe in a river, if you sacrifice a black sheep, or if someone utters words over you. A second murder will therefore be pardoned for the same price, and a third, and a hundred murders will cost you only a hundred black sheep and a hundred ablutions! Do better, wretched humans: no murder, no black sheep!

What a shameful idea, imagining that a priest of Isis or Cybele playing on cymbals and castanets will reconcile you with the Deity! And what does he think he has, this priest of Cybele, this wandering eunuch who lives off your weaknesses, that entitles him to act as mediator between you and heaven? What patents has he received from God? He takes money off you to mumble these words, and you think that the Being of Beings ratifies this charlatan's words?

There are innocent superstitions: you dance on feast days in honour of Diana or Pomona or some of the secondary gods your calendar is replete with: no problem with that. Dancing is very pleasurable; it's good for the body and delights the soul; it does nobody any harm; but don't get the idea that Pomona or Vertumnus are very grateful to you for hopping around in their honour or that they will punish you if you don't. There's no other Pomona and no other Vertumnus than your gardener's mattock and spade. Don't be so foolish as to believe that hail will flatten your garden if you've failed to dance the pyrrhic or the cordax.

There is a perhaps pardonable superstition, and one that encourages virtue: that's placing among the gods the great men and women who've benefited the human race. It would be better, no doubt, to look upon them simply as people to venerate and above all to try and imitate. Venerate a Solon, a Thales, or a Pythagoras without making it into a cult, but don't worship Hercules for cleaning the Augean stables or sleeping with fifty girls in one night.

Beware above all of establishing a cult for the rascals whose only merit is ignorance, hysteria, and filth and who have taken pride in making a virtue of indolence and beggary; do those who have been useless in life really merit apotheosis after death?

You'll have noticed that the most superstitious epochs have always been those of the most horrible crimes.

TYRANNY

(TYRANNIE)

WE call a tyrant a ruler who knows no law but his own whim, who robs his subjects and then conscripts them to go and rob his neighbours. There are no such tyrants in Europe.

Tyranny can be practised by an individual or by a group. Group tyranny would be when a body takes over the rights of other bodies and acts despotically through laws it has perverted. There is no example of this in Europe either.

What kind of tyranny would you like to live under? None; but if I had to choose, I would detest the tyranny of one person less than the tyranny of many. A despot does have his good moments, an assembly of despots never. If a tyrant does me an injustice, I can disarm him through his mistress, confessor, or page; but a company of heavy-weight tyrants is impervious to all forms of seduction. When it's not unjust it is at least harsh, and never does anyone any favours.

If I have only one despot I'm able, depending on the custom of the country, to get away with flattening myself against a wall when I see him pass by, or with bowing low, or with striking the ground with my forehead; but if there is a company of a hundred despots I run the risk of having to repeat this performance a hundred times a day, which can in the end be very tiresome if one's knees are no longer very supple. If I'm a tenant farmer and a great lord is my neighbour, I soon get squashed; if I sue one of his relatives, I soon get ruined. So what's to be done? I fear that in this world you have either to be the hammer or the anvil; happy the person who manages to avoid being either!

TOLERATION

(TOLÉRANCE)

WHAT is toleration? It is the prerogative of humanity. We're all steeped in error and weakness; let's forgive each other our follies; that's the first law of nature.

When the Zoroastrian, the Hindu, the Jew, the Muslim, the Mandarin, the Brahman, the Greek Orthodox, the Roman Catholic, the Protestant, and the Quaker all conduct business together in the trading exchanges of Amsterdam, London, Surat, or Basra, they won't pull knives on each other in order to win over souls to their faith.* So why have we been slitting each other's throats virtually without pause since the first council of Nicaea?

Constantine began by issuing a decree permitting all forms of religious worship; he ended up persecuting people. Before him Christians were attacked only because they were beginning to form a party within the state. The Romans permitted all cults, even those of the Jews and the Egyptians for whom they had nothing but contempt. Why was Rome so tolerant? It was because neither the Egyptians nor the Jews sought to destroy the ancient religion of the empire and did not run around the world proselytizing; they only thought about making money whereas, without question, the Christians wanted their religion to be the dominant one. The Jews didn't want the statue of Jupiter in Jerusalem, but the Christians didn't want it in the capitol. St Thomas is honest enough to admit that if the Christians did not unseat the emperors, it was because they couldn't. Their opinion was that the whole earth had to be Christian. So until it was converted they were necessarily the enemies of the whole earth.

Amongst themselves, on all points of controversy, they were each other's worst enemy. First of all, should Jesus be seen as God? Those who said no were anathematized as Ebionites who, in turn, anathematized the worshippers of Jesus.

When some of them wanted all property to be held in common, as they claimed it had been in the apostles' time, their adversaries called them Nicolaitans and accused them of the most awful crimes. When others aspired to a mystical form of devotion they were called

Gnostics and pilloried mercilessly. When Marcion questioned the Trinity he was called an idolater.

Before Constantine Tertullian, Praxeas, Origen, Novatus, Novatian, Sabellius, and Donatus were all persecuted by their brothers, and Constantine had hardly established Christianity as the dominant religion when the Athanasians and the Eusebians started tearing each other to pieces, and since then the Christian church has been bathed in blood right up to our own day.

The Jewish people were, I admit, a rather barbarous lot, massacring without pity all the inhabitants of an unhappy little country over which they had no more right than they had over Paris or London. Nevertheless when Naaman was cured of leprosy after jumping three times into the River Jordan, and when he wanted to thank Elisha for letting him in on the secret, he told him that out of gratitude he would worship the god of the Jews but reserved the right to worship the god of his king as well. He asked Elisha's permission to do this and the prophet had no hesitation in agreeing.* The Jews worshipped their god, but they took it for granted that other people would have their own gods. They thought it right that Chemosh should give a particular district to the Moabites as long as their god gave them one too. Jacob did not hesitate to marry the daughters of an idolater. Laban had his god as Jacob had his.* Those are examples of toleration on the part of the cruellest and most intolerant in all antiquity; we've imitated them in their absurd fits of rage, but not in their leniency.

It's clear that anyone who persecutes a man, his brother, because he does not share his opinion, is a monster. That goes without saying. But the government! The judiciary! The rulers! How will they act towards those whose faith is different from their own? If they are powerful foreigners, a prince will certainly make a pact with them. The 'Most Christian' King François I of France allied himself with the Muslims against the 'Most Catholic' Emperor Charles V, and in support of their struggle against the emperor he gave the German Lutherans money. But, as custom required, he started off by having Lutherans burned at the stake in France: he paid them in Saxony out of realpolitik, and out of realpolitik he had them burned in Paris. But what happened? Persecution creates proselytes. France was soon full of new Protestants. At first they let themselves be hanged; then they started hanging people themselves. There were civil wars. Then came the St Bartholomew Massacre, and that part of the world was soon worse than anything the ancients and moderns had ever said about hell.

Idiots! You've never been capable of offering a pure form of worship to the God who made you. Wretches! The example of the Zoroastrian Parsees, Chinese scholars, Noahides, and all the sages has never been able to guide you. Monsters! You need superstition as the crow needs carrion. If it's been said once it's been said a thousand times: if there are two religions in your country their adherents will be at each other's throats; if you have thirty they will live in peace.* Look at the Sultan: he rules over Zoroastrians, Hindus, Greek Orthodox Christians, Nestorians, and Romans. The first person who tries to stir things up is impaled, so everything is calm and tranquil.

VIRTUE
(VERTU)

WHAT is virtue? Doing good to your neighbour. Can I call virtue anything other than what does me good? I'm needy, you're generous. I'm in danger, you come to my assistance. I'm being deceived, you tell me the truth. I'm being neglected and you comfort me. I'm ignorant and you teach me. I'll happily call you virtuous. But what will become of the cardinal and theologal virtues? Some will stay in the schools.

What concern is it of mine whether you're temperate? You're just following medical advice; you'll feel the better for it, and I congratulate you. You have faith and hope, and I'm even happier for you: they will grant you eternal life. Your theologal virtues are heavenly gifts; your cardinal virtues are excellent qualities that will serve to guide you through life:* but they're not virtues as far as your neighbour is concerned. Wise individuals do themselves good; virtuous people do good to all of human kind. St Paul was right in telling you that charity is greater than faith and hope.*

What? Are the only acceptable virtues those that are useful to one's neighbour? How can it be otherwise? We live in society; so there is nothing truly good for us except what also does society good. A hermit will be sober and pious; he'll wear a hair shirt: well, he'll be made into a saint; but I won't call him 'virtuous' until he's done something virtuous that's of benefit to others. As long as he lives alone he's neither benevolent nor malevolent: he's nothing to us. If St Bruno got families to bury the hatchet, if he succoured the needy, he was virtuous; if he fasted and prayed in solitude, he was a saint. Virtue among human beings is the reciprocal exchange of benefits; those who take no part in it do not count. If this saint were in the world he would no doubt do good there; but as long as he isn't, the world will be right to deny him the accolade 'virtuous'; he will be good only for himself, not us.

But, you'll say, if a hermit is a glutton, a drunkard, and given to self-abuse in secret, he's vicious; and he's virtuous if he has the opposite qualities. I can't agree with that; he's a very unappealing person if he has the faults you mention; but in relation to society he's not vicious, wicked, and ripe for punishment, because his vile activities do it no harm. We may presume that if he rejoins society he *will* do harm, and even engage in criminal activity; the likelihood that he'll be a bad man is a lot greater than the likelihood that the other temperate and chaste hermit will be a good one; for in society faults increase and good qualities diminish.

A far stronger objection would be that Nero, Pope Alexander VI, and other monsters of that ilk did quite a few good deeds; I'd answer boldly that on those particular days they were indeed virtuous.

Some theologians say that the divine emperor, Antoninus,* wasn't virtuous; that he was an unrepentant Stoic who, not content with governing people, wanted to be admired by them too; that he drew some personal benefit from the good he did humanity; that he was all his life just, hard-working, and benevolent merely out of vanity, and that his virtues served only to deceive people: to which I reply, 'Heavens above, let's have many more such scoundrels!'

APPENDIX

TWO PORTRAITS OF VOLTAIRE IN 1764

By 1764 the 70-year-old Voltaire had become the most famous living writer in Europe. Travellers flocked to visit him at his château at Ferney, near Geneva, and many left lengthy records of their meeting.[1] The following two accounts, the first by John Morgan (1735–89), an American traveller and physician, and the second by James Boswell (1740–95), then aged 24, were both written in 1764, immediately following the publication in July of the *Pocket Philosophical Dictionary*. Neither writer mentions the *Dictionary* by name; but both are evidently aware of the work's sulphurous reputation, and they meticulously record Voltaire's every pronouncement on religion.

1. *Dr John Morgan*[2]

[16 September 1764]

Château de Fernay. Sunday, the 16th.—After dinner went to the Château de Fernay—distant about an hour's ride from town to pay our respects to Monsieur Voltaire to whom we had a letter from Mr Wm. Huet an English gentleman whom we knew at Rome.

His château as we observed it in driving into the courtyard appears new—a double house, sufficiently large to contain a great family, being three storeys high and neat with a chapel on one side of the courtyard in front, and the other which is the side by which we enter some round turrets,— which give more the air of a castle—the front side to the road being shut up. As for his theatre I did not see it to know it, being as I suppose on one side of the hall or room before the hall by which we enter from the courtyard.

Our coach having drove into the yard up to the door, Monsieur Voltaire himself received us on the steps. Having delivered him our recommendatory letter, this wrote in French yet from the characters of the superscription he knew it to come from an Englishman, and therefore addressed us in English. For the present he only looked at the beginning of the letter to learn our names and at the bottom to see who it came from. This was in the antechamber.

[1] See G. de Beer and A.-M. Rousseau, *Voltaire's British Visitors*, SVEC 49 (1967).

[2] *The Journal of Dr John Morgan of Philadelphia from the City of Rome to the City of London 1764* (Philadelphia, 1907), 216–29. Republished in G. R. de Beer, 'John Morgan's Visit to Voltaire', *Notes and Records of the Royal Society of London*, 10 (1953), 148–58; and in T. Besterman's edition of Voltaire's *Correspondence* (D12089). The text has been lightly modernized.

His reception of us was very polite. He asked why we had not come out time enough to dine with him, and why we made any difficulties, for says he, you know gentlemen that sitting together at table opens the heart and makes one more sprightly and sociable. Although at a loss sometimes for an English word, and that he used many Gallecisms, yet he took pains to articulate his words properly and accent them fully. In this he succeeded beyond what one might expect from his having been but one twelve month in England and that so many years past as in 1726. We meet with few Frenchmen who pronounce English better.

Our apology for not having come time enough to dine with him being made, he then ushered us into his salle, and introduced us to a polite Company there of gentlemen and ladies, in terms peculiar to himself. He addressed himself more particularly to a Chevalier whom we could see was a military man, and an officer of distinction, and whom we afterwards learnt from Mr Voltaire himself was the Count de Beaufremont, who was a Commodore last war, and brother to the Prince de Beaufremont in Franche Compté as well of one of the best families as one of the best officers in France.

His introduction of us was to this effect:

I beg leave to present to you two English gentlemen—O glorious nation, renowned conquerors of Canada. Though they have fought against you, and well have they fought battles by land and sea, we must now look upon them as our brave friends, since we are now at peace.

To this we replied that we hoped this peace might be lasting, that we might always regard one another in the same light of friendship. Then Monsieur Voltaire introduced us more particularly by name; we received and returned compliments with mutual respect.

Mr Voltaire then said he was very well acquainted with a gentleman of the name of Morgan* when in England in the Year 1726. Mr Beaufremont said there was a colonel of the name on the expedition against Martineco and the Havannah.* I told them that the latter was dead; that there were many of the name in England, and I could not say particularly that I knew the one Mr Voltaire meant. They replied they had often heard of the name and both of them said there was a General Morgan, Governor of Bergenopzoom, an officer of great reputation. This now indeed 200 years since his time.

A dish of coffee being presented to us, the conversation turned upon the places we had lately visited in Italy—Upon Naples, the famine and epidemical disease which lately reigned there—Upon the discoveries made at the Herculaneum etc.

A little dog happening to cross the room stopped before Mr Voltaire, wagged his tail and seemed to notice him very attentively—on which

Mr Voltaire turned to Mr Powel, and as I thought a little abruptly asked him, what think you of that little dog? Has he a soul or not, and what do the people in England now think of the soul?* This question so unexpected and before company some of whom Mr Powel was very sure at least of Mr Voltaire, that they entertained sentiments concerning the soul very different from himself and the bulk of mankind who have been taught at all to reason about the soul, was a little startled at this question put so mal a propos. To show that he was not desirous of enlarging upon this topic, his answer was that the people of England now as well as heretofore entertained very different notions from each other concerning the soul. Very true says Monsieur Beaufremont, everybody thinks after his own fashion.

Mr Voltaire however did not drop the subject entirely—says he I esteem one of your countrymen who has wrote on that subject, my Lord Bolinbroke.* He has done essential service to mankind, but there would have been still greater had he given the same matter in fewer words. Of these he is so profuse that he frequently renders the subject he handles obscure from being too copious in his expression. Have you not read this valuable author? Another question as little to Mr Powel's goût as the former—But without hesitation he told him what appeared to me sufficiently spirited—Whatever his merit may be I own I have never read him. Oh read him by all means—He is a most valuable author and let me recommend to you when you return home to get some of your friends to give an abridgement of it. It will bear to be reduced to a third of its bulk and then it will be a most excellent work.

The English added he have some fine authors, they are I swear by God himself, the first nation in Europe, and if ever I smell of a Resurrection, or come a second time on Earth, I will pray God to make me be born in England, the land of Liberty. These are four things which I adore that the English boast of so greatly—with his forefinger of the right hand counting them up, and naming each distinctly and with an emphasis—*Liberty, Property, Newton and Locke*.

Although he then spoke in English the Count de Beaufremont seemed to understand him. They tell me says he that the English have not even a word in their language which answers to the French word esclavage so little have they an idea of its state. I beg your pardon says Mr Voltaire; they speak of it in the way of opposition—English liberty and French slavery or servitude.

Here a pause ensued. To avoid being hooked in to any seeming dispute about the soul etc, I had from time to time addressed myself to a young looking gentleman who sat next me on indifferent matters, perhaps two or three and twenty years old—though all the while very attentive to what passed.

I had now time to look a little about me, and observe the company and place I was in a little more particularly.

As for Mr Voltaire himself as I have a good print of him I shall not describe him very particularly. He begins now to stoop with years or care, is thin, meagre and if straight I believe would be about five feet ten inches high. Has a very sagacious but at the same time comical look. Something satirical and very lively in his action, of which he is full as most of his nation are. His words which are very emphatical seem to be accompanied with an action little less so.

Count de Beaufremont is a well looking jolly fat man, appears under fifty, of a good appearance for an officer, one that seems to claim respect from deserving it.

Near him in one corner sat a fat French lady middle-aged*—well painted. She did not talk much, though she seemed one of the family. Her discourse seemed to be chiefly confined to a gentleman in a white broadcloth suit and silver lace, who seemed to repay her with the whole of his attention, he not bestowing a great deal on the company.

In a diagonal corner on an easy settee were placed also a middling aged but meagre French lady well smeared with paint. She did not want for discourse—at her left hand at the same settee was a younger lady perhaps aged 20, and Mr Voltaire on her right—the young gentleman with whom I conversed sometimes sat between him and myself, and Mr Powel to my right hand. These were the personages and such the arrangement of our goodly company.

The salle was elegantly adorned and had some tolerable paintings, one indeed better executed than the rest was a Mars seeming to have rose from the bed of Venus but giving her a close parting salute. His left arm supporting the weight of her body but pressing her swelling breast she turned to the right embraces him closely, whilst he gives her the parting kiss. His helmet and plume are behind him—a pair of billing doves fluttering their wings on the bed of Venus. The windows of his room which I sat just opposite to look into a fine garden. Mr Voltaire perhaps observing my eyes that way, asked do you love Greenwich gentlemen—do you love Richmond; upon answering in the affirmative says he I will show you these places.

He conducted us into the garden, and pointing to the lake of Geneva within about half a league or perhaps a little more—there says he is the Thames—and there is Richmond Hills, showing us the hills of Savoy beyond the lake—and these vineyards all round this garden and the verdant lawns are Greenwich. You see I am quite in the English taste. Look at the woods; there you see a road in the woods another in the vineyard—In the garden you have plain gravel walks or green lawns—no French gewgaws— All is after Nature.

We congratulated him upon the happiness of his situation, the judgement he had shown in the choice of his residence and the pleasing happy arrangement he had given to everything about. He prided himself in having ordered everything himself, from the building of the château to the disposition of the garden—all the gravel of the walks he had himself caused to be brought here.

I have says he six miles in circuit here, and am lord of a greater extent than the neighbouring republic of Geneva—I pay no taxes to the French king or any other—I enjoy liberty and property here and am my own master.

We told him his situation was, what it really is, most charming; and that no doubt he must have enjoyed a particular pleasure in seeing a kind of second creation rise under his hands.

Where my château is, says he, there were churches and chapels. I bought all and pulled them down to build my château. I hate churches and priests and masses. You gentlemen have been in Italy—You have been at Rome. Has not your blood often boiled to see shoescrapers and porters saying mass at a place where once a Cicero or Cato and a Scipio have thundered in eloquent harangues to the Roman people.

His soul seemed to be moved with indignation whilst he spoke it, and he accompanied this with a vehemence of action that showed to what a degree he abhorred masses and the religious.

How often when one would go fast do these fellows detain you says he. If you ask where is the postillion he is gone to mass, and you must wait with patience for half an hour till he has done.

By this time I became quite familiar with him, asked him questions with as much assurance as if I had been long acquainted with him—I asked him if he had read any accounts of electricity or was acquainted with Dr Franklin's writings* on that subject—and what he thought of him. He acknowledged him to be the discoverer and improver of electricity, that he was a man of genius of merit and a great natural philosopher.

I then asked him if he had read Mr Hume's writings or Doctor Robertson's History of Scotland as he said he often read English books.*

He told me he had, that both were men of merit, but he preferred Mr Hume, whom he said wrote more like a philosopher. He has given us a good History of England. It is not so full of minute facts as that of Rapin,* who smells indeed of the Presbyterian whilst Mr Hume throughout smells of the philosopher. He often used the word smell of, figuratively for the partake of. I know not whether it was because he delighted in the sense of smelling particularly, or for want of words to express himself better in English.

He now pulled out of his pocket a snuff box. In taking a pinch of snuff,

I observed in the inside of the lid a miniature picture of the King of Prussia, which probably was presented to him by that monarch at the time Voltaire was so great a favourite of his, and his chief counsellor.

In speaking of an intended new publication upon the history of a time which has been often wrote on he inveighed against writing on trite subjects where the author had it not in his power to bring new facts to the light or publish some new discoveries that are important and interesting— Above all authors I admire Newton and Locke—These opened our eyes to glorious objects and immortal discoveries which we did not think of.

One has dissected and laid open to us the planetary system; the other has, as I may say, dissected the soul and discovered to us all the powers of the understanding. On my knees I prostrate myself all my life before two such great men as these; to whom I esteem myself as an infant.

I then asked who Monsieur Beaufremont was. He told me of him what I wrote above.

I then asked him if the young gentleman whom I had sat next to was his son, as I had heard him call him papa; and who the young lady was.

He answered me the young lady I call my daughter,* because she was a poor orphan neglected niece of the deceased great Corneille—every nation you know has its Shakespeare—Corneille was our French Shakespeare— (because I look on myself as a soldier under the generals Corneille, Racine etc in this sort of warfare), I found out the niece of Corneille and brought her to live with me. I call her my daughter and have married her to that young man. Their children I look on as if they were my own, and take care of them all as of my own family.

Being now time to return to Geneva lest the gates of the city should be shut against us, we thanked him in the politest terms for the honour he had done us. He returned the compliment, said he should always be proud to entertain English gentlemen. Being now at the steps he ushered us in, breaking into a kind of rapture with —

'Oh Goddess Liberty; thou heaven born maid.'*

We were now within the salle, and Monsieur Voltaire as if he had been pleased with our conversation and the freedom we used with him—cries out in French to this effect—addressing himself to the company.

Behold two amiable young men, lovers of truth and inquirers into Nature. They are not satisfied with mere appearance, they love investigation and truth, and despise superstition—I command you gentlemen—go on love truth and search diligently after it. Hate hypocrisy, the masses and above all hate the priests.

Compliments being over we left the company. Monsieur Voltaire accompanied us to the door, told us he should always be proud to see us, particularly whenever we would call and dine with him; his hour was two o'clock; he would be glad to see us, and if his health permitted would dine with us but if not, his children, (meaning his adopted ones) would take care of us, nor should we ever want for company at his house who would endeavour to make themselves agreeable. We returned our thanks once more in the warmest terms, and getting into the chariot drove off.

I could not help noticing a chapel before the gate of the courtyard with this inscription over the door:

Deo
Erexit
Voltaire*
MDCCLXI

I afterwards heard that in buying this possession he was obliged to stipulate for building a chapel—of which I suppose no great use is made. Till I heard this I did not know whether it was not his theatre.

In a tavern on the road not far off these lines are penciled:

Deo erexit Voltaire
Behold the pious work of Vain Voltaire.
Who never knew a God, or said a prayer.

II. *James Boswell*[3]

Château de Ferney, 28 December 1764

My dear Temple,
[…]
And whence do I now write to you, my friend? From the château of Monsieur de Voltaire. I had a letter for him from a Swiss colonel at The Hague. I came hither Monday and was presented to him. He received me with dignity and that air of a man who has been much in the world which a Frenchman acquires in perfection. I saw him for about half an hour before dinner. He was not in spirits. Yet he gave me some brilliant sallies. He did not dine with us, and I was obliged to post away immediately after dinner, because the gates of Geneva shut before five and Ferney is a good hour from town. I was by no means satisfied to have been so little time with the monarch of French literature. A happy scheme sprung up in my adventurous mind. Madame Denis, the niece of Monsieur de Voltaire, had been

[3] *Boswell on the Grand Tour: Germany and Switzerland 1764*, ed. F. A. Pottle (London, 1953), 282–9.

extremely good to me. She is fond of our language. I wrote her a letter in English begging her interest to obtain for me the privilege of lodging a night under the roof of Monsieur de Voltaire, who, in opposition to our sun, rises in the evening. I was in the finest humour and my letter was full of wit. I told her, 'I am a hardy and a vigorous Scot. You may mount me to the highest and coldest garret. I shall not even refuse to sleep upon two chairs in the bedchamber of your maid. I saw her pass through the room where we sat before dinner.' I sent my letter on Tuesday by an express. It was shown to Monsieur de Voltaire, who with his own hand wrote this answer in the character of Madame Denis: 'You will do us much honour and pleasure. We have few beds. But you will (*shall*) not sleep on two chairs. My uncle, though very sick, hath guessed your merit. I know it better; for I have seen you longer.' Temple, I am your most obedient. How do you find yourself? Have you got such a thing as an old friend in this world? Is he to be valued or is he not?

I returned yesterday to this enchanted castle. The magician appeared a very little before dinner. But in the evening he came into the drawing room in great spirits. I placed myself by him. I touched the keys in unison with his imagination. I wish you had heard the music. He was all brilliance. He gave me continued flashes of wit. I got him to speak English, which he does in a degree that made me now and then start up and cry, "Upon my soul this is astonishing!" When he talked our language he was animated with the soul of a Briton. He had bold flights. He had humour. He had an extravagance; he had a forcible oddity of style that the most comical of our *dramatis personae* could not have exceeded. He swore bloodily, as was the fashion when he was in England. He hummed a ballad; he repeated nonsense. Then he talked of our Constitution with a noble enthusiasm. I was proud to hear this from the mouth of an illustrious Frenchman. At last we came upon religion. Then did he rage. The company went to supper. Monsieur de Voltaire and I remained in the drawing room with a great Bible before us; and if ever two mortal men disputed with vehemence, we did. Yes, upon that occasion he was one individual and I another. For a certain portion of time there was a fair opposition between Voltaire and Boswell. The daring bursts of his ridicule confounded my understanding. He stood like an orator of ancient Rome. Tully was never more agitated than he was. He went too far. His aged frame trembled beneath him. He cried, 'Oh, I am very sick; my head turns round,' and he let himself gently fall upon an easy chair. He recovered. I resumed our conversation but changed the tone. I talked to him serious and earnest. I demanded of him an honest confession of his real sentiments. He gave it me with candour and with a mild eloquence which touched my heart. I did not believe him capable of thinking in the manner that he declared to me was 'from the bottom of his heart'. He expressed his veneration—his love—of the Supreme Being, and his entire resignation to the will of Him who is All-Wise. He expressed his desire to resemble the Author of Goodness by being good himself. His sentiments go no farther. He does not inflame his mind with grand hopes of the immortality of the soul. He says it may be, but knows nothing of it. And his mind is in perfect tranquillity. I was moved; I was sorry. I doubted his sincerity. I called to him with emotion, 'Are you sincere? Are you really sincere?' He answered, 'Before God, I am.' Then with the fire of him whose tragedies have so often shone on the theatre of Paris, he said: 'I suffer much. But I suffer with patience and resignation; not as a Christian—but as a man.'

Temple, was not this an interesting scene? Would a journey from Scotland to Ferney have been too much to obtain such a remarkable interview? I have given you the great lines. The whole conversation of the evening is fully recorded, and I look upon it as an invaluable treasure. One day the public shall have it. It is a present highly worthy of their attention. I told Monsieur de Voltaire that I had written eight quarto pages of what he had said. He smiled and seemed pleased. Our important scene must not appear till after his death. But I have a great mind to send over to London a little sketch of my reception at Ferney, of the splendid manner in which Monsieur de Voltaire lives, and of the brilliant conversation of this celebrated author at the age of seventy-two.* The sketch would be a letter, addressed to you, full of gaiety and full of friendship. I would send it to one of the best public papers or magazines. But this is probably a flight of my over-heated mind. I shall not send the sketch unless you approve of my doing so.

[...]

Temple, this is a noble letter. Fare you well, my ever dear friend.

                                                                    James Boswell

————

EXPLANATORY NOTES

All modern editions of this text are indebted to the magisterial edition directed by Christiane Mervaud and published by the Voltaire Foundation in 1994 (see Select Bibliography). Readers are referred to this edition for a full account of sources. The notes which follow confine themselves to indicating Voltaire's principal sources; the headnotes to each section set out the broad polemical orientation of each article. Translations of Latin passages in the text have in most cases been taken from the edition of the Loeb Classical Library.

ABRAHAM

Voltaire opens with a withering attack on the historical veracity of the Old Testament. Abraham, first of the patriarchs of Israel, is a good place to begin, since he occupies an important place in Muslim legend as well as in the Jewish and Christian traditions. See Genesis 11–20; Qur'an 2: 127. Voltaire read the Qur'an in French translation, and also in the scholarly English translation of George Sale.

SOUL

Now Voltaire turns to a central tenet of Christian belief: to deny the immateriality of the soul was equivalent, in the eighteenth-century mind, to denying the existence of God. Voltaire had begun this flirtation with atheism in the *Letters concerning the English Nation* (Letter 13, 'On Locke'). As elsewhere, Voltaire emphasizes the limits of our knowledge, and the importance therefore of scepticism. The new emphasis here is on the Old Testament and its failure to speak of the immortality of the soul; modern theological debate according such importance to this article of faith is, he implies, a more recent development. His main sources in the present article are the article 'Âme' by the Abbé Yvon in the *Encyclopédie*, and Dom Calmet's 'Dissertation sur la nature de l'âme'. See E. D. James, 'Voltaire on the Nature of the Soul', *French Studies*, 32 (1978), 20–33.

FRIENDSHIP

This meditation on friendship is inspired by Aristotle (*Nicomachean Ethics*, 8. 3–5). Voltaire emphasizes man's fundamental sociability, something shared, he suggests, by Arabs as well as Greeks. The implication is that religion divides and pulls against man's inner (better) instincts.

LOVE

After friendship, love. Citing examples from Virgil to the Earl of Rochester, love is portrayed as a power of nature, common to all cultures. Voltaire does not need to allude to the fact that the Christian religion (in particular) had encouraged fear of sex. Taking pleasure in pleasure is a creed of the Enlightenment. After the idyll of love, Voltaire moves from the sublime to the ridiculous, and recounts the history of venereal disease. He follows the theory of the doctor Jean Astruc, *Traité des maladies vénériennes* (1740), that the disease originated in Haiti (in French, Saint-Domingue). He had already had fun with the genealogy of syphilis in *Candide* (ch. 4). The example serves the same function here, to make us question the idea that God has created 'the best of all possible worlds', another allusion to *Candide*.

18 *'Love is the same everywhere'*: Virgil, *Georgics*, 3. 244.

'*in a land of atheists . . . Almighty*': Voltaire condenses ten lines from Rochester's 'A letter from Artemisia in the town to Chloe in the country' (lines 40–9), so as to recast them in his own concise voice: 'Love, the most generous passion of the mind, | The softest refuge innocence can find, | The safe director of unguided youth, | Fraught with kind wishes, and secured by truth; | That cordial drop heaven in our cup has thrown | To make the nauseous draught of life go down; | On which one only blessing; God might raise | In lands of atheists, subsidies of praise, | For none did e'er so dull and stupid prove | But felt a god, and blessed his power in love [. . .].'

19 *Nam facit . . . vitam . . . bk. V*: 'For at times a woman may bring it about by her own doing, by her yielding ways, and the neat adornment of her body, that she accustoms you easily to live your life with her' (Lucretius, *De Rerum Natura*, 4 (not 5). 1280–2, trans. Cyril Bailey).

Rabelais dedicated his book to: in the prologue to *Gargantua*, Rabelais dedicates his work to you 'most famous drinkers, and you, most precious syphilitics'.

LOVE CALLED SOCRATIC LOVE

Homosexuality poses a problem for Voltaire (who may himself have been bisexual). On the one hand he wants to believe that we can find ethical values 'naturally' within ourselves (so that we do not need to look to the Bible for guidance). On the other hand, nature, in this case, seems to include something which he finds 'unnatural'. So he suggests that this is an aberration which youths can grow out of, and he uses historical arguments to say that in other cases the phenomenon has been misunderstood. Voltaire has fun with the salacious examples; but the subject perhaps shows his own limitations as an Enlightenment thinker.

20 *misunderstanding comes to an end*: the idea seems to come from Lucretius (*De Rerum Natura*, 4. 1052–5), and from a passage adjacent to the passage which he quoted in the previous article.

Citraque . . . flores: '[Orpheus] was the first of the Thracian people to transfer his love to young boys, and enjoy their brief springtime, and early flowering, this side of manhood' (Ovid, *Metamorphoses*, 10. 84–5, trans. A. S. Kline).

21 *Thou shalt . . . chin*: verses quoted by Plutarch in his *Dialogue on Love*, ch. 5.

Amplector hunc et illam: 'I embrace each one of them' (Théodore de Bèze, *Epigrammata*, 90), that is to say, both Audebert (the poet's male friend) and Candida (the poet's mistress).

as well he ought: Plutarch, *Dialogue on Love*, ch. 4.

SELF-LOVE

Seventeenth-century writers, like La Rochefoucauld, had been critical of the consequences of *amour-propre*. Voltaire, following Pope, here seeks to defend self-interest as a natural human attribute.

ANGEL

Voltaire shows that the idea of an angel is common to many religions and cultures. By an amusing accumulation of detail from different traditions, he relativizes—and ridicules—the Christian version of these myths. Voltaire takes most of the information in this article from Dom A. Calmet, *Commentaire littéral sur tous les livres de l'Ancien et du Nouveau Testament*, and his 'Dissertation sur les bons et les mauvais anges'. The Benedictine Dom Calmet is one of Voltaire's major sources of biblical erudition (and a contant source of mockery); his *Commentaire littéral* in twenty-three volumes appeared in 1707–16, his *Dictionnaire de la Bible* in four volumes in 1722–8.

25 *nine hierarchies or orders*: the omission of 'les principautés' from the 1764 text means that this list does not add up to nine.

CANNIBALS

Voltaire had long been interested in the phenomenon of cannibalism: he treats it comically in *Candide*. The existence of cannibals allows him to reflect on the nature of civilized man. His examples, in particular Juvenal, are hardly original; Voltaire contents himself with well-known classical references. Interestingly, he does not seem to use Montaigne's celebrated essay 'On Cannibals' (*Essais*, 1. 31), although he quotes Montaigne later, at the end of 'Limits of Human Intelligence' (p. 50).

26 *flesh of their compatriots*: Juvenal, *Satires*, 15.

privilege: Voltaire has a good memory: he had already recounted the same story to Frederick the Great in a letter of 15 October 1737 (D1376).

27 *candles from their tallow*: Voltaire has a source in John Temple, *The Irish Rebellion* (1646): but he has in effect invented this anecdote.

APIS

The wisdom of the ancient Egyptians had been a commonplace in the seventeenth century (for example in Bossuet's *Histoire universelle*). Voltaire, like

others in the eighteenth century, questions this: he is relying on Rollin's *Histoire
ancienne* (1730–8), whose source is Herodotus (*Histories*, 3. 28–9).

APOCALYPSE

This article is not primarily the work of Voltaire: for the most part, he is repro-
ducing a clandestine manuscript by the Calvinist Firmin Abauzit. Voltaire's
work consists in abridging the original text and in adding a few details of his
own. Abauzit's manuscript was published a few years later, in 1770, under the
title *Discours sur l'Apocalypse*. See M. Waterman, 'Voltaire and Firmin Abauzit',
Romanic Review, 33 (1942), 236–49. 'Apocalypse' is an alternative title of the
Book of Revelation. This article, which subjects biblical commentary to the
criterion of 'solid proof', with predictably amusing results, fits perfectly with
the style and tone of Voltaire's 'original' articles elsewhere in the volume.

  30 *Book of Revelation*: Newton's *Observations upon the Prophecies of Daniel
     and the Apocalypse of St John* were published posthumously in 1733. John
     Maynard Keynes remarked that 'Newton was not the first of the age of
     reason, he was the last of the magicians'.

ATHEIST, ATHEISM

Voltaire shows with many historical examples that the term 'atheist' is often
used merely as a term of abuse and a means of attacking dissenting thinkers
(like himself). He opposes atheism here, but on strictly pragmatic grounds:
religion is 'useful' in a civilized society, it is 'essential' that we believe in a
Supreme Being. This is a utilitarian argument for deism (and leaves wide open
the intellectual case for atheism).

  31 *malevolence*: Voltaire is not, despite the quotation marks, quoting
     directly; he is paraphrasing Plutarch's *Comparison between Aristophanes
     and Menander*.

  32 *atheism*: Voltaire approves of Michel de L'Hôpital, who in the 1560s was
     responsible for several edicts of toleration in favour of the Protestants.

     '*Homo doctus . . . atheos*': 'A learned man, but a true atheist'. Voltaire gives
     his source; but he may have found the quotation in Bayle's *Dictionnaire*,
     article 'Hospital'.

     Vanini: Lucilio Vanini was an Italian freethinker (1585–1619), who was
     condemned to be strangled at the stake in Toulouse. Voltaire thinks of this
     example all the more readily because of the link between Toulouse and the
     more recent Calas case (see Introduction).

  34 *Pierre Bayle*: Pierre Bayle (1647–1706) was a sceptical philosopher, remem-
     bered for his *Dictionnaire* as well as his *Pensées diverses sur la comète* (1682).

  36 *engraved on everyone's mind*: Voltaire spells out clearly the creed of the deist.

  37 *as a well-known author has said*: Voltaire himself, in an earlier article 'Du
     déisme' (1742).

BAPTISM

Voltaire takes on the sacrament of baptism. In his earlier *Letters concerning the English Nation*, he had shown that Quakers were Christians who did not believe in baptism. Here, he describes 'immersion' as a broader cultural phenomenon; and shows that historically baptism was not the essential article of Christian belief it has since become. Voltaire relies much on Calmet's *Dictionnaire* and on his 'Dissertation sur le baptême' (to arrive at diametrically opposed conclusions).

BEAUTIFUL, BEAUTY

Voltaire emphasizes the relativity of any artistic judgement. He may be replying implicitly to Diderot's article on the same subject in the *Encyclopédie*. The relativism which Voltaire argues for here can of course be applied to other, more controversial, domains.

ANIMALS

Descartes had claimed that animals had no soul. Arguing, on common-sense grounds, that animals do seem to share some of the feelings of man, Voltaire downgrades the uniqueness of man's supposedly immortal soul. This article is about men rather than animals.

42 *Angelic Doctor*: St Thomas Aquinas (1225–74), author of several important commentaries on Aristotle, including *On the Soul*.

say other philosophers: Voltaire relies here on Bayle's *Dictionnaire* (articles 'Rorarius' and 'Sennert').

'Deus est anima brutorum': Voltaire quotes this unidentified philosopher from Bayle's *Dictionnaire* (article 'Rorarius').

GOOD, SOVEREIGN GOOD

The classical idea of the sovereign good had become identified in a certain Christian tradition with God. So this critique of Neoplatonist metaphysics is not principally about ancient philosophy.

43 *Quid dem . . . alter*: 'What am I to put before them? What not? You refuse what your neighbour orders' (Horace, *Epistles*, 2. 2. 63, trans. H. Rushton Fairclough).

Castor . . . Pugnis: 'Castor finds joy in horses; his brother, born from the same egg, in boxing' (Horace, *Satires*, 2. 1. 26–7, trans. H. Rushton Fairclough).

Crantor: the same example (from Sextus Empiricus) is given by the Abbé Yvon in his article 'Bien' in the *Encyclopédie*.

ALL IS GOOD

Voltaire returns to the problem which had recently been at the centre of *Candide* (1759): if God is good, why is there evil in the world? The most popular eighteenth-century answer to this question of theodicy came from Leibniz (*Théodicée*, 1710): what we humans think of as evil is part of some larger good which we cannot grasp. Following Jean-Pierre de Crousaz's *Examen de l'Essai de M. Pope sur l'homme* (1737), Pope's *Essay on Man* was generally seen in the eighteenth century (wrongly, in the modern view) as a vulgarization of the ideas of Leibniz. See Steven Nadler, *The Best of All Possible Worlds: A Story of Philosophers, God, and Evil in the Age of Reason* (Princeton, 2008).

48 *Much is alleged . . . dissolve*: Shaftesbury, *The Moralists* (1709), 1. 3; republished in *Characteristics of Men, Manners, Opinions and Times* (1711). This is Shaftesbury's original, which Voltaire translates accurately.

'God sends not . . . Good': Pope, *Essay on Man*, 4. 114.

49 *Who sees . . . world*: Pope, *Essay on Man*, 1. 86–9. This is Pope's original, which Voltaire translates accurately.

LIMITS OF HUMAN INTELLIGENCE

Voltaire returns to a favourite theme: the need to accept the limits of our understanding. His later *Le Philosophe ignorant* (1766) would make explicit what is implied here: we should remain sceptical and accept the limits of our thinking, because dogmatic opinions lead to intolerance and injustice.

50 *'What do I know?'*: Montaigne, *Essais*, 2. 12.

CHARACTER

People's characters seem fundamentally fixed: the urgings of 'religion and morality' are of little effect faced by the power of nature.

52 *Naturam . . . redibit*: 'You may drive out nature with a pitchfork, yet she will ever hurry back' (Horace, *Epistles*, 1. 10. 24, trans. H. Rushton Fairclough).

CERTAIN, CERTAINTY

This discussion of the different categories of philosophical certainty is an overt reply to the article 'Certitude' in the *Encyclopédie*. The main part of the *Encyclopédie* article is by the Abbé de Prades, but the introduction and conclusion are by Diderot himself, one of the two principal editors of the enterprise. Their article, which extends the question of certainty into the field of religion, quickly became controversial.

53 *I exist, I think, I feel pain*: Voltaire reworks the Cartesian *cogito*, 'I think therefore I am.'

54 *the other writer*: Denis Diderot, who at the end of the article 'Certitude' disingenuously pretends to accept de Prades's criticism of his early *Pensées philosophiques* (1746). (See John Lough, *The Encyclopédie* (London, 1971), 242–3.) Voltaire draws attention here to the narrative games played in the *Encyclopédie* when discussing issues of religious belief—a model, of

course, for Voltaire himself, and a reminder to readers of the present volume that they need to read between the lines.

CHAIN OF EVENTS

Belief in fate, or destiny, limits free will. The seventeenth century had known religious fatalism with the Jansenists: man was doomed to obey the will of God. In the eighteenth century, a materialistic fatalism emerges: events are determined, not by the divine will, but by the relentless sequence of cause and effect, the chain of events: man was doomed to obey the immutable laws of nature. Voltaire is opposed to both forms of fatalism, and here defends free will.

55 *'sufficient reason'*: this expression had been subjected to ridicule in *Candide*.

GREAT CHAIN OF BEING

The concept of the great chain of being implied a hierarchical structure in which all forms of life were part of a continuous structure with God at the pinnacle. The idea has classical roots (Neoplatonist rather than Platonic), and it later became adopted by the Christian world. The concept is defended in the eighteenth century by Leibniz and Pope, but Voltaire is hostile to the idea, because he believes that this theory of the continuity of all beings might lend support to atheism and materialism. See Arthur O. Lovejoy, *The Great Chain of Being: A Study in the History of an Idea* (1936); and William F. Bynum, 'The Great Chain of Being after Forty Years: An Appraisal', *History of Science*, 13 (1975), 1–28.

59 *the Cassiterides*: the British Isles.

HEAVEN IN ANTIQUITY

Classical antiquity produced many poetic images of heaven (and by implication, so did the Bible); none of these poetic conceits stand up to modern scientific scrutiny.

60 *Conversations on the Plurality of Worlds*: Bernard Le Bovier de Fontenelle (1657–1757) published his *Entretiens sur la pluralité des mondes* in 1686; this hugely influential work, in dialogue form, was a model for the intelligent popularization of scientific knowledge. Fontenelle is in some respects a forerunner of Voltaire.

61 *'so that . . . starry skies'*: Ovid, *Metamorphoses*, ll. 151–3.

CIRCUMCISION

With almost exaggerated seriousness—a tone of levity creeps in only at the very end—this article deploys wide-ranging historical scholarship to show that the Jewish rite of circumcision is not unique to that tradition.

64 *Herodotus*: Herodotus, *Histories*, 2. 104.

65 *'curtus Appella'* ... *'credat* ... *Judaei'*: 'the circumcised Apella', 'may the Jew Apella believe it, the circumcised Jew'. Voltaire is rewriting Horace, *Satires*, 1. 9. 69–70 and 1. 5. 100–1.

BODY

A discussion of the philosophy of Bishop Berkeley, whose idealism brackets him with Leibniz. Both systems of belief are dangerous in Voltaire's eyes because they too easily lend themselves to credulous adherence to the unprovable. Even so, Voltaire had read Berkeley in the original English, and his understanding of his immaterialism is arguably more sophisticated than that of his French contemporaries who similarly condemn his ideas; see Sébastien Charles, 'La Figure de Berkeley dans la pensée de Voltaire', *Dix-Huitième Siècle*, 33 (2001), 367–84.

68 *Berkeley's paradox* . . . *refuting*: Voltaire's refutation of Berkeley puts us in mind of Dr Johnson's celebrated response: 'After we came out of the church, we stood talking for some time together of Bishop Berkeley's ingenious sophistry to prove the non-existence of matter, and that every thing in the universe is merely ideal. I observed, that though we are satisfied his doctrine is not true, it is impossible to refute it. I never shall forget the alacrity with which Johnson answered, striking his foot with mighty force against a large stone, till he rebounded from it, "I refute it *thus*" ' (James Boswell, *Life of Johnson*, ed. R. W. Chapman (Oxford World's Classics, 1998), 333).

a long time ago: Voltaire did indeed meet Berkeley, whom he describes in a letter as 'a learned philosopher and delicate wit' (D558). Berkeley had been in Paris in November 1713, as the Earl of Peterborough's chaplain, and he spoke good French. He was in London from 1724 to 1728, at the same time as Voltaire (1726–8).

intellectual world: Berkeley, *Three Dialogues between Hylas and Philonous*. In the following sentence, Voltaire makes a slip: it is Hylas ('matter') who should be responding to Philonous ('lover of spirit'), the spokesman for Berkeley.

a subtle philosopher: Leibniz, whose philosophy Voltaire has been satirizing since *Candide*.

grace versatile: a technical term referring to a form of divine grace which requires human will to be effective. Voltaire makes fun of such theological vocabulary in the article 'Grace'.

ON CHINA

Praise of the antiquity of Chinese civilization serves to relativize the arrogant complacency of the Europeans who believe in their own superiority. In matters of religion, moreover, there are core beliefs which seem common to all civilizations. As with the article 'Chinese Catechism' below, Voltaire is indebted to Du Halde's *Description de la Chine*.

69 *bonzes*: Buddhist priests or monks (especially in China or Japan).

the king of the country: Frederick William I of Prussia, father of Frederick the Great.

70 *Fr. Petau . . . Cumberlands and Whistons*: Denis Pétau, *Opus de Doctrina Temporum* (1627); Richard Cumberland, *Origines Gentium Antiquissimae* (1724); and William Whiston, *A New Theory of the Earth* (1696).

CHINESE CATECHISM

After trailing the idea of deism in 'Atheist, atheism', Voltaire now presents a fuller exposition of the notion in dialogue form, viewed from the defamiliarizing angle of a Chinese prince. The Supreme Being, creator of all things, judges good and evil; the existence of the soul, if not provable, is a useful social construct; happiness is linked with toleration. These precepts, ostensibly from Confucius, are presented as 'the code of all humanity': Christians take note. Voltaire draws much background information from Du Halde, *Description de la Chine*.

78 *the five Jing*: the Five Classics (in Chinese, '*wu jing*') are the five surviving sacred texts (out of the original six) supposedly edited by Confucius; in fact, only the fifth is now thought to be by Confucius. Voltaire takes his information from Du Halde.

79 *Shi-Jing*: the Shi Jing, translated by James Legge as *The Book of Odes*, and by Arthur Waley as *The Book of Songs*, is the earliest existing collection of Chinese poems and songs. Over half of these 305 poems are popular in origin, the remainder being ceremonial. The collection constitutes the first of the Five Classics (see previous note).

'the mountain . . . fertile mountains': a rewriting of Psalm 67:16.

81 *talapoin*: a small monkey or a Buddhist monk: Voltaire relishes the word's double meaning.

THE JAPANESE'S CATECHISM

As in W. S. Gilbert's *Mikado*, Japan stands here for England: Voltaire revisits the parallel existence of differing beliefs which he had earlier described in the first seven letters of his *Letters concerning the English Nation*. A dispute about the fatuity of religious disputes, viewed from the safe distance of Japan, and with religious dogmas translated into recipes. Voltaire refers to various religious groups using a series of slightly distorted names: the effect is comic and defamiliarizing: Hopsbis (bishops), Brew-he (Hebrew), Pispats (Papists), Therlu (Luther), Vincal (Calvin), Baptistanas (Anabaptists), Quekars (Quakers), Diests (Deists).

86 *thumb and first two fingers*: an allusion to the relationship between England and the Papacy before the rupture caused by Henry VIII.

a woman: Henry VIII's divorce from Catherine of Aragon and marriage to

Anne Boleyn in 1533 caused a breach with the Pope, and the beginning of
the breaking of the power of the Catholic Church in England.

86 *nearly two centuries*: an allusion to the struggles within the Church of
England.

87 *chef they like best*: this recalls Letter 5 of the *Letters concerning the English
Nation*, on the Church of England: 'England is properly the country of
sectarists. [. . .] An *Englishman*, as one to whom liberty is natural, may
go to heaven his own way' (*Letters concerning the English Nation*, Oxford
World's Classics, 26).

88 *smash into each other*: Voltaire had discussed the Quakers in positive terms
in the first four letters of the *Letters concerning the English Nation*.

89 *Recina . . . crazed*: Recina refers to the Jansenist Louis Racine, son of the
great seventeenth-century tragedian Jean Racine. The quotation is from
his religious poem *La Grâce* (1720), 4. 122–4. But Voltaire has distorted
the quotation, changing 'England' into 'Japan'. In the original poem,
Louis Racine, who died in January 1763, was criticizing religious toleration in England.

laws of Nature: an allusion to the scientific discoveries of Newton, which Voltaire had earlier described, first in the *Letters concerning the English Nation*
(Letters 14–17), and then in his *Éléments de la philosophie de Newton* (1738).

'*God . . . general laws*': a version of Pope, *Essay on Man*, ll. 145–6.

THE PRIEST'S CATECHISM

In this dialogue, Theotimus ('he who honours god') explains the role of the
enlightened priest, to encourage practical good and not to waste time on
abstract matters of theological dispute of no practical interest to his parishioners. Voltaire may be responding indirectly to Rousseau's *Émile* (1762), which
included a famous statement of the deist creed, the 'Profession de foi du vicaire
savoyard'.

91 *Molière's Misanthrope, Racine's Athalie*: Molière's *Le Misanthrope* (1666)
had been singled out by Rousseau in his *Lettre à M. d'Alembert sur les
spectacles* as an example of why theatre is pernicious (Voltaire of course
thought this view absurd). Racine's *Athalie* (1691) is a biblical tragedy,
written for the young women pupils of Saint-Cyr, a school endowed by
Louis XIV at the request of Mme de Maintenon—and so an odd target
for the Church to criticize.

CHRISTIANITY

Voltaire had a long-standing interest in biblical criticism, and in this major
article, he brings together a wide range of material, exploiting the extensive
reading he had undertaken for his universal history, the *Essai sur les mœurs*
(1756).

96 *'They are . . . widely within Egypt'*: Philo of Alexandria, *On the Contemplative Life*, chs. 2–3.

97 *AD 117*: in fact, AD 177.

100 *With five loaves . . . a dozen baskets*: Lactantius, *Divine Institutions*, 4. 15. This resumes the story told, for example, in Matthew 14: 19–21.

101 *'If I . . . cast them out?'*: Matthew 12: 24–7.

103 *'When Denis . . . anyone to do it'*: paraphrase of Eusebius, *Ecclesiastical History*, 7. 11.

105 *tauroboly*: the sacrificial slaughter of bulls. Voltaire of course disdains such pagan practices; in a letter of 1735 (D864) he had coined the pejorative word 'taurobolizer'.

CONVULSIONS

This article brings out the comic aspects of the quarrels between Jesuits and Jansenists within the Catholic Church. The papal bull 'Unigenitus' (1713) had condemned Jansenist teaching on grace and predestination, but their cause continued to enjoy a popular following and became connected with some well-publicized miracles. Most prominent were the disturbances in the churchyard of Saint-Médard in Paris (1727–32), when the number of miraculous cures led to scenes of public disorder, as women in 'convulsions' bared themselves in public. It suits Voltaire to remind us of the divisions between Jesuits and Jansenists, not least because in the years 1757–9 the two groups had come together to condemn the *Encyclopédie*.

111 *The Spirit of the Laws*: Montesquieu published *De l'esprit des lois* in 1748.

CRITICISM

This article treats literary (and not, as we might have expected, biblical) criticism. The surprising choice of subject brings a change of tone and relief. It allows Voltaire to indulge a particular interest, of course; but beyond that, the central argument of this article, in advocating the need for clear and unbiased judgement, is consistent with other articles.

112 *The shrill blast . . . forth*: Tasso, *Gerusalemme liberata*, 4. 3 (in Italian in the original).

"flashy": Boileau, *Satires*, 9. 174–5.

113 *Hatred . . . hate him*: Quinault, *Armide* (1686), 3. 2. The subject of this *tragédie en musique* (opera), set to music by Lully, is taken from Tasso's *Gerusalemme liberata*.

'ignorant architect': the east-facing colonnade of the Louvre was built by the architect Claude Perrault. His brother Charles Perrault is remembered as the author of fairy tales, and as a Modern in the Quarrel of Ancients and Moderns (and therefore an opponent of Boileau, who was an Ancient).

114 *Oft a young beauty . . . base seditious knave*: these three verses come from different poems in the *Odes* (1707) of Antoine Houdar de La Motte.

115 *A certain gosling . . . The tedious beauty . . . Too much of Quinault*: these three quotations are all taken from Jean-Baptiste Rousseau, *Épîtres*, 1. 5. 1; 1. 5. 6; and 2. 5. 11. J.-B. Rousseau was a poet and author of comedies, and a long-standing enemy of Voltaire's.

116 *The sovereign influence . . . soul's happiness*: a series of extracts drawn from the *Odes* (1723) of J.-B. Rousseau.

  genus irritabile vatum: 'the irritable race of poets' (Horace, *Epistles*, 2. 2. 102).

  fleurs-de-lys: the example is not invented: J.-B. Rousseau, *Allégories*, 2. 3.

FATE

This article picks up once more the issues raised above in 'Chain of Events'. It looks forward, explicitly, to the article 'On Free Will'.

117 *birth of Christ*: St Jerome, *Commentary on Isaiah*, 3. 8.

118 *Nullum . . . locamus*: 'Thou wouldst have no divinity, O Fortune, if we had but wisdom; it is we that make a goddess of thee, and place thee in the skies' (Juvenal, *Satires*, 10. 365–6, trans. G. G. Ramsay). The quotation is approximate, perhaps from memory.

  Cardinal d'Ossat: Arnaud d'Ossat (1537–1604), French cardinal and politician.

119 *move to the letter L*: the reference is to the later article 'Liberté' ('On Free Will'). Voltaire encourages his reader to move between different articles and to rebel against the arbitrary order of the alphabetical dictionary. In this way Voltaire emphasizes both the work's fragmented nature and its underlying thematic unity. The use of cross-references at the end of an article is reminiscent of the *Encyclopédie*.

GOD

In this encounter in dialogue form, Logomachos ('word-warrior') represents theology, while in the opposite corner Dondinac represents the simple believer. Voltaire again demonstrates the vacuity of theological disputes, the necessity of intellectual modesty, and the fundamentally simple belief in a Supreme Being.

121 *by essence*: this and the following theological arguments are taken from Thomas of Aquinas's *Summa Theologica*.

EQUALITY

This treatment of political theory is a reply to Jean-Jacques Rousseau's *Second Discourse* ('Discours sur l'origine et les fondements de l'inégalité parmi les hommes', 1755); and perhaps also to Jaucourt's article 'Égalité naturelle' in the *Encyclopédie* (vol. 5, 1755). It seems likely that Voltaire composed this text before the publication of Rousseau's *Social Contract* (*Du contrat social*) in 1762. Many of the examples of other societies have been brought to Voltaire's mind in his research for the *Essai sur les mœurs*.

124 *where they were born*: Voltaire is thinking of either Russia or Japan.

HELL

Voltaire addresses a key tenet of Christian thinking: belief in eternal damnation. He points out that historically, such a notion was alien to Jewish thought; Christians seem to have adopted the idea from other cultures, for what are perhaps essentially pragmatic reasons (with which Voltaire is inclined to agree).

127 *natural phenomena*: after the Lisbon earthquake (1755), Voltaire had ridiculed those who claimed that God was punishing the city.

   Sedet . . . Theseus: 'Hapless Theseus sits and evermore shall sit' (Virgil, *Aeneid*, 6. 617–18, trans. H. Rushton Fairclough).

128 *do believe in it*: this was also Voltaire's view, it seems. He wrote to one correspondent: 'You need hell for the rabble' (26 December 1760, D9497).

STATES, GOVERNMENTS

In considering the different forms of government, Voltaire reflects on the ideas put forward by Montesquieu. A convinced monarchist, Voltaire does not have particularly radical ideas in this area. Indeed he seems most interested, as a historian, in the flagrantly unreliable memoirs of politicians and statesmen.

129 *Abbé de Bourzeis*: the Abbé de Bourzeis (1606–72) was a writer who served as secretary to the statesman Cardinal Richelieu. But the *Testament politique*, published in 1688, long after Richelieu's death in 1642, is considered to be the work of Richelieu.

131 *virtue in a republic*: in *De l'esprit des lois* (1748), Montesquieu had distinguished three types of government, the republic, the monarchy, and despotism, characterized by virtue, honour, and fear respectively. The following remarks about climate and polygamy similarly refer to this work.

ON EZEKIEL

Different cultures require different understandings. In exploring this idea, Voltaire refers to the literary debates of the Quarrel between Ancients and Moderns (in the late seventeenth and early eighteenth centuries), and then, of course, to the Bible. This is an excuse for Voltaire to revisit his favourite example of Old Testament obscenity, in the Book of Ezekiel. But as much as an argument about biblical criticism, this article is also about language, decorum, and taste. The reference to Horace reminds us that Voltaire's own familiar tone of voice is indebted to Horatian *sermo*, a (pseudo-) conversational tone which lures us into the subject.

133 *shit*: Ezekiel 4: 12–15.

135 *in our language*: Ruth 4: 13 and Genesis 38: 18.

Nec metuo . . . recurrat: 'I have no fears while I'm fucking her that her husband will rush back from the country' (Horace, *Satires*, 1. 2. 127). Diderot's novel *Jacques le fataliste*, written some ten years later, contains a similar meditation on the use of the f-word: but Diderot writes 'foutre' in French, whereas Voltaire contents himself with the Latin 'futuo'.

FABLES

In considering the allegorical function of ancient myth and fable, Voltaire might seem on safe ground. But in taking one example from the Old Testament and another from Hesiod, he relativizes the uniqueness of the Bible. And as a final insult, at the end of this article there is a jibe against some contemporary fiction: the Bible is just one form of storytelling among many others. And Voltaire doesn't like modern fiction much either.

136 *as Hesiod retells it*: Hesiod, *Theogony*, 178–200.

FANATICISM

In this attack on religious fanaticism, the name of Christianity is never mentioned, merely the name of notorious Christian criminals acting in the name of religion. Voltaire's argument is in the end a moral one: fanaticism makes people ugly, while 'philosophy' (i.e. reasonable and reasoned behaviour) 'brings peace to the soul'.

137 *enthusiast*: Juan Díaz (*c.*1510–46) was a Spanish Protestant theologian; his brother Alfonso (died *c.*1555) was a Spanish lawyer at the court in Rome.

smash the ornaments: Corneille, *Polyeucte*, 2. 6 and 3. 2.

Duc François de Guise . . . Henri IV: the Duc de Guise was killed by the Protestant Jean Poltrot de Méré (1563); William of Orange by Balthazar Gerard (1584); Henri III by Jacques Clément (1589); and Henri IV by Jacques Ravaillac (1610).

mass: the St Bartholomew's Day Massacre (1572) was the bloodiest event of the French Wars of Religion: the king ordered the killing of a group of Huguenot leaders, an act which unleashed a wave of killings leaving many thousands dead. Every year on the anniversary of the massacre, Voltaire became physically sick.

138 *The plumage . . . injury*: an extract from a poem, 'La Défense de l'amour accusé par M. D. P.' by bishop Jean Bertaut (1552–1611).

FALSENESS OF HUMAN VIRTUES

This brief article is an attack on Jacques Esprit's *La Fausseté des vertus humaines*, first published in 1678 (translated into English in 1706 as *Discourses on the*

Deceitfulness of Human Virtues). Esprit was familiar with La Rochefoucauld (*Maximes*, 1665), who had argued that man's motives were egotistical, and virtues forms of disguised pride. Esprit takes this idea and gives it a Christian twist: if it is true that man is basically egotistical, charity alone, a good done for the love of God, is the one ethically sound motivation. Voltaire is anxious to show that an ethical code can be developed independently of Christian doctrine.

139 *None shall have virtue . . . friends!*: adapted from Molière, *Les Femmes savantes*, 3. 2.

END, FINAL CAUSES

A more 'purely' philosophical article. The argument from design says that the existence of God can be proved from the evidence of order, purpose, and design that we perceive in nature. This is also called the teleological argument (Greek *telos* means 'end'), or (by Kant) the physico-theological proof. The argument is made in classical antiquity, and continues today in modern discussion of 'intelligent design'. Put at its simplest, God is the watchmaker: 'The universe confuses me, and I cannot believe that this watch can exist and have no watchmaker' (Voltaire, *Les Cabales*, 1772). Many philosophers (like Hume) dismiss such arguments out of hand as worthless. Voltaire senses the potential weakness of the case, and tries here to find a middle path between simplistic teleology and mere hedonism. See B. E. Schwarzbach, 'Coincé entre Pluche et Lucrèce: Voltaire et la théologie naturelle', *SVEC* 192 (1980), 1072–84. See also Thomas McPherson, *The Argument from Design* (London, 1972). Richard Dawkins argues against this theory in *The Blind Watchmaker* (Harlow, 1986).

140 *glasses*: an echo of *Candide*, ch. 1.

MADNESS

Philosophers in the 'age of reason' are (or should be) concerned with madness and the seeming lack of reason. Diderot writes about seeming madness at length in his contemporary satire *Le Neveu de Rameau*. Voltaire ponders why God would give man sick souls: might madness be an argument against the existence of the soul? . . .

142 *Erasmus' book*: Erasmus, *Praise of Folly* (1511). Voltaire respected Erasmus as a humanist who defended religious toleration.

FRAUD

Established religions use 'fraud', 'fables' to teach their truths; but simple belief in the Supreme Being can do without such rhetoric. Voltaire had explored the theme earlier in a play, *Le Fanatisme, ou Mahomet le prophète* (1741), in which a religious impostor leads his followers into fanaticism; but whether the setting is Islam, as in this play, or China, as in the present dialogue, the message is universal, and Voltaire's true target Christianity.

GLORY

Voltaire mocks the idea that man imagines God in his own image; a modest man admits that the Supreme Being is unknowable. He also has fun at the expense of the Jesuits.

148 *"Ek allhà . . . gloriam"*: this formulation is not of course Muslim, but by the Jesuits. Their order had just been suppressed in France, in 1761, and their schools closed. On the chapel which Voltaire constructed at Ferney (1761), he had the simple inscription: 'Deo erexit Voltaire' ('Voltaire built this for God'): no mention of 'glory' here; and Voltaire's name was larger than God's.

   chiaus: a messenger or servant at the Ottoman court.

WAR

Voltaire writes in the context of the Seven Years War (1756–63); he had already raged against war in *Candide* (see ch. 3). And as in *Candide*, he draws a distinction here between metaphysical evil (earthquakes, famine, pestilence), and moral evil, the evil caused by man (war, persecution).

151 *Polyeucte and Athalie*: *Polyeucte*, by Corneille, and *Athalie*, by Racine, are both seventeenth-century tragedies based on biblical themes.

   Massillon: Jean-Baptiste Massillon (1663–1742), bishop and celebrated author of sermons.

   Bourdaloue: Louis Bourdaloue (1632–1704), Jesuit preacher and author of sermons. He has given his name to a French chamber pot shaped like a gravy-boat and used by ladies in church; the object became necessary, so the story runs, on account of the length of his sermons.

GRACE

Voltaire again targets the jargon of theologians, and again, as in 'God' above, Thomas of Aquinas's *Summa Theologica* is the principal source. His trick is to take the highly technical vocabulary concerning notions of grace, and to place it out of context in everyday situations, with predictably ridiculous effect. The Jansenist notions of grace still familiar in the eighteenth century seem to deprive the individual of free will, and for that reason alone would not recommend themselves to Voltaire.

152 *Marcus Aurelius*: the wise Roman emperor of the first century AD and Stoic philosopher; his *Meditations*, on duties of government, was a favourite book of Frederick the Great; and needless to add, he is not the author of the passage attributed to him here.

HISTORY OF THE JEWISH KINGS AND CHRONICLES

The change from theocracy to monarchy is a key moment in Jewish history. It is told in 1 Samuel 8, when the people of Israel tell Samuel that they desire a king. Voltaire points up the paradox that the Jewish people wanted to be like other nations in having a king as their leader, yet still considered themselves God's chosen people. The historian Voltaire also has some fun with the notion of God himself as the historian of the Jewish people. At several moments in this article, Voltaire is replying to Dom Calmet's *Commentaire littéral*. On the question of Jewish theocracy, see Antonio Gurrado, 'Théocratie et monarchie judaïque: Voltaire entre exégèse et politique', *Revue Voltaire*, 8 (2008), 443–7.

154 *Chronicles ... chronology*: in the Vulgate, the two books of Samuel followed by the two books of Kings are together called the four books of Kings. They are followed by the two books of Chronicles.

155 *David killed ... Remaliah*: these murders are all described in Samuel, book 2, and the two books of Kings.

IDOL, IDOLATER, IDOLATRY

The length and detail of this article are explained by the fact that Voltaire first wrote it in 1757 to appear in the *Encyclopédie*; publication of further volumes was banned in 1758, so Voltaire recycles the piece here. He uses wide-ranging historical scholarship to show that we tend to use the term 'idolatry' to denigrate religions other than our own; the Christian use of images and statues could equally seem 'idolatrous' to outsiders who were not sensitive to their spiritual meaning. The wide research carried out for the *Essai sur les mœurs* informs this article.

156 *Trévoux Dictionary*: the *Dictionnaire de Trévoux* was a Jesuit dictionary and encyclopedia (1704, and re-edited all through the eighteenth century).

159 *'I was once ... god'*: Horace, *Satires*, 1. 8. 1–3.

'They will ... want them to be': André Dacier, a French classical scholar, produced an edition of Horace with commentaries, *Œuvres d'Horace [. . .] avec des remarques critiques et historiques* (1681–9).

Qui finxit ... deos: 'He who shapes sacred lineaments in gold or marble does not make gods: he makes them who prays' (Martial, *Epigrams*, 8. 24. 5–6, trans. Walter C. A. Ker).

Colitur pro Jove forma Jovis: '[Thus it is that men know the gods whom the lofty aether conceals;] they worship in Jupiter's stead the likeness of Jupiter' (Ovid, *Ex Ponto*, 2. 8. 62, trans. Arthur Leslie Wheeler).

160 *Nulla autem ... gaudet*: 'No image is there, no shape of deity committed to metal; she joys to dwell in minds and hearts' (Statius, *Thebaid*, 12. 493–4, trans. D. R. Shackleton Bailey).

Estne Dei ... aer?: 'Has [the Creator] any dwelling-place save earth and sea, the air of heaven?' (Lucan, *Pharsalia* (*The Civil War*), 9. 578, trans. J. D. Duff). The passage from which this extract is taken is worth quoting in full: 'We men are all inseparable from the gods, and, even if the oracle be dumb, all our actions are predetermined by Heaven. The gods have no need to speak; for the Creator told us once for all at our birth whatever we are permitted to know. Did he choose these barren sands, that a few might hear his voice? Did he bury truth in this desert? Has he any dwelling-place save earth and sea, the air of heaven and virtuous hearts? Why seek we further for deities? All that we see is God; every motion we make is God also. Men who doubt and are ever uncertain of future events—let *them* cry out for the prophets: I draw my assurance from no oracle but from the sureness of death.' From such authors, Voltaire can argue that his deism has origins independent of Christianity.

164 *'I wanted . . . god'*: Ovid, *Fasti*, 4. 269–70.

165 *'Contemplate . . . visible to him'*: Voltaire has borrowed this quotation from Bishop William Warburton, *Divine Legation of Moses demonstrated on the Principles of a Religious Deist*, 2 vols. (1737–41), which Voltaire read in English. Warburton was bishop of Gloucester from 1759.

166 *'God . . . cease to live'*: Epictetus, *Discourses*, 2. 18 and 3. 64.

'The soul . . . God': Marcus Aurelius, *Meditations*, 12. 26.

Moreri's dictionary: Louis Moreri's *Grand Dictionnaire historique* went through some twenty editions from 1671; it defends orthodox Catholic views.

JEPHTHAH, OR ON HUMAN SACRIFICES

This biblical story can be relativized by comparison with other fables of classical antiquity; or it can be treated as a strict historical record, in which case it reflects badly on the society which originated it. Neither reading is comfortable for orthodox Christianity.

FLOOD

Voltaire has a double target in this short article. He ironizes about miracles as articles of faith beyond rational grasp (a subject to which he will return later). And in the particular case of the miracle of the universal flood, he confronts the biblical account with the findings of modern science.

JOSEPH

Voltaire retells the story of Joseph in his own words. He points out that it has the hallmarks of an 'oriental' tale, and comparisons with Homer and the Qur'an put the biblical scholars in their place. But his admiration for the narrative style and structure of this tale is not (altogether) ironical. To his friend Mme Du Deffand, who wrote asking him what novels she should read, he replied suggesting the Old Testament, along with three or four cantos of Virgil, all of Ariosto, and part of the *Thousand and One Nights* (17 September 1759, D8484).

171 *come down to us*: Genesis 37–47.

172 *in the Qur'an*: 12: 6–7.

interpretation of dreams: Voltaire's own tales (*contes*) make use of the device
of the dream (for example *Le Crocheteur borgne, Le Blanc et le Noir*) or of
a dream-like atmosphere: Candide on two occasions remarks that he feels
he is in a dream (chs. 7 and 27).

ON FREE WILL

If Voltaire was mistrustful of determinism (see 'Chain of Events', above), he
thought long and hard about the question of free will. He was much influenced
by Locke's views on the question, and has expounded them on previous occasions, notably in his *Éléments de la philosophie de Newton*. See E. D. James,
'Voltaire on Free Will', *SVEC* 249 (1987), 1–18.

174 So *liberty . . . what I want?*: a position close to that of Locke.

175 *'my will . . . wish?'*: Juvenal, *Satires*, 6. 223.

ON LAWS

Montesquieu had written a celebrated philosophical treatment of the laws,
De l'esprit des lois (1748), with much of which Voltaire agrees, for example his
criticism of the disproportion between punishment and crime (12. 4). See also,
above, notes to pp. 111 and 131. But where Montesquieu's approach is broadly
philosophical, Voltaire's approach to the law is strictly practical and common-
sensical. His experience of the Calas affair has taught him the absurdity of the
fact that different regions of France operated different systems of justice. And
at the end of the article, there are allusions to the local legal disputes occupying
him in Ferney and the pays de Gex.

178 *I was told . . . France*: the 'I' who speaks is not of course Voltaire (who never
    travelled to India): this is a reminder not to take other 'I's in this work as
    representing Voltaire.

180 *Mentzel*: Chodorlahomor was a contemporary of Abraham (Genesis 14:
    1–17); Menzel was an Austrian solider in the War of 1741.

royal army: an allusion to the English execution of Admiral Byng, following his failure against the French in the battle of Minorca (1756). Voltaire
had already referred to the incident in *Candide* (ch. 23).

CIVIL AND ECCLESIASTICAL LAWS

Continuing the discussions of 'On Laws' above, Voltaire reflects on the need
for the civil laws to operate independently of ecclesiastical interference. This
is an important part of Voltaire's 'republican' legacy in France, where by the
law of 1905 Church and State are formally separated. Beccaria's *On Crimes
and Punishments* (*Dei delitti e delle pene*) appeared in Italian in 1764, and would
further influence Voltaire's thought in this area; he published a *Commentaire* on
Beccaria in 1766.

LUXURY

The eighteenth century brought to perfection the production of a whole range of luxury consumer goods; in parallel, there was a debate about luxury: this trade produced wealth and employment, or did it just encourage the idle rich to be idler still? Voltaire had earlier addressed this question in two poems *Le Mondain* (1736) and *Défense du Mondain, ou L'Apologie du luxe* (1737). Voltaire's nuanced defence of luxury in this article seems to be a reply to Jean-Jacques Rousseau's 'First Discourse' (*Discours sur les sciences et les arts*, 1750), in which he argued that progress in the sciences and arts corrupted human morality.

185 *Know this . . . destroyed*: Voltaire quotes his own *Défense du Mondain*, 53–4.

   Est modus . . . rectum: 'There is measure in all things. There are, in short, fixed bounds, beyond and short of which right can find no place' (Horace, *Satires*, 1. 1. 106–7, trans. H. Rushton Fairclough).

MATTER

Arguments about the nature of matter are important, in so far as materialism (the belief that only matter exists) is equated in the eighteenth century with atheism. Voltaire shows that he is conversant with many of the arguments; and at the same time, he shows his total contempt for metaphysical speculation of all kinds, 'chatter round a dinner-table'. The deist can leave it to the Supreme Being to worry about creation and matter, and concentrate instead on practical issues of morality.

187 *'chaos was what existed first'*: Hesiod, *Theogony*, 116.

   Sic ubi . . . secuit: 'When god, whoever he was, had so divided up and distributed the mass of matter' (Ovid, *Metamorphoses*, 1. 32–3).

   the divine power: Voltaire is paraphrasing the Bible, where the image is found in both Old and New Testaments: Jeremiah 18: 6 and Romans 9: 21.

188 *Zoroaster and Manes*: Zoroaster and Mani, founder of Manichaeism, taught that the world was divided between the two powers of good and evil, light and dark. Voltaire's source here is Isaac de Beausobre, *Histoire critique de Manichée et du manichéisme* (1734–9).

WICKED

Voltaire shares the eighteenth century's general optimism about human nature. Man is naturally good, everywhere. This relativizes Christianity's claims to exclusivity; and there is a hint that religion is often the cause of misfortunes and crimes.

190 *the Philadelphians and the Banians*: the Philadelphians are the Quakers: they founded Pennsylvania, whose capital is Philadelphia; they were famous for their pacifism and spirit of tolerance. The Banians are members of an Indian (Brahmanic) sect.

MESSIAH

This learned article is the second that is not entirely the original work of Voltaire (see above, 'Apocalypse'). Voltaire had earlier recruited Antoine Noé de Polier de Bottens, *premier pasteur de Lausanne*, to write articles for the *Encyclopédie* (and he also helped to recruit another Swiss Protestant pastor, Élie Bertrand). Polier de Bottens contributed altogether nine articles, all of them highly unorthodox: Voltaire decribed him approvingly as 'a priest by profession, an unbeliever by common sense'. One of his articles was 'Messie' ('Messiah'), but due to delays caused by the banning of the publication of the *Encyclopédie*, it could not be published until 1766. In the meantime, Voltaire decided to include the article in his own *Dictionnaire*, albeit in an edited form: he shortens and condenses the original version, and makes a small number of additions (for further detail, see the Voltaire Foundation edition, appendix II, vol. 2, pp. 588–617). The article begins with the fact that Jews do not give to Jesus the status of Messiah which Christians do; and shows how many different messiahs have been proclaimed at different times, in different cultures. A year after first publication, in 1765, Voltaire adds a note at the end of this article: 'This article is found almost word for word in the *Encyclopédie*. It is by a man of worth who has become pastor in a Protestant church.'

METAMORPHOSIS, METEMPSYCHOSIS

The idea that souls pass from one body to another seems prevalent in many cultures: examples from classical antiquity and the Old Testament are put on the same cultural footing. This further fragilizes the Christian notion of the unique human soul.

200 *in his admirable work*: for the references which follow, see Ovid, *Metamorphoses*, 6. 305–12; 10. 56–64; 8. 695–8; 13. 652–4; and 4. 576–603.

metamorphoses: for the references which follow, see Genesis 19: 26 and 24–8; John 2: 1–11; Exodus 7: 10; and Genesis 18: 2–8.

In his epistle . . . colaphiset: 2 Corinthians 12: 7.

MIRACLES

Voltaire stages a debate between Christians and philosophers about the existence of miracles: why would God wish to circumvent his own rules? Voltaire's sympathies are obvious from the start, and he tries, not very convincingly, to present both sides of the argument. The debate about miracles was a key plank of Enlightenment debate. David Hume is uncompromising on the subject: his essay 'Of Miracles' (1748), first published as section 10 of *An Enquiry concerning the Human Understanding*, was one of his most controversial works: 'A miracle is a violation of the laws of nature, and as a firm and unalterable experience has established these laws, the proof against a miracle, from the very nature of the fact, is as entire as any argument from experience can possibly be imaged' (*Enquiries*, ed. L. A. Selby-Bigge, 114). Gibbon later pours sarcasm on miracles in *The Decline and Fall of the Roman Empire* (1776–89). Voltaire borrows most of his examples from the English churchman (and deist) Conyers Middleton, who writes in his *Free Inquiry concerning the Miraculous Powers which are supposed to have subsisted in the Christian Church* (1749): 'The History of the Gospel, I hope may be true, though the History of the Church be fabulous. And if the ecclesiastic Historians have recorded many silly fictions, under the name of miracles, as they undoubtedly have, the blame must be charged to the writers, not to their religion.'

204 *'Cur . . . mundus'*: 'Why is it, they say, that these miracles you boast of no longer occur now? It is because, I could reply, they were necessary before the world believed, in order to make it believe' (St Augustine, *The City of God*, 22. 8).

205 *Ospiniam, p. 230*: the reference is to Rudolph Wirth (Rodolphus Hospinianus), *Historia Jesuitica* (1619). Few readers were (or are) likely to check a page reference to a book as obscure as this: but Voltaire enjoys parading the apparatus of Latin scholarship. In fact, Voltaire himself had most likely never read the book (which is not in his library at Ferney); the detail is lifted—along with the preceding allusion to a 'learned Jesuit' (José de Acosta) and the following reference to St Francis Xavier—directly from Conyers Middleton.

grace versatile: see note to p. 68.

MOSES

The Pentateuch is the name given to the first five books of the Old Testament. In Judaism, these books constitute the Torah: they are the founding legal and ethical texts of the faith, and are attributed to Moses. Mosaic authorship began to be questioned by Christian theologians from the seventeenth century. An important source for Voltaire is Jean Le Clerc, *Sentiments de quelques théologiens de Hollande sur l'histoire critique du Vieux Testament* (1685) in which the Swiss Protestant theologian argues against Mosaic authorship of the Pentateuch.

ONE'S COUNTRY

Voltaire considers different political systems: he regrets the patriotism that causes wars, but his pessimism about human nature ('human beings are very rarely capable of self-government') makes him conservative and lean towards monarchy. He seems to find the 'monarchical republic' as typified by Poland, Sweden, and England as the least bad alternative.

211 *a bell around the cat's neck*: the allusion is to La Fontaine, 'Conseil tenu par les rats', *Fables*, 2. 2.

PETER

Jesus named Peter the leader of the Church, and although he did not have the title of pope, Catholics recognize him as the first pope. Protestants, on the other hand, find no evidence in the New Testament that Jesus established the Papacy or appointed Peter to it. A discussion of the historical uncertainties surrounding the figure of Peter, 'first bishop of Rome', leads into a wide-ranging critique of the secular power of the Papacy.

212 *the kingdom of heaven*: Matthew 16: 19.

bound in heaven: Matthew 16: 19.

213 *'Kill and eat'*: Acts 10: 9–16.

substance of the people: Voltaire is summing up passages from William Wollaston, *The Religion of Nature Delineated* (1722). This exposition of deism was hugely popular in England: an eighth edition appeared in 1750. A French translation, *Ébauche de la religion naturelle*, was published in 1726.

214 *Conringius*: Hermann Conring, *Dissertatio academica de majestate civili* (1677). Conring was a professor in north Germany descended from Lutheran clergy.

215 *parricide*: an allusion to Joseph I, king of Portugal 1750–77. A conspiracy to assassinate the king and his powerful minister, the marquis de Pombal, led to the expulsion of the Jesuits from Portugal in 1759.

Sturbinus: Voltaire presumably means the Protestant Jean Sturm (1507–89), whose Latinized name Sturmius has become mangled.

PREJUDICES

Voltaire warns us against adherence to inherited and unexamined ideas: prejudice leads to persecution. Cautiously (or disingenuously?), he allows that 'some prejudices . . . are necessary': rather than unfettered reason, he advocates judgement as our guide.

216 *John Law's bank*: John Law, a Scottish economist, set up the Mississippi Company in Paris under the Regency; after a rapid rise, stock prices collapsed in 1721, ruining many investors.

RELIGION

In this wide-ranging survey of religion, Christianity is treated as one belief among many others. Voltaire is developing a form of comparative religion, so that even if his examples are not new, his overall strategy is. He will further develop this approach in his *Philosophie de l'histoire* (1765), published after the present work, but begun earlier.

219 *Providence*: *The Divine Legation of Moses*: see note to p. 165.

220 *only one Supreme Being*: the allusion seems to be to Nicolas Fréret. The whole passage is indebted to Fontenelle's *De l'origine des fables* (1724).

221 *'Will not you . . . we possess'*: Judges 11: 24.

223 *Origen says*: Origen, *Contra Celsum*. Celsus was a second-century Greek philosopher who opposed Christianity.

224 Voltaire means para. 374.

225 *Prologue to Amphitryon*: Molière's comedy (1668), based on Plautus, in which Jupiter undergoes various metamorphoses.

RESURRECTION

Not only is Christian theology unclear about the origin and uniqueness of the doctrine of resurrection, but in addition other cultures in other periods seem to have been equally interested in the concept. Here, as elsewhere, Voltaire relies heavily on the biblical commentaries of Dom Calmet.

SOLOMON

An all-out assault on the Old Testament: Voltaire focuses on the historical difficulties concerned with the authorship of certain books, and on the poetic nature of some of the writing.

231 *third book of the Kings*: see note to p. 154.

breasts are better than wine: Song of Solomon 1: 2 and 4: 10–11.

betwixt my breasts: Song of Solomon 1: 13.

232 *tower of Lebanon*: Song of Solomon 7: 3–5.

inclose her: Song of Solomon 8: 8–9.

curtains of Solomon: Song of Solomon 1: 5

flagitiosus: reference taken from Dom Calmet's *Commentaire littéral*.

233 *colour to the glass*: Proverbs 20: 2 and 23: 31.

SENSATION

Unlike Descartes, who believed in innate ideas, Locke, as an empiricist, believed that our knowledge derives from the senses. Voltaire is a follower of Locke, whose ideas he had first expounded in the *Letters concerning the English Nation* (Letter 13). The idea seems a safe one: but Voltaire pushes it to the limits of questioning the existence of the soul.

235 *I don't know enough about it*: Voltaire feigns ignorance just at the point where the argument is becoming dangerous, where he floats the possibility that the immaterial soul might not exist.

236 *sensation*: the same idea is found in Helvétius, *De l'esprit* (1758), 1: 1.

Condillac: Étienne Bonnot de Condillac (1714–80) was a disciple of Locke and the greatest 'technical' French philosopher among Voltaire's contemporaries. But this quotation from his *Traité des sensations* (1. 7. 2), first published 1754, is tendentious: Condillac actually wrote 'sensation envelops all the faculties of the soul'; Voltaire's rewriting of the sentence might hint that Condillac was questioning the existence of the immaterial soul (which he was not).

DREAMS

The subject of dreaming is of interest to understanding the connection between body and soul; but treating dreams like oracles or predictions of the future is mere superstition. Voltaire is much influenced by La Mothe Le Vayer, 'Du sommeil et des songes' (*Œuvres*, 1662).

237 *Somnia quae . . . facit*: 'It is not the shrines of the gods, not the powers of the air, that send the dreams which mock the mind with flitting shadows; each man makes dreams for himself' (Petronius, *Fragments*, 30, trans. Michael Heseltine). The quotation is approximate. This is one of several influential classical statements about dreams: see Manfred Weidhorn, 'The Anxiety Dream in Literature from Homer to Milton', *Studies in Philology*, 64 (1967), 65–82.

238 *interpreting it*: Daniel 2: 1–47.

SUPERSTITION

Voltaire stops short of applying the criterion of reason to all religious beliefs, defining superstition as 'everything that goes beyond worship of the Supreme Being'. The subtitle places this article under the protection of classical antiquity: Cicero, *On Divination*; Seneca, *On Superstition* (the work is lost, but quoted in Augustine's *City of God*); and Plutarch, *On Superstition*.

239 *Et nigras . . . mittunt*: 'They [...] slay black cattle, and send down oblations to the departed ghosts' (Lucretius, *De Rerum Natura*, 3. 52–3, trans. W. H. D. Rouse).

   O faciles. . . aqua!: 'Fond fools alack! To fancy murder's gruesome stain by river water could be washed away!' (Ovid, *Fasti*, 2. 45–6, trans. James George Frazer and G. P. Goold).

TYRANNY

Voltaire returns to politics: monarchy, even a bad monarchy, he seems to say, is the lesser evil. Voltaire's personal experience of being a courtier had been unhappy: he had never succeeded in finding a role at the court of Louis XV, who disliked him; and his sojourn at the Prussian court with Frederick the Great ended in disaster. As patriarch of Ferney, and as a wealthy lord of the manor, he had finally found a way not to be 'either . . . the hammer or the anvil'.

TOLERATION

Voltaire's *Traité sur la tolérance* (*Treatise on Toleration*) appeared in 1763, a year before the *Dictionary*. The perspective here is comparative and historical.

242 *souls to their faith*: This image of the trading exchange, where commerce levels the differences between cultures and so brings men together, first appeared in the *Letters concerning the English Nation* (Letter 6). The

implication is that trade unites where religion divides. The free trade in ideas goes hand in hand with free trade in commerce.

243 *no hesitation in agreeing*: 2 Kings 5: 14–19.

as Jacob had his: Genesis 29 and 31: 19

244 *live in peace*: this is silent self-quotation: Voltaire is referring back to Letter 6 of the *Letters concerning the English Nation*: 'If one religion only were allowed in England, the government would very possibly become arbitrary; if there were but two, the people would cut one another's throats; but as there are such a multitude, they all live happy and in peace' (ed. Cronk, p. 30).

VIRTUE

Voltaire concludes on a note of secular pragmatism: never mind what the theologians say, virtue consists in doing good to fellow humankind.

245 *guide you through life*: in Christian thinking, the three theological virtues (faith, hope, and charity) are associated with salvation; the four cardinal virtues are prudence, justice, temperance, and courage.

faith and hope: Corinthinans 13: 13.

246 *Antoninus*: probably Marcus Aurelius.

APPENDIX

248 *gentleman of the name of Morgan*: it has been suggested that this might be the English deist Thomas Morgan, but this seems improbable. See Jan van den Berg, 'Did Voltaire Meet the Deist Thomas Morgan (d. 1743) during his Stay in England in 1726?', *Notes and Queries*, 57 (2010), 108–9.

Martineco and the Havannah: Lieutenant-Colonel Hugh Morgan served in Havana in 1760.

249 *dog. . . now think of the soul?*: Voltaire poses again the question he had asked in the *Pocket Philosophical Dictionary*, in the article 'Animals'. Samuel Powel, also of Philadelphia, was accompanying John Morgan on his Grand Tour of Europe.

Bolinbroke: Henry St John, Viscount Bolingbroke was a freethinking Tory aristocrat associated with the Jacobite cause. He lived as an exile in France during the Regency, when Voltaire visited him frequently at La Source, near Orléans. Later, when Voltaire came to England, Bolingbroke introduced him to his cultural and political circle. Voltaire had many of Bolingbroke's works in his library at Ferney, including the five volumes of his *Philosophical Works*.

250 *fat French lady middle-aged*: this must be Mme Denis, the lady of the house, Voltaire's niece and (as we now know) his mistress since the 1750s.

251 *Dr Franklin's writings*: John Morgan is perhaps the first American visitor to Ferney, so it is natural he should ask Voltaire about Benjamin Franklin who

at this date was famous for his experiments with electricity and in particular his proposal for an experiment to prove that lightning was electricity by flying a kite in a storm. A French scientist, Thomas-François Dalibard, successfully carried out this experiment in 1752. In 1756, Franklin had been elected a Fellow of the Royal Society in recognition of his scientific work. In 1778 Franklin became the first American ambassador to France, and in February that year he called on Voltaire in Paris, only months before the writer's death.

English books: Voltaire read English fluently, and his library at Ferney contained both David Hume's *The History of England* (1754–62) and William Robertson's *The History of Scotland* (1759). Voltaire would later acquire Robertson's *The History of the Reign of the Emperor Charles V* (1769), the preface of which praises Voltaire as a historian.

Rapin: Paul de Rapin-Thoyras is a French historian remembered for *L'Histoire d'Angleterre* (*History of England*), published at The Hague in seven volumes in 1724, with a dedication to George I.

252 *I call my daughter*: Marie-Françoise Corneille, great-granddaughter of the uncle of Pierre Corneille, the eminent seventeenth-century dramatist. Hearing that she was living in poverty, Voltaire took her in and arranged her marriage in 1763 to a local man of wealth, Pierre-Jacques-Claude Dupuits de la Chaux.

'Oh Goddess . . . born maid': Voltaire parodies the 'Ave Maria', the prayer for the intercession of the Virgin Mary.

253 *Deo Erexit Voltaire*: 'Built for God by Voltaire'. What John Morgan does not say is that Voltaire designed the inscription so that his name was larger than God's. When Flaubert visited Ferney in 1845, he reported that these infamous words had been effaced by 'bad people'. They have since been re-engraved and Voltaire's inscription is visible once more. See also note to p. 148.

255 *age of seventy-two*: actually, 70.